Well-Dressed Role Models

The Portrayal of Women in Biographies for Children

Gale Eaton

The Scarecrow Press, Inc.
Lanham, Maryland • Toronto • Oxford
2006

SCARECROW PRESS, INC.

Published in the United States of America
by Scarecrow Press, Inc.
A wholly owned subsidary of
The Rowman & Littlefield Publishing Group, Inc.
4501 Forbes Boulevard, Suite 200, Lanham, Maryland 20706
www.scarecrowpress.com

PO Box 317
Oxford
OX2 9RU, UK

British Library Cataloguing in Publication Information Available

Library of Congress Cataloging-in-Publication Data
Eaton, Gale, 1947–
  Well-dressed role models : the portrayal of women in biographies
for children / Gale Eaton.
    v. cm.
  Includes bibliographical references and index.
  Contents: Rediscovering Elizabeth—1946 : private women and
the public good—1971 : public work and private loss—1996 :
objectivity and the culture wars—Pocahontas : four political fictions.
  ISBN-13: 978-0-8108-5194-8 (pbk. : alk. paper)
  ISBN-10: 0-8108-5194-6 (pbk. : alk. paper)
  1. Biography as a literary form. 2. Women—Biography—Juvenile
literature—History and criticism. 3. Children's literature, American
—History and criticism. 4. Children's literature, English—History
and criticism. I. Title.
CT21.E2155 2006
920.72—dc22   2006007043

♾™ The paper used in this publication meets the minimum requirements of
American National Standard for Information Sciences—Permanence of
Paper for Printed Library Materials, ANSI/NISO Z39.48-1992.
Manufactured in the United States of America.

To GLE,

who attempted a high kick in a hobble skirt,

and to all who love her

Contents

Acknowledgments

Family, friends, colleagues, and students have supported me throughout this project. They egged me on. They brought relevant books and ideas to my attention. They read and critiqued and proofread and encouraged. They listened—and for a writer who would rather be telling stories, that was the greatest gift of all. I owe more than I can say to my parents and grandparents, who surrounded me with books and stories but resisted getting a television; to my friend Mary Woodcock Kietzman, who started the argument about Tudors and Stuarts when we were in grade school; to Paula Grey and Rachael Hungerford, whose proofreading goes far beyond mere line editing; to my colleagues at the University of Rhode Island Graduate School of Library and Information Studies; to Jim Carmichael, Mariellen Eaton, Ingrid Graff, Nora Hall, William Hudson Hunt, Sally Leahy, Marybeth McGreen, Frances Martindale, Marilyn Miller, Emily Eaton Moore, Mary Ellen Reilly, John Richardson, Jim Seymour, Linda Sherouse, Carol Sonduck, Ben Spence, Jessica Wilson, and the 4Rs; and to editors Shirley Lambert (for the courage to acquire a work in process), Susan Easun (for the patience to let it evolve), and Martin Dillon (for active help in bringing it to fruition). I am especially grateful to the graduate assistants who helped me in different ways each year; to the University of Rhode Island, for a half-year sabbatical to launch the project; and to the librarians of the Mashantucket Pequot Research Center, the Peacedale Public Library, and the University of Rhode Island Library. If I have forgotten anybody, or fallen short of their excellent suggestions, it is for lack of wits rather than gratitude.

Introduction

Biographies for Girls, 1946-1996

Back in the 1950s, two eleven-year-old girls in Bangor, Maine, had an ongoing debate. Mary, my best friend, was a Catholic; I was a Protestant, named Elizabeth; and our argument was staunchly partisan. Was the beautiful Mary Queen of Scots an innocent victim, unfairly imprisoned and finally executed by that shrewish virago, Elizabeth Tudor? Or was Elizabeth I a wise and tolerant monarch, driven to harsh measures only by the underhanded plotting of her charming but wicked cousin, Mary Stuart?

The debate had murky origins and unspoken rules. We both seemed to feel that one of those queens had to be right, and the other wrong; there had to be a clear-cut solution. It was difficult to see the solution or even the problem clearly; the books were so discreet. This was a time and place when polite folks did not discuss religion or politics in public, let alone expose children to explicit information about sex. Not knowing that there was such a thing as illegitimacy, I was baffled by the succession controversy: how could people think the king's niece had a better claim to the throne than his daughter? But we both assumed that the important issues, under all the glamour, were moral. Perhaps both of us felt, too, that reasons of state could be used to excuse a king's ruthlessness, but not a queen's.

To sustain the discussion, we ranged beyond home encyclopedias to the public library's collection of biographies for children: solid books with five-inch by eight-inch pages, thick with print and relieved by an occasional line drawing. (They left me in the dark about illegitimacy.) We read everything we could find for ammunition, and argued earnestly for weeks or months, but by the time we entered junior high school we had left the debate behind us. I was left with an abiding interest in Tudor history, romantic ideas about Elizabeth's wardrobe and her swashbuckling privateers, and (although I could not have admitted it to Mary) an uneasy sense of moral ambiguity. Those reticent books held enough contradictions to make me suspect that the answers were not so clear as I had thought.

Mary and I, hunting moral truth in biographies, were following a timeworn path. Biography has been a didactic genre at least since Plutarch examined the lives of the great Greeks and Romans. In the nineteenth century, adults were reading Samuel Smiles's popular lives of engineers; like today's celebrity biographies, they were rags-to-riches stories, chronicling the success of hard-working, intelligent men who triumphed over obstacles (Nadel 1984). "Historically, the purpose of biographies was to bring the good news, to paint a life that was exemplary," Zinsser (1986) observes; and Altick (1965) states that "until well past the middle of the nineteenth century, the universal justification of biography was its didactic usefulness."

In traditional biographies for children, the moral elements were even more pronounced, and remained prominent longer. As Shavit (1986) has shown, change in adult genres is slow to reach children's books. Adult biographies might aim for careful scholarship (at one extreme) or sensational popularity (at the other), but in many juvenile biographies edification still took precedence. Children's writers omitted embarrassing episodes and augmented their narratives with didactic legends. American children heard Parson Weems's tale of honest little George Washington, who hacked at his father's beloved cherry tree with his hatchet but bravely confessed, "I cannot tell a lie." British children heard equally apocalyptic tales of King Alfred, who gently accepted a peasant woman's scolding after he had let her cakes burn, or Canute, who showed his flattering courtiers that even a king cannot turn back the tide. British educator Pamela Mays (1974) comments approvingly on this use of legend: "One is teaching [children] about human nature, its reactions to certain predicaments, its wickedness, its goodness, and also tacitly imparting the values of our own time."

Juvenile biography is in some ways a conservative genre, still trying to provide good role models for young readers. Some of the efforts are blatant. There is a perennial market for short biographies that link each subject to a prevailing trait. Thus the Rosen/PowerKids Press, in the late 1990s, included titles like *Learning about Compassion from the life of Florence Nightingale* and *Learning about Determination from the life of Gloria Estefan* in a series of Character Building Books.

Child's World reissued the Value Biographies series in a boxed set in 2002; volumes include *Compassion: The Story of Clara Barton* and *Bravery: The Story of Sitting Bull.*

Such didacticism is far from universal; but it is pervasive. The moral of a biography may be conservative, enshrining and perpetuating the virtues of the forefathers; or it may be progressive, encouraging young readers to question past injustices and work toward a better future. In the 1830s, for instance, Lydia Maria Child "created a series of popular biographies about outstanding women of the past," writing "about women who went to jail for their heretical opinions, women who fought against tyrants, women who had wit, talent, learning, and love for beauty which they tried to use for good ends" (Meltzer 1994, 139-140). Words like "inspire" and "inspirational" were common praise in juvenile biography reviews in the 1940s and 1950s. Biographer Jeannette Eaton (1942) described the biographer's vicarious experience of "how mighty beings of the spiritual world work through earthly means," an experience that offered hope to writer and readers alike.

Throughout the twentieth century, critics applauded trends toward greater accuracy and away from didacticism and what Nesbitt (1953) called the "legendary approach." Children's literature critics say the genre has improved: "Today," observed Giblin (1997), "the chief goal of a young people's biography is not to establish a role model but rather to provide solid, honest information about a man or woman worth knowing for one reason or another." Yet, textbooks have been saying so for decades. Anne Thaxter Eaton (1940, 226) commented on the "artistry and care" that replaced the "dull prosaic little books" of earlier years, and Arbuthnot (1947, 471) said that the new juvenile biography offered "an honest reporting of a man's life," where an older book would have turned him into a "prig." In the 1940s we might have thought those "dull prosaic" biographies, with their old-fashioned didacticism, were relics of the 1920s; by the 1990s, we could imagine them as leftovers from the 1970s.

At the same time, we still want juvenile biographies—as a group, if not book by book—to instill moral values and ameliorate both the lives of individual children and the future of society at large. For instance, there have been repeated calls over the decades for more inclusiveness and diversity. It is widely asserted that children, in the process of constructing healthy identities, need to see themselves in the books they read; they need role models of their own race and gender. Such a claim is intuitively convincing, and the choice of subjects has indeed widened over the years. The 1946 edition of II. W. Wilson's *Children's Catalog* recommended biographies of 190 subjects, including only 31 women (16.3%) and 5 members of racial minorities in the United States or Canada (2.6%). By contrast, the 254 subjects of biographies recommended in the 1996 edition included 80 women (31.5%) and 65 members of racial minorities (25.6%). The message of encouragement seems to be simple: men and women from every kind of background have achieved great things, and the world is open to the fresh achievements of today's girls and boys. Young readers should dare great things.

Yet, a closer scrutiny of the books reveals other, less direct messages. Some of them have to do with the choice of content. While many of the newer biographies are frank and even courageous, giving lively "warts and all" portrayals of their subjects, highlighted achievements still tend to be those that fit most easily into society's status quo. Biographies of Helen Keller, for instance, tell children that she overcame deafness and blindness—but not that she became a socialist and advocated radical political change (Loewen 1995). Favorite subjects for African American biography are often nineteenth- or mid-twentieth-century reformers whose messages have already been accepted into the mainstream, or late-twentieth-century entertainers and sports stars—less often figures who are politically controversial now. So, while children are encouraged to make a difference, they are rarely incited to challenge the rules of the world they inherit.

There may also be subtle messages inherent in the form. The books Mary and I read in the 1950s were considered biographies, but they were fictionalized so we could identify with the subjects much as we identified with characters in storybooks. We could imagine ourselves in their worlds, seeing through their eyes, and feeling as they felt about things; if they had moral effects on us, it was partly by means of this immersion. Of course, the subjects were all very different, but one thing they had in common seemed to be an impressive unity of character and purpose. I thought that was what being a grown-up would be like. As a child, I was confused, and I knew that other children, too, could be self-contradictory and confused; but I expected to grow up, by some magic, into one of those dependable people who make sense. Looking back, I wonder how much of that expectation came from the solid heroes I met in biographies.

In some ways, one would expect the form of newer biographies to intensify the unified, coherent impression given by the old story biographies. One noted publisher and biographer, explaining why a successful 1974 book for young readers would not have been published in the same form a scant dozen years later, said that newer juvenile nonfiction exhibited "four key features":

> a close focus on one significant aspect of a topic that will serve to reveal other aspects; a concise, tightly written text that will catch and hold the interest of young readers; a built-in emphasis on illustrations, whether they are photographs or drawings or a combination of the two; careful attention to the overall design of the book to make sure it is visually inviting. The visual look of nonfiction is especially important today, when books have to compete with so many other media for a young person's attention (Giblin 1987).

Great brevity precludes completeness in the telling of a life; writers are forced to emphasize selected episodes or traits. In picture book biographies that make their subjects the exemplars of single virtues, brevity and oversimplification may indeed give a monolithic impression of adult character. On the other hand, the careful factuality of many newer books, and their use of multiple viewpoints, may evoke greater complexity and even fragmentation of character. As generic conventions evolve, both in style and in content, juvenile biography offers children different ways of imagining what life will hold.

In the mid-1990s, almost forty years after Mary and I set aside our debate over the Tudor succession, I found myself returning to the old biographies with new questions. How is it possible that one generation of children's literature critics after another, with equal credibility, can accuse old juvenile biographies of fusty didacticism and claim that new ones have overcome this tendency? Has there really been a consistent trend toward less moralistic, more accurate biographies? Or are we just less likely to perceive didacticism in messages we approve, and more likely to approve the messages of our own times? How have juvenile biographies of women really changed over the past half century? What do they tell readers about how to be human?

Background: General Trends in Biography

It is not only juvenile biography that has evolved as a genre; changing moral beliefs and literary forms have shaped biography for adults, as well. Traditional biography told the public stories of successful men, whose lives sometimes had to be shoehorned into the formula. The biography of individual accomplishment dovetailed neatly with the old political histories that centered on the activities of kings and generals.

Carlyle (1895) said in 1840 that "Universal History, the history of what man has accomplished in this world, is at bottom the History of the Great Men who have worked here." The traditional focus was on public achievements and significance; biographers skimmed tactfully over their subjects' private lives. Altick (1965) notes that some of Boswell's contemporaries felt his "penchant for verisimilitude and the significant detail was not in good taste" (72); that Harriet Beecher Stowe was excoriated for revealing the story of Lord Byron's incest; and that nineteenth-century biographies of Charles Lamb skirted his sister's madness, her murder of their mother, and the "equally troublesome . . . problem of drink" (167). He speculates that growing numbers of women readers in the nineteenth century led to a "tendency toward domesticity and antiheroism in literature," including biography, where the trend was met with "concern over the deepening threat . . . to individual, or family, privacy" (151).

Some have argued that women, as biographical subjects, deserve the same veil of privacy that traditionally covered men. By the early twentieth century, however, Freud was a major influence. Popular interest in personality grew, and the privacy of both male and female subjects was threatened by the advent of psychobiography, which gained currency in the 1920s (Weinberg 1992). Another challenge to privacy, especially since the 1970s, is the biography of living subjects, often by investigative reporters rather than academics, and often incorporating elements of psychobiography (Weinberg 1992). Both trends help meet a demand (which some critics attribute to women as readers) for personal details:

> Readers wanted to know whether the subject, like them, had spent hours in front of bathroom mirrors, playing dress up in her mother's clothes, experimenting with lipstick and mascara. They wanted to know about her battle to maintain a consistent weight, about her sexual and psychological health. Women readers . . . demanded different kinds of information, and, as a result, the role of the biographer changed dramatically (Wagner-Martin 1994, 4).

Such emphasis on the personal and psychological has been criticized as trivial. Shortland and Yeo (1996, 4) find Stanley Weintraub's 1987 biography of Victoria "more preoccupied with the Queen's medical details, with sex, pregnancy and depression than with any public activities like wars, elections and Acts of Parliament"; and there are those who feel that the lives of women, so long confined to the private domain, need to emphasize their public roles. But quotidian details illumine character and add depth to biography (Wagner-Martin 1994; Codell 2000), and the private has its own dignity.

Quotidian details were also prominent in biographies influenced by social history. In the 1960s and 1970s, America's professional historians were debating a shift in emphasis from political to cultural history, or from a top-down focus on "the determinative behavior of elites" to a bottom-up examination of "the lives of common people" (Fitzpatrick 2002). This "new" history, which retrieves the forgotten textures of everyday life, was not really so new. It had been influential in Europe at least since the 1930s, when the seminal *Annales* journal was founded and Marc Bloch outlined the social history of the Middle Ages (Cantor 1991). Even earlier, in the United States, important work on cultural history was done in the late nineteenth century and by the Progressive historians (Fitzpatrick 2002). Because it privileges the everyday, and explores the meaning of unsung lives, social history is obviously useful for the study of women and minorities.

Feminist Critiques of Biography

The traditional biography of achievement, the psychobiography, the investigative biography, the biography informed by social and cultural history—each constitutes a subgenre, with its own evolving conventions; and in each case, the generic conventions affect the way an individual's story may be told and the moral implications that will emerge from the telling. Feminist critics of biography as a genre have been concerned with these conventions, and the ways they may exclude or misrepresent the lives of women. Heilbrun (1988, 13) argues that women's lives are more difficult than men's to fit into standard narrative patterns of quest and conflict. Women have been "forbidden . . . anger, together with the open admission of the desire for power and control over one's own life (which inevitably means accepting some degree of power and control over other lives)." To seek greatness, as a man might, was unwomanly, and women whose independent accomplishments made them famous would portray themselves as having been called rather than as having selected their own missions. It was more difficult for the biographers of women to cast their narratives as unified success stories or heroic quests, both because their actual lives were constantly interrupted and fragmented, and because public sentiment nudged subjects and biographers alike to mute the sustained ambitions that might have given their stories unity.

Still, women's lives can be squeezed into formulae, as men's can. Cloud (1996), after examining television and print biographies of Oprah Winfrey, concludes that their conventional rags-to-riches plots both falsify Winfrey's individual experience and serve to reinforce social injustice: the "biographical narratives construct a token 'Oprah' persona whose life story resonates with and reinforces the ideology of the American Dream, implying the accessibility of this dream to black Americans despite the structural economic and political barriers posed in a racist society to achievement and survival." Cloud's critique raises questions about the legitimacy of biography as a genre concerned with individual achievement and success.

In the late twentieth century, biographers of women experimented with alternative narrative forms and expository conventions, often drawing on social, economic, and cultural history as much as on political history. Arguing that the old archetypal patterns "may create inappropriate expectations and blur our ability to see the actual shape of lives," Bateson (1990, 5) looked at women's lives as improvisatory art, fluid, discontinuous, and composite, like patchwork. Ulrich (1990) used a "checkered weave" as a metaphor for the partially intersecting lives of men and women, doctors and midwives, in the early United States. By definition, a biography tells the life of an individual; but Ulrich and Bateson suggest that new formulae could be developed, emphasizing the individual's embeddedness rather than separateness from her community.

Biographies for Girls

Juvenile biography, as a limited subgenre, has been shaped both by trends in biography for adults and by assumptions about what is appropriate to children. The very structure of Victorian children's history books incorporated Carlyle's perception that history was the cumulation of great men's lives. *Little Arthur's History of England*, for instance, is essentially a series of short lives of the English kings. It was an approach that lent itself easily to simplification and moral judgment:

> Henry the Sixth grew up to be a very good but very weak man. He was married to a beautiful lady called Margaret of Anjou, who was very fierce and cruel, and who behaved more like a man than a woman. She wanted to govern the kingdom entirely herself. . . (Calcott 1884, 119).

Calcott's strictures on feminine ambition were by no means unique. Opportunities for great public achievement were closed to most women, and women who did achieve great things were often regarded with suspicion and distaste. Both the lack of achievement and the reluctance to offer ambitious women as role models to girls limited the supply of juvenile biographies of women. Mary and I encountered much the same dearth at the Bangor Public Library in the 1950s that feminist scholar Carolyn Heilbrun had found at the New York Public Library in the 1930s and early 1940s:

> I was profoundly caught up in biography because it allowed me, as a young girl, to enter the world of daring and achievement. But I had to make myself a boy to enter that world; I could find no comparable biographies of women, indeed, almost no biographies of women at all (Heilbrun 1988, 27).

The biographies of successful men—great engineers, great scientists, great generals—far outnumbered the biographies of queens, saints, consorts, and seamstresses.

Meanwhile, the psychobiography influenced books for older girls. As early as 1929, Jeanette Eaton's biography of a French revolutionary, Madame Roland, highlighted an unconsummated romance which did not become publicly known until a decade after her daughter's death. Eaton stressed Roland's virtuous self-abnegation, as she stood loyally by her husband and child, denying the great passion of her lifetime. The sacrifice of romance to duty was a recurrent theme in girls' biographies of women as different as Queen Elizabeth and Emily Dickinson. Vicinus observed it in children's books on Florence Nightingale: early in the twentieth century they emphasized her devotion to nursing, but later they began to focus on her sacrifice of romance. The new formula carried "both feminist and literary contradictions":

> If an author added romance to the narrative, the heroine's identity became defined by her desire. Once romance was admitted, a woman could not be portrayed as a whole person if she had rejected a suitor (Vicinus 1990, 103).

Although the treatment of private lives was rarely as sensational in juvenile as in popular adult biographies, a focus on romance could function to distract readers from a woman's public achievements, or to warn girls against ambitions that could cost them lives of loneliness.

On the other hand, juvenile biography was open to the perceptions and formal innovations associated with social, intellectual, and cultural history. Foster, in a series including *George Washington's World* (1941), anticipated the emphasis on how individuals are embedded in their communities when she looked at what was happening everywhere else in the world at various stages of her subjects' lives. By the 1960s and 1970s, when the "new" social history was capturing academic attention, the civil rights and women's movements drove demand for more juvenile biographies of minorities and women; and between the 1970s and the 1980s, newly available printing technologies contributed to a dramatic change in the look of children's nonfiction. Thus, Thomson (1995) threaded the story of Navajo sheepherder Katie Henio among expository sections about her work, tools, and traditions, and punctuated the book with affectionate stories told by Henio's young grandson. The shifting viewpoints, the alternation between narrative and exposition, and the colorful photographs convey the complex texture of a life that, in an earlier decade, would probably not have been written—not so much because of Henio's race and gender as because her story does not fit the established patterns of the old genre.

External Constraints on Juvenile Biography as a Genre

Within an evolving genre, it seems that individual writers have broad freedom to choose both their material and their approaches; no central authority dictates what is permissible. Still, some choices are better rewarded than others. Hunt (1991) diagrams many influences on the production and transmission of children's books: authors are affected by their peers, by conventions of the genres in which they work, and by general social expectations; publishers are swayed by economic considerations; children read in a social and informational environment that shapes their understanding. Hunt, whose publisher once rejected an experimental novel because aspects of both style and content were likely to make it unpopular with readers and their parents, had first-hand experience of these constraints as they apply to fiction.

Nonfiction is similarly constrained. The children's biographer, in choosing a perspective or discerning major themes and patterns in a subject's life, strives for a portrayal that is not only accurate but also meets public assumptions about what morals, comforts, or insights young readers should take from their books. In some cases, the public demand comes before the author's interest in the subject. Meltzer (1994, 182) notes the "great prominence of the promoted book, that is, the book that is not the author's own idea, but that he has been persuaded or directed to write by a publisher or an agent because there seems to be a market for it." When authors compromise with economic necessity to write "not for love, but for money"—as must happen often in the series that now account for a majority of children's biographies—the books' morals are likely to be more predictable, more supportive of popular taste and the status quo, than otherwise.

Thus, although individual writers are bound to have unique insights and approaches, market constraints should operate to keep juvenile biography responsive to public needs and tastes. This emboldened me to scrutinize girls' books for evidence of changing assumptions about what constitutes a worthwhile role model for girls, and how such a model's life should be presented.

Overview of This Book

Chapter 1

I began my exploration with a survey of juvenile material on Elizabeth Tudor published in England and the United States between 1852 and 2002, scrutinizing all the full-length juvenile biographies I could obtain (and a few histories and collected biographies as well) for trends in both content and rhetoric. The resulting sample of thirty-four books, although not exhaustive, was comparable in scope to similar longitudinal studies. Klatt (1992), focusing on just three books, found that the d'Aulaires presented Abraham Lincoln to children in 1939 as a "deified martyr," Judson in 1950 as a "flesh and blood hero," and Freedman in 1987 as "a man with warts." Gardner (1991) surveyed thirty-three biographies of Columbus published between 1932 and 1991, and found that the "rhetoric of domination" had been moderated, but not eliminated. Vicinus (1990) discussed developments in girls' books on Florence Nightingale between the 1880s and the 1950s.

The advantages of confining a study to biographies of a single individual are great. One can read much of what is known about the subject, and thus may recognize more easily what has been added to and subtracted from juvenile biographies. One can see how writers' contemporary concerns affect interpretations of a subject: in the 1950s, more than one author compared England's rivalry with Spain to the Cold War. One can spot the moral sensitivities that move biographers to omit details, or resort to euphemisms: by the 1990s, writers had become more open about sex, but more squeamish about English involvement in the slave trade.

Comparing juvenile to scholarly biographies of Elizabeth, I was struck by how often children's writers have managed to omit much of her life from her life story, while still giving an impression of completeness—and even a vivid sense of some aspects of her character. At the beginning of my exploration, I focused on three aspects of the children's books. First, how accurate were their facts? Second, how much did they omit? And third, what kind of rhetoric did they use to tell their stories? Under the heading of "rhetoric," at first I asked whether writers evaluated character with abstract adjectives (like "noble" and "cruel"), or revealed it through the protagonist's action; but soon I became interested in the different ways biographers structured the story. It was not only the fictionalized versions that used novelistic devices like foreshadowings and recurring motifs; even quite factual accounts could be shaped as cautionary tales or as triumphal fairy stories, depending in part on where the writers chose to stop.

There are fashions in such rhetorical devices, but a longitudinal study focused on just one biographical subject—or even a cluster of similar studies—has built-in limitations for tracing shifts in the genre. For one thing, only perennial subjects like Louisa May Alcott, Elizabeth Blackwell, Nellie Bly, Joan of Arc, and Harriet Tubman would be available for inclusion; these stars would not constitute a truly representative sample of biographies for girls half a century ago, let alone now. In 1996, one girls' biography in three featured a living subject—and two were still teenagers when the books went to press.

The characters and lives of the old favorite subjects were unique, and the available biographical sources were, too. Biographies of Phillis Wheatley were based largely on a memoir by her owner's cousin, downplaying the inhumanity of her bondage; biographies of Nellie Bly on her own reporting, which was less accurate than we might have thought; and biographies of Queen Victoria on diaries expurgated by her daughter. Various as they are, the sources for most nineteenth-century women's lives were limited by the expectation that they should be private. The biographers of late twentieth-century athletes and celebrities drew on different sources, shaped by different attitudes toward publicity on the part of their subjects' contemporaries. The intellectual habits of the subjects' own times affect what biographers can say about them. Juvenile biographies could also be influenced by the work of magisterial scholars on their subjects, whose interpretations and choice anecdotes might be cited for decades.

Chapters 2 through 4:
Biographies of Women in 1946, 1971, and 1996

In an effort to compensate for these limitations, I broadened my investigation by taking a "snapshot" approach, looking at biographies published in three selected years instead of biographies published about a few selected women. For this, too, there are precedents. Witucke (1985), replicating a study she had carried out five years earlier, did a citation analysis of eighty juvenile biographies published in 1983. She found that 31 percent were about women (compared to a quarter in 1978), and that the women were "strong, significant characters like Eleanor Roosevelt, Golda Meir, Margaret Mead, and Amelia Earhart." There were fewer ephemeral, pop culture biographies than five years earlier, and more featured people from the past (or at least over fifty years old); but there were "still too many stodgily written, inadequately researched books." Fewer were fictionalized, so perhaps some distortion or misinformation had been avoided; but too few had found "other means" to "make people seem alive and interesting."

The work reported in chapters 2 to 4 of this book is neither a citation analysis nor a strict content analysis, but a qualitative exploration, based on close readings of juvenile biographies of women that were published in the United States in the years 1946, 1971, and 1996. These years, at quarter-century intervals, mark distinct moments in women's history. In 1945, World War II ended, and in 1946, after years of war work in traditionally male jobs that seemed to prove "Rosie the Riveter" could do anything, women were laid off in favor of veterans; the active propaganda campaign to lure them into the workplace was superseded by an active campaign to encourage their return to the kitchen. In 1969 and 1970, a "great media blitz" ensured that Americans were aware of second-wave feminism—or at least had seen pejorative images of bra-burners and women's libbers (Rosen 2000, 296); and by 1971, trade publications like *School Library Journal* and *College English* were calling for more and better books about women and girls. In 1996, many women took the feminist gains of the 1970s for granted, but the movement was splintered and there was a significant backlash; the role of women had become an issue in the culture wars. The bitter polarization of this time was reflected in many publications, ranging from reports on "how schools cheat girls" (e.g., the Sadkers' 1994 *Failing at Fairness*) to "scathing indictment[s] of the feminist movement" (e.g., Christina Hoff Sommers' 1995 *Who Stole Feminism?*).

Thus the political, social, and economic expectations of women were dramatically different in these three years, and I anticipated interesting differences in how women were selected as the subjects of juvenile biographies and how they were treated. Against the background of societal change, the world of children's literature experts—writers, editors, librarians, and teachers—was also changing. The flavor of professional discourse was generally idealistic, but the patriotic optimism of 1946 gave way to greater skepticism, concern for multiculturalism, and willingness to celebrate worldly success. As context for my readings of the three years' biographies, I scanned contemporary children's literature textbooks (which laid out standards for juvenile biographies and other nonfiction) and essays in *The Horn Book Magazine* and other professional journals.

For purposes of this investigation, I defined a juvenile biography as a book devoted to the whole or partial life of an individual, and reviewed as nonfiction for readers in elementary, middle, or junior high school. I excluded those that were reviewed only for high school or "grades nine and up"; autobiographies; chapters in volumes of collected biographies; and documentary accounts of private individuals intended to represent different nations or life circumstances. My three years' samples consisted of all qualifying juvenile biographies I could find reviewed in published bibliographies or in the 1946, 1947, 1971, 1972, 1996, and 1997 issues of standard library selection tools—*Booklist*; *Bulletin for the Center of Children's Books*; *The Horn Book Magazine*; *Library Journal*, or the newer *School Library Journal*; and *Voice of Youth Advocates*. In all, I examined twelve books published in 1946, twenty-six in 1971, and fifty-one in 1996.

This sampling process may have missed a few relevant titles, but I believe that it caught most of them, and that any bias is toward the most widely read. First, the majority of published children's books are reviewed. Anderson found that about three quarters of those published in 1955 were reviewed by at least one of my sources (Sutherland 1967); in 1971, when 1,991 new juvenile titles were published (American Book Title Output 1972), *School Library Journal* alone reviewed 2,088 juvenile and 445 young adult books (Book Review Media 1972), including some published the previous year; and Bishop and Van Orden (1998) reported that *School Library Journal* reviewed 96 percent of sampled titles published in 1996. Second, children's book selectors throughout the period relied heavily on reviews; Van Orden (1978) found that 151 of 222 media center personnel rated favorable reviews as the most important factor in book selection, and most reviews are indeed positive

(Evans 1995). Reviews increase the probability that books will be held by libraries. Third, until recently most children's books were sold to libraries and schools, not directly to families and children; Schuman (1973) stated that librarians were "the market for over 80 percent of the new children's books published." Although some of the older books are no longer widely owned, all were accessible through interlibrary loan.

The Template:
Semantic, Syntagmatic, and Pragmatic Criteria

To systematize my observations on the sampled biographies, I used a template based on library selection criteria for children's nonfiction, which are commonly listed in children's literature textbooks and in collection development policies. They refer to accuracy and authenticity, prose style and illustrations, organization, support for school curricula, appeal to children, and other considerations. With some additions and changes of emphasis over the years, they have been remarkably consistent; they have given a comforting air of objectivity to book selection practices and have been invoked as defenses against censorship. Yet, they have proved flexible enough in application to allow the selection of remarkably different books.

This is possible in part because so much of what book selectors know and act on is unexpressed. The criteria themselves are not true "criteria," or tests which one book will demonstrably pass and another fail. Rather, they are lists of open-ended considerations. Some textbooks list them in the form of questions, to which the correct answers are assumed—for instance, "Is the book well designed?" The questions may remain the same; what changes over time is the selector's implicit sense of what the right answers look like.

Also unexpressed, much of the time, are the ways criteria interact with each other. A selector's sense of what constitutes graphic excellence may change in response to her belief that children raised on color television will not find black and white illustrations appealing. Or, she may believe strongly that children's books must be accurate, while at the same time assuming that too much accuracy in controversial areas would be inappropriate.

My template groups the major criteria in three categories— semantic considerations, having to do with truthfulness, representational adequacy, or a text's relation to the reality it describes; syntagmatic considerations, having to do with literary and graphic excellence, or the text's relation to others of its kind; and pragmatic considerations, having to do with usefulness and appeal, or the text's relation to readers. I use these terms for convenience, to clarify relations among the numerous and often overlapping selection criteria listed in children's literature textbooks. Conflicts can occur both within and across categories.

Semantic criteria: Officially, most youth librarians are taught to value accuracy first in the selection of nonfiction. Arbuthnot (1947) put historic authenticity at the head of her standards for biography, and it has remained there since. Children's book author Bruce McMillan (1993), calling for more rigorous elimination of error by authors, publishers, and reviewers, described the outrage of elementary school children on discovering a sea lion misidentified as a seal in a critically esteemed book on zoos. The children assumed that a book of nonfiction should be trustworthy, and they wrote, "it is TERRIBLE that children all over the nation are reading information that is not true." Most of us would automatically agree.

Accuracy, however, is only one of several semantic criteria. Others that fall naturally into this group include authenticity, currency, and objectivity. Several familiar standards are really surrogates for accuracy: the author's qualifications, the publisher's reputation, and the copyright date, for instance, are useful chiefly insofar as they help estimate the reliability and currency of an item to be selected. Other semantic criteria, like fairness and support for critical thinking, supplement accuracy and authenticity.

We might expect that semantic criteria would not change. Truth is truth, and historical facts are set. Yet, social changes do influence our interpretations. To adopt fairness and balance (or "avoidance of stereotypes" and "positive images of cultural diversity") as criteria for biographies is to recognize that a set of accurate facts may not tell the whole truth; it suggests that truth may be found at the intersection of multiple viewpoints, and may be intersubjective rather than completely objective. This approach is compatible with the civil rights and women's movements, making audible the voices of groups once excluded from full participation in American society. Similarly, to apply standards like "support of critical thinking" or "encouragement of further inquiry" is to assume that the truth is dynamic rather than static, and that young readers should be encouraged to explore it rather than to learn it by rote. This is consistent with constructivist theories of learning.

These criteria have philosophical implications. As modern and postmodern historians debate whether the past can be known, philosophers question whether any external reality can be known. To the commonsense idea that there is an objective world out there, possible to discover and identical for all of us, critics have opposed a model of reality as something relative, something constructed by witnesses whose view depends on where they are situated. And of course, semantic choices have political implications as well. To look at historical facts from the viewpoint of the colonized or the enslaved may undermine a child's secure identification with the interests of a dominant class; and to consider historical fact as something that has been constructed may predispose a child to question both precedent and the status quo.

None of this makes it easy for nonspecialists to assess the accuracy, authenticity, fairness, and balance of individual books. I could not compare the eighty-nine juvenile biographies in these samples to the historical realities they report. As a poor substitute, I read adult biographies of the subjects; in some cases I also found and read primary sources (published diaries and collected letters). This gave me at least some sense of the general reliability of the children's books—and of how juvenile biographers had handled the sources available to them.

Syntagmatic criteria: A second group of criteria has to do with the relationship or comparison between a book and others of its type: Is the book well written? Is it beautifully illustrated? Is it well organized? We do not answer these questions in a vacuum, but in a familiar context, measuring excellence against what we already know. I have called these "syntagmatic" criteria. Atkinson (1984, 111) described as syntagmatic the relationship between elements in a citation, where each element influences the way other elements are read, or, as he put it, "any element necessarily functions as the intertext of its neighbors." *Webster's Third New International Dictionary* defines "syntagm" as "a systematic collection of writings" (Gove 1961), and thinking of the biography collection as a systematic whole may help as we consider the real effect of these stylistic criteria. A single excellent book has an impact; it compels our attention. The effects of the collection as an "intertext" may be harder to observe, but the books we have read shape our habitual expectations and guide our attention in future reading.

Between the 1940s and the 1990s, both the graphics and the rhetoric of juvenile nonfiction changed. At mid-century, the typical well-organized biography was a single, continuous narrative. It was fictionalized, with invented conversations and episodes, and its style was novelistic, borrowing many of the devices that made fiction so readable. It did not have many illustrations. Good book design meant adequate margins and attractive, legible typefaces. The book as an object was modest, not diverting attention from the story. A fluent reader was likely to become immersed, experiencing a subject's "life" from within.

By the 1990s, full-color illustrations were no longer rare, and the varied illustration and design of books had become major factors in evaluation. Photographs, reproductions, maps, and charts created an impression of authenticity. Most biographies were still organized as sequential narratives, but the style was journalistic, establishing a claim to credibility by the inclusion of specific, verifiable facts—exact dates, exact quantities of men or ships—and sometimes narrative was supplementary, enlivening and supporting the exposition. Content was increasingly distributed among main text, captions, and sidebars, creating what Dresang (1999) has called "handheld hypertext." Indices became more important as the organization and design of books suggested that they were intended, not to be read straight through, but to be mined for relevant information.

Changes in book design are more than cosmetic; they affect the ways readers approach books and take meaning from them. The sustained narratives of earlier decades invited reader immersion and implied that a successful life, like a good story, was a unified whole. More recent books, presenting a colorful smorgasbord of anecdotes, quotations, and boxed sidelights, encourage readers to take a more critical stance as they integrate the fragmented aspects of the biographees' characters and experiences for themselves. Like the gradual evolution in semantic criteria, these changes in syntagmatic criteria have philosophical and political implications. Books with distributed texts may be better suited to constructivist than rote learning, and biographies that rely on short factual sections rather than continuous narratives support a different approach to understanding and developing identity.

Pragmatic criteria: Criteria such as curriculum relevance, age appropriateness, and support of character development are more directly concerned with the relationship between the book and its users. These are the most overtly political considerations, and in controversies over what should be taught to children, and how, pragmatic criteria trump the rest. When the books Mary and I read blurred the facts of Tudor history, it was in service of pragmatic criteria. By tactfully withholding some information, or sometimes even by substituting discreet fictions for awkward facts, biographers contrived to preserve our innocence and inspire us to virtue. The truth they told us was not allowed to interfere with the purposes for which it was told.

This conflict between facts and morals, veiled by apparent consensus in the 1950s, has become louder in recent decades. The civil rights movement of the 1960s was rapidly followed by a newly energized women's movement, and advocates for African Americans, women, and other marginalized groups analyzed the omissions and distortions of their stories in children's literature and called for redress. Inclusiveness, multiculturalism, and gender equity all seemed like self-evidently good ideas to liberal librarians, but resistance was signaled by an upswing in complaints about library materials. Between 1990 and 2000, the American Library Association's Office for Intellectual Freedom recorded 6,364 book challenges. The most frequent objections had to do with sexuality, offensive language, and inappropriateness to age groups, but other reasons for challenge included violence, racism, the promotion of occultism or religious viewpoints, or "anti-family" content (American Library Association 2005). By the 1990s, when a set of National History Standards developed with support from both the Department of Education and the National Endowment for the Humanities was rejected by Bill Clinton, Bob Dole, and ninety-nine members of the U.S. Senate, the "Culture Wars" were fully joined, and children's books were deployed on either side (Nash, Crabtree, and Dunn 1997).

In such controversies, the central issue is pragmatic: what is the purpose of our children's education? Morshead (1995) roots curriculum theory in ethics. Whether a curriculum is classical or vocational, progressive or performance based, he says—and whether or not its proponents are fully conscious of their own philosophical assumptions—it can only flourish in the context of a prevailing ideology. Thus he claims that the vocational curriculum depends on acceptance of both capitalism and utilitarian ethics, and that the progressive curriculum, critical of both, declined as fear of Soviet collectivism increased.

The supply of juvenile biographies is influenced by many of the same forces that shape school curricula. Definitions of "truth" or "accuracy" are affected by our intuitions of their pragmatic effects; we understand, tacitly, that the purpose of education must help determine whose stories are to be told, and how. Acceptance of multicultural ideals, for instance, may extend our list of semantic criteria to include "fairness" as well as "accuracy." Even without changes to the list of criteria, multiculturalism may be advanced by the influence of recent historical scholarship: the "new" social history lends itself to a greater representation of women, minorities, and ordinary people. In these and other more or less subtle ways, a selector's pragmatic commitment to desirable social outcomes may influence the application of semantic criteria, as perceptions of a book's historical accuracy are filtered through hope or fear of its contemporary effects.

Chapters 5 and 6: Emergent Themes

Within each of the three categories, my template had a number of sub-headings. Among the semantic considerations, for instance, I wrote notes on each book's accuracy (how did it compare to adult biographies of the same subjects?), but also fairness and balance (how did the writer treat the subject's character, choices, and relationships with family, friends, and work?). My notes on pragmatic considerations included the book's own purpose (sometimes explicitly stated in a series note, some-times implicit in organization and focus), but also its handling of purposes commonly advocated for the genre (introducing history, or pro-viding inspirational role models).

One major subheading concerned the treatment of diversity issues, which of course changed dramatically. In 1946, African Americans appeared as minor characters in some of the fictionalized biographies; their dialect added local color, and their sad plight allowed beneficent heroines to show generosity. By 1996, such insensitive portrayals would have been unthinkable, and strong African American women were the subjects of a dozen biographies. It made sense to me to treat this impor-tant material in a separate chapter. But the only subject who appeared in all three sample years was a Native American, Pocahontas. Her treat-ment in those three years became the basis for chapter 5.

My original headings seemed comprehensive, but when I began to read, I quickly discovered a cluster of others. Unexpectedly important in all the 1946 and 1971 books, and most of the 1996 books, were clothing and appearances. Only a little less salient were the women's attitudes toward privacy or publicity. From reclusive Emily Dickinson, dressed in white and hiding her poetry away in drawers, to twentieth-century divas, glittering in front of the microphone and hiding their private selves behind media-friendly personae, comments about clothes and privacy were often related to women's roles in their communities.

These three themes—appearances, the private versus the public, and embeddedness in or isolation from community—teased at me until they became the basis for my concluding chapter. They are integral to the way we construct and experience identity, and much of what writers have said about them is accurate and well documented: George Eliot's experience of being ugly, and Emmeline Pankhurst's confidence in her own beauty, surely affected their lives and the ways in which they fit their environments. Yet, because questions of appearances, privacy, and community have not attracted the same level of attention we give to diversity issues in children's books, their handling may be subject to more subtle generic fashions; and it is possible that they exert subtle influences on readers in turn. In the end, a biography clothes the truth, concealing a bit here, revealing a bit there, and creating an aesthetic impression that does more or less justice to the character that wears it.

References

Altick, Richard D. 1965. *Lives and letters: A history of literary biography in England and America.* New York: Knopf.

American Library Association. Office for Intellectual Freedom. 2005. Challenged and banned books. www.ala.org/ala/oif/bannedbooksweek/challengedbanned/challengedbanned.htm#backgroundinformation.

Arbuthnot, May Hill. 1947. Chapter 17, Biography. In *Children and books*: 470-501. Chicago: Scott, Foresman.

Atkinson, Ross. 1984. The citation as intertext: Toward a theory of the selection process. *Library Resources and Technical Services* 28: 109-119.

Bateson, Mary Catherine. 1990. *Composing a life.* New York: Plume.

Bishop, Kay, and Phyllis Van Orden. 1998. Reviewing children's books: A content analysis. *Library Quarterly* 68 (2): 145-182.

Book Review Media. 1972. In *The Bowker Annual of Library & Book Trade Information 1972*, 17th ed., ed. Janice Johnson and Frank L. Schick. New York: R. R. Bowker.

Calcott, Lady. 1884. *Little Arthur's history of England.* New York: Thomas Y. Crowell.

Cantor, Norman F. 1991. *Inventing the Middle Ages.* New York: William Morrow.

Carlyle, Thomas. 1895. *On heroes, hero-worship and the heroic in history.* New York: Scribner.

Cloud, Dana L. 1996. Hegemony or concordance? The rhetoric of tokenism in "Oprah" Winfrey's rags-to-riches biography. *Critical Studies in Mass Communication* 13: 115-137.

Codell, Julie F. 2000. Victorian artists' family biographies: Domestic authority, the marketplace, and the artist's body. In *Biographical passages: Essays in Victorian and modernist biography*, ed. Joe Law and Linda K. Hughes. Columbia: University of Missouri Press.

Dresang, Eliza T. 1999. *Radical change: Books for youth in a digital age.* New York: H. W. Wilson.

Eaton, Anne Thaxter. 1940. Chapter 11, Men and manners of the past. In *Reading with children*, 220-226. New York: Viking.

Eaton, Jeanette. 1929. *A daughter of the Seine: The life of Madame Roland.* New York: Harper & Brothers.

Eaton, Jeanette. 1942. A biographer's perilous joy. *The Horn Book Magazine* 18 (March/April): 120-125.

Evans, G. Edward. 1995. *Developing library and information center collections.* Englewood, CO: Libraries Unlimited.

Fitzpatrick, Ellen. 2002. *History's memory: Writing America's past, 1880-1980.* Cambridge, MA: Harvard University Press.

Foster, Genevieve. 1941. *George Washington's world.* New York: Scribner.

Gardner, Susan. 1991. My first rhetoric of domination: The Columbian encounter in children's biographies. *Children's Literature in Education* 22: 275-290.

Giblin, James Cross. 1987. A publisher's perspective. *The Horn Book Magazine* 63 (January/February): 104-107.

Giblin, James Cross. 1997. Writing biographies for young people. *The Writer* 110 (April): 7-9.

Gove, Philip Babcock, Ed. 1961. *Webster's third new international dictionary of the English language, unabridged.* Springfield, MA: G. & C. Merriam.

Heilbrun, Carolyn. 1988. *Writing a woman's life.* New York: Ballantine.

Hunt, Peter. 1991. *Criticism, theory, and children's literature.* Cambridge, MA: Blackwell.

Klatt, Beverly. 1992. Abraham Lincoln: Deified martyr, flesh and blood hero, and a man with warts. *Children's Literature in Education* 23: 119-129.

Loewen, James W. 1995. *Lies my teacher told me: Everything your American history textbook got wrong.* New York: New Press.

McMillan, Bruce. 1993. Accuracy in books for young readers: From first to last check. *The New Advocate* 6 (2): 97-104.

Mays, Pamela. 1974. *Why teach history?* London: University of London Press.

Meltzer, Milton. 1994. *Nonfiction for the classroom: Milton Meltzer on writing, history, and social responsibility.* Ed. E. Wendy Saul. New York: Teachers College Press.

Morshead, Richard W. 1995. *Patterns of educational practice: Theories of curriculum.* Ann Arbor, MI: Pierian Press.

Nadel, I. B. 1984. *Biography: Fiction, fact, and form.* New York: St. Martin's Press.

Nash, Gary B., Charlotte Crabtree, and Ross E. Dunn. 1997. *History on trial: Culture wars and the teaching of the past.* New York: Knopf.

Nesbitt, Elizabeth. 1953. Events and people: History and biography [1820-1920]. In *A critical history of children's literature*, ed. Cornelia Meigs, 392-398. New York: Macmillan.

Rosen, Ruth. 2000. *The world split open: How the modern women's movement changed America.* New York: Viking.

Sadker, Myra, and David Sadker. 1994. *Failing at fairness: How America's schools cheat girls*. New York: Scribner.

Schuman, Patricia. 1973. Concerned criticism or casual cop-outs? In *Issues in children's book selection: A* School Library Journal/Library Journal *anthology*, 191-197. New York: R. R. Bowker Company.

Shavit, Zohar. 1986. *The poetics of children's literature*. Athens: University of Georgia Press.

Shortland, Michael, and Richard Yeo, eds. 1996. Introduction. In *Telling lives in science: Essays on scientific biography*, 1-44. Cambridge: Cambridge University Press.

Sommers, Christina Hoff. 1995. *Who stole feminism? How women have betrayed women*. New York: Touchstone/ Simon & Schuster.

Sutherland, Zena. 1967. Current reviewing of children's books. In *A critical approach to children's literature*, 110-118. Chicago: University of Chicago Press.

Thomson, Peggy. 1995. *Katie Henio: Navajo sheepherder*. New York: Cobblehill Books/Dutton.

Ulrich, Laurel Thatcher. 1991. *A midwife's tale: The life of Martha Ballard, based on her diary, 1785-1812*. New York: Vintage Books.

Van Orden, Phyllis. 1978. Promotion, review, and examination of materials. *School Media Quarterly* 6, 120-122, 127-132.

Vicinus, Martha. 1990. What makes a heroine? Girls' biographies of Florence Nightingale. In *Florence Nightingale and her era: A collection of new scholarship*, ed. Vern Bullough, Bonnie Bullough, and Marietta P. Stanton, 90-106. New York: Garland.

Wagner-Martin, Linda. 1994. *Telling women's lives: The new biography*. New Brunswick, NJ: Rutgers University Press.

Weinberg, Steve. 1992. *Telling the untold story: How investigative reporters are changing the craft of biography*. Columbia: University of Missouri Press.

Witucke, Virginia. 1985. Trends in juvenile biography: Five years later. *Top of the News* 42, 1 (Fall): 45-53.

Zinsser, William. 1986. *Extraordinary lives: The art and craft of American biography*. New York: American Heritage.

Chapter 1

Rediscovering Elizabeth

Most biographers agree that Elizabeth Tudor's hair was red or red-gold, although Vance (1954) gave her a "mop of black curls." They disagree wildly about her eyes—Trease (1953) said they were "striking blue," Linington (1961) said "pale hazel-green," and Hanff (1969) said "brown." Her complexion was described as "clear olive" or "milk-white," and after her bout with smallpox either pitted or unscarred—but in any case masked by cosmetics that contained poisonous lead. Such descriptions, like many portraits painted during her lifetime, hardly seem to represent the same woman. She apparently did not like to sit for her likeness, but "well understood the usefulness of portraits in creating [her] image," and attempted to control their quality by having them copied from approved patterns (Hibbert 1991, 102).

About her character there is even more disagreement. The outward facts of her life are better known than those of almost any woman before her, but she kept her inner life private. Famously unwilling to "make windows into men's hearts and secret thoughts," she certainly allowed few into her own, and interpretations of her motives vary.

The opacity of her character has ensured that her biographies vary even more than her portraits. For children's writers, especially, freedom of interpretation has been essential, as Elizabeth's personality was in many ways ill-adapted to the conventions of juvenile biography. Biographical subjects are expected to be role models for young readers, but absolute monarch was a role to which middle-class girls could not aspire. The things Elizabeth did to keep not only her power but her life were things nice girls could not be encouraged to do, like delaying, equivocating, playing kings and councilors off against each other, throwing temper tantrums, and, when all else failed, ordering the executions of dangerous enemies. In the 1950s juvenile biographies tended to promote reader identification with subject by novelistic techniques, but Elizabeth was a subject who called for distancing—historically important, but not safe to identify with. It may be helpful here to summarize her life, with emphasis on details that required sensitive handling in children's books.

Hardly a Model Life

She was controversial from birth, and in general the controversies centered around the men in her life, starting with her father. Henry VIII had withdrawn England from allegiance to the Catholic Church so that he could marry Elizabeth's mother, Anne Boleyn. Catholics did not recognize the annulment of his marriage to Catherine of Aragon, and considered that Elizabeth (the Little Whore, child of the Great Whore) had no legitimate rights in the royal succession. To be a Catholic, Elizabeth would have had to confess herself a bastard; so she was necessarily Protestant, and Protestants, at home and abroad, expected her support. Before she was even born, Henry had embroiled her in Reformation politics, making her the enemy of her sister Mary and giving a religious justification to any Catholic who might claim her throne.

Henry had Anne beheaded, on the pretext that she had taken lovers, before Elizabeth was three. There were four stepmothers: Jane Seymour, who died after the birth of Edward; Anne of Cleves, quickly divorced for ugliness and kept on as a kind of royal sister; Katherine Howard, beheaded for infidelity, like her cousin Anne; and Katherine Parr, reputedly the most motherly to Henry's children, who survived him but died after bearing a child to Thomas Seymour. Elizabeth (like most royal children) spent most of her time in manor houses away from court, where she may have seen happier marriages, but never a royal marriage that was easy on a queen. As a child of eight, she reportedly announced that she would never marry, and later her sister's alliance with Philip of Spain may have sealed her intention. A husband expected to rule his wife, and Elizabeth preferred to rule in her own right.

After Henry's death, Katherine kept Elizabeth in her household and married Thomas Seymour. Uncle to the new king and brother to the Lord Protector, Seymour had ambitions of his own and a way with women. While Elizabeth was a ward in his house, he treated her with suggestive familiarity, slapping her buttocks and bursting into her chamber to tickle her in bed. On at least one occasion, Katherine joined the tickling; on another, she held Elizabeth while Seymour shredded her gown with scissors. Eventually, however, she called a halt to the game. Elizabeth was then fourteen. Katherine sent her away with a warning about the dangers of scandal, and died of puerperal fever before they could be reunited. Seymour may have sexually abused Elizabeth (Starkey 2000); rumors then and since have hinted that she bore his child. As usual with Elizabeth, there is no proof.

Seymour, meanwhile, was angling for influence over three royal children: Elizabeth; his ward Jane Grey, whom he hoped to marry to his nephew, King Edward; and the young king himself, whom he attempted to abduct. He was sent to the Tower and executed for treason. Also jailed were Elizabeth's governess, Kat Ashley, and her cofferer, Thomas Parry, who were suspected of collusion in Seymour's plot to marry Elizabeth without permission of King or Council. Elizabeth herself was closely questioned. She kept her poise, gave away nothing, and went on the offensive with a barrage of letters to Somerset, the Lord Protector. Her reputation had suffered; gossips held that Seymour had got her with child. She demanded that Somerset clear her name by proclamation, by allowing her to show herself at court, and by reinstating her servants lest it should be thought that they had indeed taken part in a conspiracy for which she was pardoned only because of her youth (Hibbert 1991). At fourteen, she was no longer a protected child, but a householder assuming responsibility for her dependents. Keeping a low profile and adopting chaste Puritan dress, Elizabeth survived her brother's Protestant reign.

In those days, a country's religion was the religion of its monarch. Mary, succeeding Edward, was determined to restore England to the Catholic fold, and negotiated a marriage with her cousin Philip of Spain. English Protestants objected. Before the marriage could take place, Sir Thomas Wyatt led a rebellion in Elizabeth's name. Although there was no proof that she approved the uprising, Elizabeth was again suspected of treason and this time confined to the Tower. Ironically, it was Philip who protected her from harsher punishment for the Wyatt uprising and for later plots, in which her involvement was clearer (Starkey 2000). With Mary childless, the alternative heir would have been Mary Stuart, Queen of Scots, who would have tipped the balance of international power to her French in-laws, against Spain.

When Elizabeth finally ascended the throne, Catholics plotted on behalf of Mary Stuart much as Protestants had conspired on her behalf. The situation became more dangerous when Mary fled Scotland and begged sanctuary in England; Elizabeth imprisoned her for nearly twenty years before reluctantly ordering her execution. Elizabeth disliked extremes and considered bloodshed wasteful. She was often asked to support religious warfare, aiding Dutch Protestants in their rebellion against Philip of Spain and Huguenots against the Catholic Guise faction in France; but she preferred diplomacy whenever possible.

One of her favorite diplomatic maneuvers was the marriage negotiation. It was taken for granted that she would marry; to be a woman in Renaissance Europe was to be considered weak and in need of male protection. Moreover, her councilors were determined that Elizabeth should marry quickly to ensure a Protestant succession. The question seemed to be not whether she would marry, but whom—and as one perspicacious councilor told the Spanish ambassador, there was really "no one she could marry outside the kingdom or within it" (Starkey 2000, 314). Marriage to a subject would have risked civil war; marriage to a foreign prince, making England a tool of some other power, would have alienated her people. Dangling the possibility of marriage was a good way to manipulate foreign princes, however, as it gave them the hope of controlling England without the expense of invasion. Elizabeth was able to draw out such negotiations until she was well into her forties, breaking them off as needed with the excuse of religious incompatibility. The last French prince to woo her, the Duc d'Alençon, was short, pockmarked, and half her age. She called him her Frog, and sometimes appeared quite fond of him; but it was also said she danced for joy when he finally left her.

Meanwhile, Elizabeth ruled as monarch in her own right, taking an active and informed interest in state affairs (to the occasional annoyance of strong-minded councilors like Sir William Cecil and Sir Francis Walsingham) and flirting with courtiers (to the scandalized pleasure of half Europe). She was in love, people said, with Sir Robert Dudley, and when his invalid wife fell down a flight of stairs to her death, people said she'd been pushed. Elizabeth never married Dudley. She made him Earl of Leicester and proposed him as a suitable match for her cousin Mary, Queen of Scots, but went into a snit when he married somebody else. He died in 1588. She kept his last letter in a coffer by her bedside, but continued to flirt. Her last great flirtation was with Dudley's stepson Robert Devereux, Earl of Essex, more than thirty years her junior. Like Seymour, Essex was handsome, rash, self-serving, and treacherous.

After he tried to rouse London for a coup against her administration, Elizabeth ordered his execution in 1601. She was still believed to be grieving for him when she died in 1603.

Juvenile Biographies: Precedents, 1852-1940

Elizabeth's life violated the norms for children's books in the 1950s. It was shaped by the passionate convictions and hostilities of Catholics and Protestants; children in the 1950s were told that nice people did not discuss religion in public, for fear of controversy. Elizabeth's life began in a murderously dysfunctional family; from Dick and Jane up, children in the 1950s were given books that presented the family as a safe, pleasant sanctuary. As a young teen, Elizabeth was subjected to sexual harassment and possibly molestation by her guardian; if such things happened in the 1950s, they were unmentionable. And while things done to her as a child could hardly be mentioned in polite children's books, things she herself did when she had the power were even more problematic. Her flirtations with d'Alençon and Essex violated the expectation that women will always be younger and less powerful than men in a relationship. The executions of Mary Stuart, Essex, and others—however reluctantly Elizabeth authorized them—violated the expectation that women should be more merciful than men, putting tender feeling before political necessity. Perhaps worst of all was her creative understanding of political necessity. She did not leave politics to the men, but practiced statecraft with unforgivable competence.

Of course, all this violated the norms for women in her own time and the intervening centuries, too. Popular and scholarly opinion on her has always been partisan, and some of her detractors seem to have been genuinely revolted by her unwomanly behavior; others, opposing her on different grounds, may simply have used gender stereotypes as convenient weapons against her. In any event, there is a long tradition of hostile portrayals. In the 1790s, a teen-aged Jane Austen railed against "that pest of society, Elizabeth . . . the destroyer of all comfort, the deceitful Betrayer of trust reposed in her, & the Murderess of her Cousin" (Austen 1993). Froude attributed "all the achievements of her reign to her advisers and especially to William Cecil" (Ridley 1987), and Strachey (1928) accused her of succeeding "by virtue of all the qualities which every hero should be without—dissimulation, pliability, indecision, procrastination, parsimony":

Only a woman could have shuffled so shamelessly, only a woman
could have abandoned with such unscrupulous completeness the last
shreds not only of consistency, but of dignity, honour, and common
decency, in order to escape the appalling necessity of having, really
and truly, to make up her mind.

Erickson (1983) showed a pathetically vain and shrewish Elizabeth,
erupting in unreasonable anger at the ladies of her court.

Biographers, like historians, deal in narrative; they must create
believable stories, explaining and connecting details and producing the
illusion of completeness. It is widely agreed that historical discourse
should be accurate in reporting individual facts and their logical connections, but Hayden White argues that it must go beyond accuracy,
transforming events into "intimations of patterns of meaning that any
literal representation of them as facts could never produce." Historical
narrative is allegorical; it "endows sets of real events with the kinds of
meaning found otherwise only in myth and literature" (White 1987, 45).
Going beyond the mere chronicle of events as they occurred, a historian
selects those that are important and arranges them to show how they
affect each other. To impose this kind of orderly plot requires some
principle or theory to guide the selection and arrangement. Biographers
for adults may have pragmatic objectives in their shaping of plot;
White's example is a passage from Marx. Biographers for children almost certainly have pragmatic objectives, as they consider how their
communication of historical events will influence young minds.

Elizabeth's life provided more than one good plot. A friendly biographer could make a Cinderella story of her girlhood: the unwanted
daughter who should have been a son survived childhood dangers and
captivated the English. Starkey (2000) states that few biographers have
focused on Elizabeth's early years, but juvenile biographers have routinely done so, ending their books with her triumphant accession to the
throne. Others have stressed the public accomplishments of her reign,
framing stories of robust nationalism and adventure: fiercely devoted to
her people, the queen refused to marry but ruled wisely, supporting
explorers, privateers, and Protestant artisans who fled Catholic rule.
Her reign culminated with the glorious defeat of the Spanish Armada in
1588, and in the last chapter there was room to mention Spenser, Marlowe, and Shakespeare. By emphasizing more personal considerations,
other "friendly" biographers have produced tales of romantic sacrifice
and renunciation, or psychological portraits of a traumatized child.

An unfriendly biographer could dwell on Elizabeth's faults and
gloat on the griefs of her old age. Agnes Strickland, a nineteenth-

century chronicler of English queens who was especially partial to Mary, Queen of Scots (Lee 1922), saw Elizabeth as a monster combining the worst of both sexes. Elizabeth's "animosity" toward Mary was "sustained by a sorry feminine spite and vanity," but at the same time, Elizabeth was a "masculine and powerful rival":

> During the reign of Mary, her whole life was one ceaseless peril and adversity. These harsh trials, however, which are generally so beneficial and mollifying to the heart, made no permanent impression on the unfeminine mind of the energetic princess; and when, in her turn, she obtained the power of persecuting and oppressing, she manifested to another Mary a far greater extent of hate and cruelty than she herself had ever experienced (Strickland 1852, 272).

Satirically minimizing Mary Stuart's provocations (she had been "weak enough to commit the . . . offence of assuming the arms of England, and quartering them upon all her equipages and liveries"), Strickland explained Elizabeth's actions in personal terms, and encouraged readers to judge them on moral grounds.

Biography was a moral genre; and children's histories, written as series of linked biographical sketches, could be just as moral. Calcott wrote with a strong Protestant bias, believing that to "teach the love of our own country is almost a religious duty" (Calcott 1884, viii). Nevertheless, in spite of Mary's "wicked" plotting to make "the English all Papists again," Calcott thought her execution wrong: "This is a very bad thing: and I cannot make any excuse for Elizabeth" (176). Both Strickland and Calcott seemed to feel that Elizabeth, as a woman, should have had higher standards; she should have put mercy and compassion before political considerations.

Strickland communicated her moral stance most strongly through emplotment. She proportioned her text to scant Elizabeth's youth and the successes of her reign, lingering instead over the mortification of her vanity in old age: her grief for Essex, her weeping and insomnia, the filing of her coronation ring from her swollen finger, and even a malicious account of how her ladies-in-waiting mocked her by painting her nose red. The narrative suggested a cautionary tale, in which a queen's cruelty was justly punished by the greater cruelty of time.

The cautionary tale was a popular genre in the nineteenth century, and children's writers exploited its didactic strategies to ensure that young readers would draw the proper conclusions from imperfect examples. Thus E. S. Brooks (1891, iii), in a collection of biographical sketches of famous women and girls "who by their actions and endeavors proved themselves the equal of the men of their time in valor, shrewdness, and ability," twisted his story of the fifteen-year-old Elizabeth to accommodate a lesson in ladylike behavior. His apparent feminism was of its times, sentimental about "the real girl-nature, that has ever been impulsive, trusting, tender, and true."

He introduced Elizabeth as a girl with a "heedless and impetuous" expression, who bragged about outriding Admiral Seymour and, "with a sly and sudden push of her dainty foot," knocked over her friend Dudley when he attempted to help her dismount. This fictional princess was rude, and young readers should not emulate her poor behavior:

> Self-willed and thoughtless—even rude and hoydenish—we may think her in these days of gentler manners and more guarded speech. But those were less refined and cultured times than these in which we live. . . (Brooks 1891, 178).

Brooks had to depend on overt moralizing to make his point; it was not inherent in his plot, where Elizabeth faced dangers arising, not from her rudeness, but from the suspicion that she was involved in Seymour's treason against her brother. On the other hand, fictionalizing Elizabeth's faults and placing them in the context of her early life enabled him to imply that she overcame them: "through it all, the young princess grew still more firm of will, more self-reliant, wise, and strong, developing all those peculiar qualities that helped make her England's greatest queen, and one of the most wonderful women in history" (190). His emphasis was thus on character, which he defined with sweeping confidence, rearranging events to support his interpretation. This kind of treatment may have appealed to a writer more concerned with the moral than with the historical instruction of the young, but it could make for oversimplified and belittling sketches.

Stereotyped portrayals of Elizabeth as a bossy, vain old spinster— often meant to be jocular—were to persist through the twentieth century. Examples can be found in *Kings & Things* (Marshall 1937), *Van Loon's Lives* (Van Loon 1942), and *The Terrible Tudors* (Deary and Tonge 1993). Juvenile biography as it developed in the twentieth century, however, has been strongly biased toward positive images of its subjects, and recent children's writers have usually relied on the work of more sympathetic historians. Ridley (1987, xii) noted that J. E. Neale, doyen of Elizabethan historians in the 1950s, portrayed her as an astute stateswoman "whose acts of cruelty must be excused by the period in which she lived, and whose apparent hesitations and vacillations were cunning and brilliant diplomatic manoevres." Ridley himself saw her "as a very religious and conscientious woman, a convinced Protestant, determined to do her duty . . . to God and her people," and "overwhelmed by her sense of responsibility as a Queen, which she did not enjoy. . ." (xii). Levin (1994) analyzed her deft manipulation of feminine images in an age when only men expected to wield power. Drawing on the work of such scholars, recent juvenile biographies credit Elizabeth with political intelligence and genuine love of her people.

Two sympathetic juvenile biographies in the first half of the twentieth century—one by Tappan (1902) and the other by King (1940)—set useful patterns for many that came after. Eve March Tappan, Ph.D., focused on Elizabeth's political achievements. The introduction recognized her flaws but called for balance and a judgment based on public accomplishment: "no one should forget that the little white hand of which she was so vain guided the ship of state with most consummate skill. . . ." Indeed, Tappan's own skill showed to best advantage in her discussion of public life. Her chapters on Elizabeth's childhood were marred by expository conversations among speakers who had to be improbably ignorant at some points and knowledgeable at others, and by a sentimental focus on Elizabeth's innocence and powerlessness as "the little offender," "the anxious child," or "the poor little girl" (Tappan 1902, 39-40). To mitigate the horrors of the Tudor household, Tappan highlighted or invented evidence of forgiveness, reconciliation, and family affection wherever possible: Mary forgave Anne Boleyn, everybody loved Elizabeth, and little Edward, not liking to see his beloved sister cry, interceded with their angry father. Imagined episodes softened the harsher facts of private life.

In her chapters on Elizabeth's reign, however, Tappan used fictionalization to dramatize political issues and to place them in historical context. Elizabeth spoke to Sir John Hawkins, whose trading with the colonies landed him "in trouble" with Spain, with a broad irony signaling her collusion with her privateers—not quite open enough to justify Philip in declaring war, "for no one could expect a pirate to obey his queen. . ." (Tappan 1902, 209-211). Similar encounters with Frobisher and Raleigh illustrated the queen's active and intelligent support of her sailors. Economically and without pedantry, Tappan's imagined conversations between historical figures suggested the variety of Elizabeth's political activities.

At the same time, fictional speakers—courtiers, merchants, sailors, or onlookers at processions—evoked the climate of public opinion within which Elizabeth worked. In frequent vignettes, unnamed citizens commented and speculated about the activities of the great, the queen's feelings for Leicester, the likelihood of war with Spain, or the reasons Elizabeth should or should not order Mary's execution. Combined with direct exposition, such passages explained complex material in a lively way. Tappan was informative about the lives of ordinary Elizabethans, from their homes (made pleasanter by the adoption of chimneys) to their homelessness (as peasants were driven from old farmlands newly devoted to sheep). Like the chorus in a Greek play, her nameless but opinionated citizens created an impression of a vital community involving high and low.

Tappan based her account on thorough research, although she never lumbered her text with footnotes or other scholarly apparatus. She had a fine eye for colorful detail. While their parents were murmuring against Mary's wedding plans:

> the children played a game called "English and Spaniards." Philip was one of the characters in this play, and there was always a pretence of hanging him (Tappan 1902, 85).

Her use of invented conversations to convey a realistic, sophisticated view of Elizabeth's life and times demonstrated that fictionalization need not falsify history; but the invented episodes in her early chapters, softening the unpalatable or creating a gentler example of family life for modern youth, corresponded better to Victorian genre requirements than Elizabethan facts.

By contrast, in 1940 the jacket copy on Marian King's partial biography promised that the author made "no attempt at imaginary conversation or episode. Every remark and every happening in this account of a young girl's strange and exciting life is authentic." Aiming at both authenticity and liveliness, King relied heavily on quotations from letters and other documents by Elizabeth's contemporaries. This, too, was firmly in the tradition—nineteenth-century biographers used documentation, and especially letters, to reveal the personalities and moral characters of their subjects—and indeed Tappan had quoted or paraphrased some of the same sources. A decade after King, Nolan (1951) used some imaginary conversations in her life of Elizabeth for younger readers, but showed which remarks had historical documentation by scrupulously boldfacing the quotation marks.

King's avoidance of imaginary conversation did not extend to interior monologues, however. Tappan had enlisted sympathy for Elizabeth through the conversations of those who loved and admired her, but King invited the reader share Elizabeth's own thoughts:

Perhaps hurried thoughts raced through her mind as she thought of the Tower. Was she to suffer the same fate as her mother, Anne Boleyn, who had been imprisoned in the Tower, to walk later to the scaffold? Was she, Elizabeth, to follow in the footsteps of Lady Jane Grey and others who had been innocent victims of the executioner's ax? No, Mary could not do this! (King 1940, 111-112).

The shift from imagined conversation to imagined inner soliloquy paralleled a shift in emphasis from Elizabeth's public, political maturity to her more private youth; King's narrative covers Elizabeth's life only until her accession to the throne.

Tappan and King's biographies, though they now seem dated, were among the best in their generations. Both were recommended in multiple editions of *Children's Catalog* (overlapping in 1941 and 1946). Both incorporated extensive historical research in coherent, sustained accounts. Both offered positive views of Elizabeth, avoiding Strickland's scathing personal criticisms. Yet they plotted their narratives very differently, leaving sharply contrasted examples for the writers who followed. King's approach, with its interior monologues and focus on Elizabeth's individual development in youth, emphasized her psychology and her relationships to fellow royals and aristocrats. By contrast, Tappan's chapters on her productive maturity gave a more extraverted, public view of her significance to people at all levels of society; Tappan's Elizabeth was a progressive heroine, paving the way for democracy. Since 1950, some children's biographers, like King, have emphasized Elizabeth's private life—her emotions, her family life, and her possible romances—while others, like Tappan, have focused on her public significance and the achievements of her reign. Almost all have shown her as a sympathetic character.

The following discussion is based on books found in an extensive but not exhaustive search for individual juvenile biographies of Elizabeth published for children in the second half of the twentieth century. There were many relevant entries in collective biographies, as well. Of these, I have referred extensively only to Trease (1953), whose chapter on Elizabeth is longer and more thorough than many whole books published since. I deliberately omitted books that were recommended only for grades 9 and higher, and books that were plainly classified as fiction—although the line of demarcation between juvenile fiction and nonfiction in 1950 was less strict than it has since become. *Elizabeth I: Red Rose of the House of Tudor* (Lasky 1999), omitted from this account, is arguably more factual than some earlier books that were categorized as biographies. I did include a few of the social histories, or "life and times" books, that became more common in the 1980s and 1990s.

Juvenile Biographies: 1951–1970

As a subject for juvenile biography in the 1950s, Elizabeth was both inevitable and problematic—inevitable because she was known as one of the greatest women in history and because her namesake ascended to the throne in 1952, and problematic because so many aspects of her life could not be discussed with children. In 1953, a desire to protect the innocence of childhood led the Kansas State Board of Review to withhold approval from *The Moon Is Blue*, a film which included such words as "pregnant," "seduce," "virgin," and "mistress"—words which the board's lawyer argued would not be used "in ordinary conversation with children of high school age" (West 1988, 58-60). A complete biography of Elizabeth could use all of those words, and the relationships they connote are important for an understanding of her story.

Writers leapt to the challenge. The Farjeons (1953) revised their verse list of English monarchs. *Compton's Pictured Encyclopedia* updated its entry on Elizabeth: she was now Elizabeth I (Compton 1953). Nolan, Malkus, Vance, and Winwar all published biographies of her— and Trease a collective biography of English queens—between 1951 and 1954. Nolan and Malkus may have been writing for fluent readers in third or fourth grade, and Winwar and Trease for slightly older children, but there was little differentiation by age level. Fluent reading ability was assumed, and emotional content was not inappropriate for bright elementary school children. In general, the authors of the early 1950s focused on the public side of Elizabeth's life or—if they were more introspective, like Vance—concentrated on her childhood.

A psychological emphasis became more common in the fictionalized biographies of the following decade, when Plaidy (1961) published an account of Elizabeth's childhood and youth, and Linington (1961), Cammiade (1962), Bigland (1965), and Hanff (1969) published full-life biographies. Most relied on the conventions of fiction, from Bigland's relatively minor stage business (pacing, sighing, and caressing jewels) to Hanff's more structural foreshadowings. Cammiade's documentary, with its brevity, objectivity, and double columns punctuated by photographs and reproductions, was a forerunner of more recent practice in children's nonfiction.

Another trend during this decade was toward increased differentiation of audiences for juvenile biography, as children's and young adult markets began to diverge. Linington, Cammiade, Bigland, and Hanff, all writing for slightly older readers than their 1950s predecessors, devoted relatively less attention to Elizabeth's sea dogs and more to her court. Cammiade emphasized public affairs—she even summarized the career of economist Thomas Gresham—but Linington, Bigland, and Hanff directed attention inward, playing up the element of pathos in Elizabeth's sacrifice of romance for patriotic duty.

Naturally, there is far too much material on Elizabeth's life to be contained in any one biography for young readers; much has to be omitted or simplified. Biographers of the 1950s and 1960s used a number of techniques to simplify the story, including euphemism; diverting attention from less acceptable aspects of a story by highlighting more attractive bits; emplotment (for instance, framing Elizabeth's childhood and youth as a rags-to-riches story, ending with her ascension); fictionalization; and explanations of events based on the innate characters rather than political motivations of historical figures. These techniques were all more or less effective in covering gaps left by the omission of facts and issues too troublesome, too morally sensitive, or simply too complex to discuss in children's books. All were at least occasionally used as well to emphasize preferred meanings in the story (such as patriotism or the virtue of self-denial), or to tame Elizabeth's image (accentuating her feminine kindness, vanity, deviousness, or dependence on Cecil and her other councilors while glossing over her courage, assertiveness, and political skill).

Euphemisms and Sir Thomas Seymour

Children's writers in the 1950s generally avoided controversial material. This included religion, an area they were more likely to skirt than their forerunners. Calcott (1884) had given a partisan impression of religious politics in Renaissance Europe, and Edwards (1920) repeated approvingly the old belief that Elizabeth "was Protestant at heart" and would end Mary's "cruel persecutions." In the 1950s, Protestant chauvinism was no longer so open in children's books, and Trease apologized for discussing religious issues:

> It is impossible to write of the sixteenth and seventeenth centuries without stirring tragic memories of religious strife: one can only do

one's best to record events fairly and, at the same time, indicate how they affected people of both sides who were caught up in them and could not see as clearly as can the modern historian with all the facts before him. One tries to hold the balance evenly, and hopes that no present-day reader will see offense to his own faith where none is intended (Trease 1953, 11-12).

Malkus simply did not mention religion at all—an accomplishment that Elizabeth, whose choices in life were always constrained by religious considerations, might have envied.

Children's writers were delicate in their language. Especially reticent about sex, they tended to gloss over Henry VIII's marital history. King (1940) had used the word "disloyalty" as a euphemism for "adultery," and "outcast" for "bastard" or "illegitimate." Plaidy (1961, 32) explained that Katherine Howard had "loved others before the King, so they say"; that ambiguous "before" could be taken to mean "previous to" or "more than." Malkus presented her summary as the child Elizabeth's musing, and left out two wives, two divorces, and two beheadings, while highlighting the child's empathy for her father and appreciation of her stepmothers:

> The Princess Elizabeth . . . thought of her father. Sometimes it must be hard for him to be a king, and lonely, too. Perhaps that was why he had married so often. His first wife had been a Spanish princess. She was the mother of Elizabeth's half sister, Mary. Then the King had married a beautiful girl named Anne Boleyn, who was Elizabeth's mother. Next he had married Lady Jane Seymour, the mother of Elizabeth's little half brother, Edward. Now she was dead, like the others, and lovely Catherine Parr was the Queen (Malkus 1953, 13).

Even more than the women in Henry's life, writers glossed over the men in Elizabeth's. Gossips in her own day speculated about her feelings for Thomas Seymour; Robert Dudley, whom she created the Earl of Leicester; François, the Duc d'Alençon; and Robert Devereux, the Earl of Essex. Juvenile biographers did not fan the flames.

A look at the role of Seymour, whose activities embroiled Elizabeth in a dangerous political crisis, illustrates the problem. Biographers have suggested that Seymour's behavior had profound psychological effects on Elizabeth, and certainly if a modern foster-father treated a teenaged girl that way, it would be considered sexual harassment or abuse. Midcentury children's writers tended to pass it off lightly. Winwar suggested, by adroit juxtaposition and sequencing of "rumors" (some of them true), that there was little substance to the story:

[T]here was an ugly rumor that Sir Thomas . . . probably poisoned his wife. There was another rumor that Sir Thomas might be thinking of marrying Princess Elizabeth to get nearer to the throne. There was still another, that . . . he had tried to gain personal control over the boy King (Winwar 1954, 41).

Trease (1953, 79) called the slashed gown a "joke" and added judiciously, "Fun and games of this type . . . may have been quite innocent, but they caused a great deal of gossip." Vance (1954, 86) had Seymour tear Elizabeth's sleeve in a "frolic"; Plaidy (1961, 73) summed it all up as "too much romping." Cammiade (1962, 9) blamed Seymour for spoiling "what might have been a very happy arrangement by behaving with complete lack of dignity and common-sense."

These euphemisms veiled the sexual aspects of Elizabeth's experience. At the same time, minor elisions and inaccuracies in some accounts concealed the strength of her political response. Some mid-century biographers emphasized this as an early insight into Elizabeth's character: she argued clearly and forcefully, with a fierce sense of royal prerogative, and Cammiade (1962, 11) noted that her political baptism by fire must have "left a deep mark." Bigland (1965) stressed Elizabeth's loyalty, shown in her readiness to protect her servants, and Trease (1953, 80) pointed to her "controlling caution," the cool-headed political astuteness that checked her warm-blooded flirtatiousness. But other writers elided over her courage and assertiveness, as if they were shameful traits. Nolan (1951, 10), in a misleading bit of fictionalization, stated that when her beloved governess was dismissed from her service, "Elizabeth did not complain. She knew that Edward was only a boy, and a sick one. . . ." This compliant girl, making sympathetic excuses for the injustice done to her, sounds more like a model of 1950s femininity than the historical Elizabeth.

Highlighting the Achievements of Men

The lives of women and girls in the 1950s and 1960s were still supposed to be private, rather than public, and it was their job to be sympathetic. They might be high achievers, but they typically deferred to men and boys. Elizabeth did not defer. Several writers, however, placed her political accomplishments in the background, along with her romantic interests, and highlighted instead either her reliance on councilors or the activities of Drake, Raleigh, and others away from court.

Most 1950s biographers focused on the sailors. Perhaps Elizabeth's work at court did not make a good enough story for children; her surroundings glittered, but the drafting of laws, negotiation of treaties, and the management of Parliament were not so exciting as naval combat. Worse, court politics could not be made fully comprehensible without reference to Elizabeth's flirtations. It was easier to deflect attention from court life, and to focus instead on the more wholesome outdoor activities of men like Hawkins, Drake, Frobisher, and Raleigh—the famous slave traders, privateers, explorers, and promoters who made England a sea power.

Winwar's *Queen Elizabeth and the Spanish Armada* was in many ways typical. Scrupulously factual, Winwar sketched important religious, political, and cultural developments in an understandable context. But she minimized the importance of Dudley, and never mentioned d'Alençon or Essex at all. After devoting the first half of the book to Elizabeth's youth, Winwar allowed Francis Drake to upstage her in the second half: a full chapter described his piratical voyage around the world, and he figured prominently in three chapters on the Armada. This material was traditional, as were the proportions Winwar gave it. It may have been supposed to appeal to boys, and the triumphalist saga of war with Spain fit the nationalistic temper of the Cold War era. Elizabeth herself, however, was absent from a large section of her life; reading it, a young girl in the 1950s could imagine her as a kind of glamorous cheerleader for English naval adventurers.

In the 1960s, biographers writing for an implied audience of adolescent girls were more likely to set most of their narratives at court, and consequently to say more about courtiers. Elizabeth's first and best known councilor was Sir William Cecil, later Lord Burghley, who served her from 1558 until his death in 1598. Many early twentieth-century historians credited him more than the queen for the success of her reign; with sound authority, young people's biographies in the 1960s emphasized her feminine dependence on his wisdom. Linington (1961) imagined Cecil meeting Elizabeth furtively at Edward's court, advising her patience, discretion, and rejection of foreign marriages, and following up later with secret messages in times of danger. Hanff (1969) said that sending Essex to Ireland in 1599 "was the kind of mistake William Cecil would have kept Elizabeth from making."

Bigland (1965), who portrayed Elizabeth as nervous, temperamental, and high-strung, appeared to sympathize with the problems Cecil and other councilors faced in managing her: "Cecil had the utmost difficulty in making her see things in their right proportions" (84). On the one hand, Bigland valorized Elizabeth's strength and commitment, delighting in the way "this imperious young woman" confounded her Lords of the Council by showing them "that she knew a great deal more about the nation's affairs than they did themselves" (49-50). On the other hand, she described how Elizabeth's "meddlesome ways irritated Walsingham," who told Cecil "how much simpler" it would be if Elizabeth left intelligence operations "to those best capable of understanding them, as other Princes did" (101). By emphasizing the role of advisors, Bigland made Elizabeth seem more feminine—and perhaps less responsible for any unpalatable exercise of power during her reign.

Framing: The Innocence of Youth

Another way to avoid discussing Elizabeth's use of power was to write a partial biography. Like a carefully cropped picture, a selected episode or life passage can stand as an aesthetically pleasing whole, as Strachey demonstrated in his disquieting examination of her last years, *Elizabeth and Essex* (1928). Writers for the young naturally focus on Elizabeth's youth, avoiding discussion of the moral ambiguities and equivocal choices of her adult life. To wield and maintain power, Elizabeth sacrificed innocence, but her first twenty-five years have an attractive rags-to-riches balance: the unwanted and unjustly suspected princess survived to become queen. Elizabeth herself, entering at her ascension the Tower where she had once been held prisoner, noted the satisfying symmetry, and Plaidy concluded her book with a direct quote:

> Some . . . have fallen from being princes of this land to be prisoners
> in this place; I am raised from being a prisoner in this place to being
> a prince in this land . . . (Plaidy 1961, 133-134).

Partial biographies can end with the coronation pageantry, or with a glimpse of the triumphant future. Plaidy suggested it briefly: "This bright young girl, with her dedicated air, would bring peace and prosperity to their country; under her rule England would be merry again" (134). King (1940, x) foreshadowed Elizabeth's 1588 review of her troops in preparation for the Spanish invasion: "She loved her sturdy English people, and they in turn loved her, but never before had they shown it so much as now. . . ." These accounts made her first twenty-five years a patriotic Cinderella story without a prince, and suggested that she did live happily ever after.

Even whole-life biographers in the 1950s tended to draw a discreet veil over Elizabeth's last years, when her friends died and her popular-

ity waned. After the climactic defeat of the Spanish Armada, the rest
was denouement. Trease (1953, 10) explained that he gave more space to
the queens' girlhoods than their old age for the sake of readability: "those
early years are likely to be of more interest to general readers, though not
perhaps to political historians." Vance (1954) covered Elizabeth's last
thirty-five years in 14 of her 157 pages; she mentioned Elizabeth's
brooding over the treason and death of Essex, but softened the episode
by deathbed recollections of happier times. Winwar's final ten pages
began with the post-Armada rejoicing and ended with Elizabeth's death,
passing over her "few personal sorrows" to dwell on her public "triumph and glory" and advances in the arts, exploration, and prosperity
during her reign (Winwar 1954, 175). Sidney, Marlowe, and Shakespeare covered the omission of Essex as effectively as Drake and the
sea dogs covered the omission of Dudley and d'Alençon. By de-
emphasizing the last years, and by focusing on literature rather than
politics, Winwar made a moral success story from material that Strickland, a century before, had molded into a cautionary tale. Rather than
showing young readers how life punishes failings like Elizabeth's, the
writers of the 1950s obscured both failings and punishment.

Fictionalizing

Awkward questions could also be smoothed over by the use of fictional
techniques, from substituting invented episodes for facts to simply ma-
nipulating the narrative point of view. At its best, fictionalization added
verve and color to the story. Nolan and Cammiade had pictures on almost every doublespread, but other books of the 1950s and 1960s were
illustrated sparsely if at all; words had to suggest the color and atmosphere of an unfamiliar era. For descriptions of christenings, coronations,
royal progresses, or Elizabeth's refusal to enter the Tower by the Traitors'
Gate, there was contemporary documentation. The generally accepted
sources were not always reliable; Elizabeth was not actually made to
enter by the Traitors' Gate, for instance, but biographers often relied on
a colorful anecdote appended to John Foxe's *Book of Martyrs* rather
than the Tower diarist (Starkey 2000). In repeating such anecdotes,
juvenile biographers produced accounts that, while not wholly accurate,
were still largely consistent with current scholarship. But many went
further, inventing conversations, episodes, and even new characters to
advance the story.

The writers used third-person narration, usually by an omniscient narrator, but occasionally from the restricted viewpoint of one character or another. Some followed Tappan's example by occasionally showing Elizabeth through the eyes of adoring crowds, emphasizing her popularity and legitimizing her as Henry's English daughter. Malkus, who omitted more factual material than most and also fictionalized more, used a shift in narrative stance much as others used partial biography: the first part of her story was told from Elizabeth's point of view, but after Elizabeth's ascension to the throne the viewpoint was that of two fictional children. As innocent outsiders, they achieved a vagueness about affairs of state that would have been unbelievable from Elizabeth or an omniscient narrator; their presence helped camouflage the omission of sensitive matters such as sex, religion, and politics by turning the book into a historical adventure tale.

Other writers presented Elizabeth's supposed thoughts as indirect discourse throughout their books. Thus Linington often detailed Elizabeth's insomniac musings and unspoken opinions of the people around her. This served both to develop a sense of Elizabeth's personality (astute, wary, and unable to trust) and to sum up other personalities. Through Elizabeth's fictionalized consciousness they almost all appeared foolish and weak, from her brother Edward, a "very spoiled and unpleasant little boy," to "the vain and foolish young Earl" of Essex (Linington 1961, 26, 187).

The more overt fictionalizations went beyond manipulations of viewpoint, framing not only character but historical events to fit 1950s conceptions. Malkus flung a swashbuckling Hollywood glamour over her narrative, using stock motifs such as the messenger scene. Of course the Elizabethans did rely on horsemen to carry urgent news, but Malkus defied plausibility. In at least seven passages, messengers rushed in with news eerily relevant to whatever was being thought or said. Just as Elizabeth was having a tantrum because her father hadn't called her to court since she was three, a messenger arrived with the summons. Just as she reassured Cecil that Drake, missing three years, would return, "the bells began to toll" and "a messenger knelt before the Queen" to announce Drake's sail "clear around the world" (Malkus 1953, 137).

Almost as many messengers galloped through Linington's book. She, too, had a Hollywood way of setting up scenes. Messengers slipped notes through hedges or arrived, "wet and muddy," through dark and stormy nights, their horses "in a lather" (Linington 1961, 38, 42, 44), offering a picturesque contrast to the princess who watched from her window or sat with her embroidery by the fire. Cumulatively, these scenes built a passive image of Elizabeth, who had to await news.

Linington and Malkus, although they fictionalized far more than Trease and Winwar, belonged to much the same extraverted tradition. Like Tappan's, their fictions dramatized the chauvinistic excitement of nation-building, cheering plucky little England against imperial Spain. There was a partisan sentimentality about Malkus's invented characters and the colorful stock figures that Linington made of historical persons. Elizabeth's governess, Katherine Ashley, was the daughter of Sir Philip Champernon and an educated woman; her correspondents included Cambridge scholars (Starkey 2000). Linington (1961) portrayed her as a "kindly housekeeper" (18), a "fluttery" person (20) whose snobbery and servant-class diction added a comic note, and gave a misleading sense of Elizabeth's intellectual isolation. At the same time, she romanticized the common masses: "honest and patriotic Englishmen" (111), "humble honest people of Scotland" (106), "sturdy, brave little English ships" (125), "brave and patriotic" businessmen and sailors (126), "brave, stalwart, bold young Englishmen like Sir Francis Drake" (155). Elizabeth's romance with the English people really was a mainstay of her reign, but Linington's emotional tone suggests an anti-intellectualism quite untypical of the Tudors, especially Elizabeth.

Vance, Plaidy, and Hanff, with their emphasis on psychological development, fictionalized in somewhat different directions. Vance (1954) portrayed Elizabeth as hungry for mothering and affection, pathetically jealous of Katherine Parr's attentions to Jane Grey. Careful descriptions, not only of settings and people but of physical gestures, emphasized her warmth and vulnerability, making her poignantly corporeal. The book opened with Elizabeth, not yet three, chuckling innocently at the sound of the cannon that announced her mother's execution: "Boom, boom!" (14). The historical record suggests that she was a more articulate child. Stripped of her title before she turned four, she reportedly objected, "How haps it, Governor: yesterday my Lady Princess, and today but my Lady Elizabeth?" (Hibbert 1991, 20). But Vance's Elizabeth, naïve and unattuned to court politics, did not learn her mother's fate until a full year after Henry had another wife, Katherine Howard, beheaded as well:

> To the sensitive mechanism of a nine-year-old girl's nature, the shock
> of what she had heard, added to the probing, nameless suspicions that
> had nagged her consciousness for months or longer, was devastating.
> To this wretched sense of insecurity and horror in childhood may be

traced the main cause for Queen Elizabeth's contradictory nature in later years (Vance 1954, 42).

Vance's omniscient narrator sounded authoritative; but Elizabeth was surely more astute at nine. Even more than Linington, Vance downplayed Elizabeth's intellectual gifts, showing her as a girl who referred to her lessons with distaste, and later illustrating her queenly judgment and ability not by her laws, treaties, or skillful handling of the powerful, but by her tactful reception of an overly generous banquet. Her greatness was the product of dedication rather than skill:

> She had ruled for forty-four years, perhaps not always wisely but to the very best of her ability and with a singleness of purpose that defied failure. A blind devotion to any cause . . . must inevitably bring success (Vance 1954, 156).

To succeed in life, girl readers might infer, one must rely not on one's dubious feminine intelligence but on persistent effort.

Plaidy (1961) showed a more intelligent young Elizabeth, and compensated her for motherlessness by developing the role of Katherine Ashley. Kat was her governess from the time Elizabeth was four, and in Plaidy's book her presence as a stable and encouraging adult mentor accounted plausibly for Elizabeth's self-confidence and drive. Less plausible, although not impossible, was Elizabeth's childhood empathy for her sister:

> Indeed, Mary did look unloved; that was why Elizabeth suddenly . . . put her arms around her and looked up into her face beseechingly.
>
> "Mary," she said, "I am so happy to be with my brother and sister" (Plaidy 1961, 26).

When Mary failed to share her compassion for Katherine Howard, eight-year-old Elizabeth knew "that there would be occasions when she and Mary would be the bitterest enemies"; but Plaidy (like Tappan, Nolan, and others) softened family conflict wherever possible. Her portrait showed the young Elizabeth warm in sympathy as well as in anger.

Fictionalized passages served many functions in these books. Conversations and interior monologues were used in exposition of events as well as in the development of character; invented episodes could illustrate everyday life in Tudor England as well as Elizabeth's behavior. What they did contribute to an understanding of her character varied from book to book, as the authors' interpretations varied.

Too often, however, deviations from the historical record brought Elizabeth closer to a mid-twentieth-century feminine ideal. In order to shield her from the accusation that she was (as the Victorian Strickland had called her) too masculine, some authors used fictional passages to downplay her real competence. Vance's hurt, jealous child and Linington's scornful, hypervigilant queen both were less intellectually able than the historical Elizabeth; Somerset (1991, 20) quotes Elizabeth's tutor Roger Ascham, who claimed she had "a mind 'exempt from female weakness, and . . . endued with a masculine power of application.'" In later years she continued to read Greek, and took pleasure in speaking fluent Latin at need.

At the same time, fictionalization could endow the young Elizabeth with stereotypically feminine virtues she may not have had. Nolan and Plaidy made her sympathetic and forgiving of those who hurt her; Hanff, romanticizing her in a way that might appeal to teenage girls, emphasized her sacrifice of personal fulfillment for the good of her country. In general, these simplified portrayals minimized her political achievements, which depended on her responsible and sometimes shocking exercise of power. By softening and domesticating her image, they minimized her distance from the mid-twentieth-century norm for girls and made her a safer role model.

Character as Explanation: The Two Marys

The novelistic emphasis on character in fictionalized biographies of this era was consistent with a tradition, in older historical writings for adults as well as for children, of explaining major historical events by the character traits of individuals involved. This enhanced readability, and there was usually good justification for it. Although the major crises and decisions of Elizabeth's life had complex roots in (and implications for) the national and international politics of her time, politics were intensely personal.

The Protestant Duke of Northumberland, for instance, succeeded Somerset as Edward's Lord Protector, married his son to Lady Jane Grey, and crowned her queen instead of the Catholic Mary Tudor. When writers attributed his plot solely to evil ambition and failed to mention his religious motives, they avoided tedious explanations of the spread of Protestantism under Edward, or the increasingly polarized convictions of the people, or the legitimacy of Henry's daughters. Northumberland was a minor character in Elizabeth's life, and treating his plot as merely personal was economical; it left space for more important matters. At the same time, a biography emplotted in personal terms may be better suited to convey moral lessons. Northumberland, like many of Elizabeth's adversaries, was characterized as "cruel" and "ambitious," and came to a bad end. The fates of villains like Seymour and Northumberland warned young readers against reprehensible faults like ambition and selfishness.

"Cruelty," along with religious fanaticism, was often made the explanation for Elizabeth's treatment by her sister Mary. Their family circumstances alone almost guaranteed the sisters' enmity; at Elizabeth's birth, Henry declared seventeen-year-old Mary illegitimate, dissolved her household, and sent her to wait on her baby sister. But even if they could have risen above this history, their religious loyalties made conflict inevitable when Mary came to the throne. Mary's Catholicism was deep and genuine. Throughout the Protestant reigns of her father and brother she had relied for support and advice on her cousin, the Emperor Charles, and when she married his son Philip she was not forging a new alliance but cementing an old one. It was a marriage which many Englishmen opposed, for both economic and religious reasons; Elizabeth may not have approved the Protestant uprising in her name, but she was inevitably suspected of it and imprisoned, first in the Tower (where Jane Grey had just been beheaded) and then at Woodstock.

Malkus (1953), who said little about public policy of any sort, implied that all opposition to Elizabeth was personal. She portrayed Mary as "sullen," "sallow," "cross and unhappy" (Malkus 1953, 18) and showed her behaving "coldly" and "cruelly" to Elizabeth (54). Other writers did more to place the sisters' conflict in political perspective. Vance (1954, 123) pointed out that Elizabeth's position was dangerous because she was the Protestants' "hope for deliverance." Trease (1953) and Hanff (1969) used Cold War parallels to explain the international ramifications of religious choice. Yet even writers who mentioned political reasons for the sisters' estrangement often preferred to emphasize the personal, and several portrayed Mary as a religious crank: "a grim, gloomy woman" who "tried to comfort herself with prayers and masses" (Nolan 1951, 12); "[f]anatically religious" (Vance 1954, 24); a "tiresomely religious" girl who as a woman was even made "insane" by "fanatical devotion to her religion" (Linington 1961, 13, 68).

The harsher accounts implied that Mary's religion was a compensation for her unhappiness as a woman. She was "silent, sallow, and unhealthy-looking" (Vance 1954, 24). Not "lovable," her "stern, unattractive face seldom lighted by a smile," the "faded, unattractive Queen" was outshone by Elizabeth from the beginning (Winwar 1954, 47, 61). Linington (1961) repeatedly called Mary "ugly"—"so ugly," in fact, that "no one could possibly love her," and she was a fool to marry Philip (64). Philip was "unable to endure his ailing wife's stupid infatuation," and busied himself away from England (Bigland 1965, 44).

Mary's age and faded looks might not deserve the punishment of neglect and loneliness, but seemed to explain it. They also made her a foil for Elizabeth. Hanff's description of the sisters' arrival in London prepared the reader for a story of personal rivalry based on the disparity in looks and popularity instead of political and religious differences. Mary was prematurely aged, "plain and pale," while the twenty-year-old Elizabeth had her father's coloring and "all his charm"; it was Elizabeth the crowds cheered most, and Mary saw it (Hanff 1969, 35). Their contemporaries indeed contrasted the looks and personalities of the two sisters, and Mary's age and poor health, like her religious devotion, are well documented. Yet the unfriendly, dismissive tone of some juvenile biographies suggested a fairy-tale reading of history, with Mary as the ugly stepsister, jealous of Elizabeth's beauty and charm.

Such a reading was also supported by flattering descriptions of Elizabeth, who (as the Spanish ambassador warned Mary) had a dangerous "spirit full of incantation" (Hibbert 1991, 44) or "a power of enchantment" (Trease 1953, 68). She developed her mystique with great care (Levin 1994), and would probably have been delighted to know that children's books centuries after her death would repeat the story of Henry's affection for her, her resemblance to him, and her power to move English hearts. In fairy-tale terms, she was the right sister, the one destined to rule from the beginning.

In these books, Henry's affection for Elizabeth was not constant; after her mother's death, he sometimes neglected her and once, in a rage, exiled her from court. Starkey (2000) argues that Elizabeth's exile was caused, not by Henry's disfavor, but by historians' sentimental misreading of a letter from Elizabeth; in effect, it never happened. In children's biographies, however, there were reconciliation scenes, in which Henry's admiration for Elizabeth's spunk and intelligence validated her future right to rule. Malkus (1953, 23-25) showed Henry greeting the nine-year-old Elizabeth with delight after a long absence: "My own child!" he cried. "Honest and fearless!" Vance's Henry loved Elizabeth for her "spirit, Tudor spirit, the stuff kings are made of!"; dying, he remembered her as a boy, the one who should have been his heir (Vance 1954, 35, 59). According to Plaidy (1961, 30), Henry preferred Elizabeth to Mary because of her bright presence: "Poor Mary! thought Elizabeth. If only she would laugh and be gay and lively!"

In these books, what Henry most appreciated in Elizabeth was her resemblance to himself. "You're a Tudor, Bess—you're like me! If you'd been a boy, I'd know I left England in good hands!" (Linington 1961, 15). The English people agreed, and midcentury writers followed Tappan's lead by having anonymous members of the crowd comment on her likeness: "Aye, old Harry's daughter she be!" (Linington 1961, 24). Her red hair, political intelligence, classical learning, gift for languages, sudden rages, and above all her concern for the people linked her to Henry and legitimacy. To writers in the 1960s, her physical grace and personal charm, too, were signs of the inward qualities that destined her for greatness. Hanff (1969, 55) spoke of her "strange, bright face," and Bigland (1965) of her "shining, incandescent quality" (48), the "eerie brilliance about that slim, erect figure" (117), and even in age the "ethereal illusion" of "remote, supernatural beauty" (140).

Such fairy-tale conventions cut the other direction in the conflict between Elizabeth and her younger cousin, Mary Queen of Scots, whose beauty was famous. Many writers had implied that their antagonism was motivated chiefly by Elizabeth's jealousy. The personal contrasts between the cousins were dramatic and could be used both to overshadow the question of legitimacy and to organize an effective exposition. Trease, in an extended comparison based on the events and actions of their lives, protested one interpretation of their personalities:

> Elizabeth's life, though hardly without incident, pales into dullness beside Mary's. From babyhood Mary was accustomed to wild escapes, sudden alarms, violence, and conspiracy. She ended her days on the scaffold, after long captivity, whereas Elizabeth plodded along the path of duty into old age. It is easy to depict Mary as the lovely victim, Elizabeth as the scheming villainess. Plenty of people did so then, and have done so since.
>
> This picture hardly squares with the facts (Trease 1953, 100).

Yet Mary threatened the stubbornly unmarried Elizabeth much as Elizabeth had threatened her childless sister; she was not only the likely heir, but also the natural center of Catholic plots.

While Trease explained that Mary, as a Catholic, honestly believed in her right to the English throne, other biographers fell back on flaws in her character either to explain her actions or to excuse Elizabeth's. Perhaps she was "dishonest and deceitful by nature, or perhaps she had so many enemies that she grew desperate and confused," said Nolan (1951, 26). She "had begun life as a creature of singular sweetness and spirituality," but had become "a woman without conscience or moral principle," said Vance (1954, 139). She was unfit to rule:

> Oh, Mary was a charming and lovely woman—everyone said so—but
> she was also a vain and stupid woman. And she was a bad Queen, for
> before anything else she thought of her own desires and feelings. She
> cared nothing for her people at all . . . (Linington 1961, 99).

Bigland implied that Mary's "sinister web of plots" was motivated at
least in part by Elizabeth's stinginess in supplying her wardrobe, but
found Elizabeth superior in both morals and patriotism:

> They shared two qualities, vanity and ambition; otherwise their
> characters were poles apart . . . . Elizabeth could be both cunning and
> scheming—but only when the necessity arose; Mary was never happy
> unless she was planning the destruction of her enemies . . . . .
> Elizabeth's strongest emotion was her overwhelming pride in and
> love of her country, England; Mary detested Scotland, which she
> regarded as a poor, uncouth land (Bigland 1965, 80).

Elizabeth's biographers spotlighted Mary's faults; even the reticent
Malkus alluded to the murder of Darnley, Mary's second husband, by
Bothwell, who quickly became her third.

Meanwhile, they justified Elizabeth: too "merciful by nature" to
send Mary back to Scotland, where her own outraged subjects might
have executed her (Trease 1953, 101), she was too cautious to send her
to France, where she might have rallied support for an invasion of
England. Elizabeth was not "cruel to Mary" (Linington 1961, 164); for
years, she refused to allow her execution. Even after signing the
warrant, she was bitterly distressed at news of Mary's death, and
blamed her councilors. Still, it was difficult to make the queen look like
the innocent victim of her lovely young prisoner. Full-life biographies
often concluded with some variation of the old theme: Elizabeth had
her faults, she was vain and jealous and a shocking flirt, but her
dedicated love of England paid for all. Was she a role model for girl
readers? That use of the books was suggested by their emphasis on
character, their omissions of sensitive material, and their use of
novelistic techniques to promote reader identification with the subject.

Narrative Tradition in the 1950s and 1960s

Of course, that wasn't their only function. These biographies exhibited
considerable variety in form and content. Trease, Winwar, and Cammiade
avoided fictionalization; Malkus, Vance, Plaidy, and Linington used it
liberally. Nolan, Malkus, Winwar, and Linington, with their patriotic
anecdotes and expansionist outlooks, were well suited to the traditional
elementary history curricula that aimed at creating first impressions of

historical events, stimulating interest and curiosity, and nurturing good citizenship. Vance and Plaidy, focused on Elizabeth's childhood and psychological development, might nourish empathy. Cammiade and Bigland's political biographies emphasized events at court and Anglo-French relations; like Trease, with his careful exposition of political alternatives and relative frankness about the darker aspects of Elizabethan life, they encouraged critical thinking.

Balancing an introduction to the historical era with the presentation of Elizabeth as a role model, all the writers made her a sympathetic or at least understandable personality. With shifts in setting, political perspective, and the age of the implied reader came shifts in the portrayal of her character and responsibility. Writers of the 1950s, less overtly moralistic than those of the nineteenth century, displayed her adult character through public ceremonies and speeches; they tended to fictionalize her childhood development, concentrating on the kinds of filial and sisterly affection that middle-class children could emulate.

One thing these books had in common was their reliance on narrative. The best of them flowed seamlessly and persuasively, guiding readers' perceptions without resorting to the intrusive authorial voice of earlier generations. Even when they did not fictionalize, they borrowed the devices of the novel: vivid descriptions, lively anecdotes, and touches of humor helped readers imagine Elizabeth's life and the world she lived in. Unified and coherent, they invited a leisurely, immersed style of reading. The next generation's books, forecast by Cammiade's documentary, were very different.

Juvenile Biographies: 1979-2002

From 1980 on, the number of books on Elizabeth increased, many of them clustered around the four hundredth anniversaries of the Spanish Armada (1588) and her death (1603). Of ten biographies discussed in this section, seven (Zamoyska 1981; Turner 1987; Frost 1989; Greene 1990; Sabin 1990; Stanley and Vennema 1990; Green 1997) are for elementary school students and the other three (Bush 1988; Thomas 1998; Price-Goff 2001) to junior high school. Also discussed here are five histories or life-and-times books with extensive biographical coverage of Elizabeth (Hodges 1980; White-Thomson 1984; Deary and Tonge 1993; Lace 1995; Greenblatt 2002).

As a group, these books differ from their predecessors in content (they are more open about sexuality, more explicit about differences between sixteenth- and twentieth-century expectations for women, and more extensive in their coverage of social history); in format and organization (texts are shorter, chronological order is less likely to be the main organizing principle, and the presence of numerous picture captions and sidebars interrupts sequential reading); and in rhetoric (narrative gives way to a more expository style, marked by the rhetorical devices of persuasive journalism and by quotations giving many points of view). Nonfiction for young adults, and even for children, carries more scholarly apparatus than it used to; most of these books include bibliographies, and since the late 1990s endnotes as well. Indexes and frequent subheadings within chapters suggest that information is to be retrieved.

The New Openness, Seymour, and Alençon

By the 1980s, children's biographers could write more frankly about sex and death. Zamoyska (1981, 8), explaining how Elizabeth's mother won her father, noted that "Anne's older sister had been Henry's mistress, but Anne was shrewd enough to hold out for a more secure position." Later, after a briskly circumstantial account of the Seymour affair, she pointed out that Elizabeth "could not afford to have a tainted reputation. People had not forgotten that [her] mother, Anne Boleyn, had been accused of adultery and immoral behavior" (16). In a thirty-two-page account for younger readers, Turner (1987, 6) explained that Anne "was accused of being unfaithful to Henry" and that Elizabeth "was declared illegitimate"; a glossary defined "illegitimate" as "Illegal; born of parents not legally married" (31).

Not every book addressed Elizabeth's romances and marriage negotiations in any detail. Frost and Sabin wrote partial biographies, focused on her youth, and Greene's 1990 primer-level text passed over the love of her life in two age-appropriate sentences: "She liked Dudley a lot. But she knew he wasn't the right man to marry" (20). Seymour was even less prominent than he had been in the 1950s. Zamoyska, Bush, Frost, Thomas, and Greenblatt discussed him, but many writers omitted or barely mentioned him. This may have been for the sake of brevity; but perhaps, too, at a time when there was both heightened awareness of parental abuse and growing pressure for a return to family values in children's books, it was tempting to avoid material that could hardly be discussed without offending one faction or the other. Greenblatt's quick summary of the "scandal" was both brief and inoffensive:

> Suspected of having an affair with Seymour, the fifteen-year-old
> Elizabeth declared that she had nothing to hide and presented herself

at court as "a virtuous maid" dressed in simple clothes of black and white. Her behavior quickly won her the good opinion of the English people (Greenblatt 2002, 10).

The words "scandal" and "affair," in contrast to the careful euphemisms of the 1950s, create an impression of factual openness; but little is revealed. Most writers who mentioned the Seymour affair concluded with a comment on what Elizabeth learned from it—the importance of appearances, for instance. For some, the moral lesson trumped politics:

> Elizabeth had learned a lot from this sad episode. She realized that she had been a foolish girl, playing at love with another woman's husband. She now knew that, in her position, men might play with her feelings in order to take her power for themselves (Frost 1989, 21).

One reason for brevity in discussing Seymour was that the proportions of full-life biographies had shifted, so that relatively less space was devoted to Elizabeth's youth and more to her reign. Biographers were likely to say more about François, the duc d'Alençon, who had gone unmentioned in the 1940s and 1950s. Alençon, the last of Elizabeth's foreign suitors (and the first who came to woo her in England), was the younger brother of the king of France. Historically, Spain had been England's ally against France, but the alliance was no longer secure, and Elizabeth maneuvered constantly to maintain the balance of power between her two strong Catholic neighbors. In 1572, after the St. Bartholomew's Day massacre of French Protestants, she had broken off marriage negotiations with Alençon's older brother. In 1579 she was well into her forties, over twenty years older than her new suitor.

Nobody can be sure how Elizabeth really felt about Alençon, an "unattractive" man less than five feet tall, with a large pocked nose, who "had been reared in the corrupt French court" (Thomas 1998, 145). Bush (1988) argued that Elizabeth had two possible reasons for marrying him. First, he had allied himself with the Dutch Protestants in their war against Philip, and England could not be safe with the Netherlands under either Spanish or French domination; marrying Alençon would limit the threat more effectively than open military involvement—or as Zamoyska (1981, 52) put it, "She probably thought that if Philip were busy trying to keep his own empire under control he would have less time and money to invade England." Second, as the French envoy Simier cleverly told her, Leicester had secretly married; Elizabeth may have wanted "to distract herself from Leicester's betrayal and to get back at him" (Bush 1988, 76). Thomas (1998, 145), emphasizing Elizabeth's ability to manipulate appearances, called the "fling" a "theatrical ploy for her own personal and political purposes."

Stanley and Vennema (1990, n.p.) pointed to another reason: "if she was ever to have children—and give England an heir to the throne—she must do it now. At forty-six her time was running out." It had probably run out already. Elizabeth's loyal subjects, who for twenty years had urged her to marry, now opposed the idea. She appeared devoted to her "Frog," as she called Alençon; she banished Sir Philip Sidney from court and had a tactless Puritan sentenced to lose his right hand as punishment for their arguments against the marriage, "but," as Turner (1987, 24) remarked, "no one could ever fathom her real feelings." Was she in love, or was she spinning out marriage negotiations to avoid war with France? Stanley and Vennema told young readers, "It was all a matter of politics and religion, but then, that's all a queen's marriage was about."

Greater attention to Elizabeth's marriage negotiations and the activities of her court meant less space given to the exploits of Drake and her other sea dogs. This made it easier for biographers to omit a detail which seemed fully as horrifying in the 1990s as extramarital sex and illegitimate births in the 1950s: the slave trade. Earlier writers had touched on it with disapproval. Tappan (1902, 153) had explained that it "was looked upon as an honorable business and a valuable source of wealth for England." The Spanish were already transporting Africans to their colonies, where demand for cheap labor outpaced supply; in 1562, when John Hawkins kidnapped a cargo in Africa, he found an eager market in the West Indies. "Strangely enough, these shocking doings were not considered wrong either by Queen Elizabeth or by the majority of her subjects," said Winwar (1954, 106). Cammiade (1962, 30) argued that only the Spanish were upset by England's violation of their monopoly; even "the negroes—mostly captives who would otherwise have suffered an even harder fate—were resigned."

By the 1980s, any excuse for the slave trade sounded shocking, and most writers simply ignored it. The difficulty was to explain sixteenth-century attitudes without sacrificing the reader's sympathy; and for the sake of proportion, little space could be given to the issue in a life of Elizabeth. Thomas (1998) did mention it, burying it (much as Winwar had buried Seymour's designs on Elizabeth) in a paragraph on the growth of sea power, between the Roanoke colony and the import of New World crops: "Sir John Hawkins would join the slave trade that had been firmly established by other nations for fifty years" (142).

Feminism and Elizabeth's Character

More central to Elizabeth's story than her contemporaries' views on slavery were their views on women. These had not seemed to need much explanation in the 1950s, but newer writers were more explicit. Trease (1953) had explained Henry's need for a son: doubt about the succession had kindled "the War of the Roses, the bloodiest civil war in English history" (46), and nobody wanted a repeat. In their accounts of Elizabeth's birth or of her decision not to marry, 1980s biographers gave much the same explanation: a monarch was expected to marry in order to assure the succession, but a foreign husband might act against England's interests, and raising an Englishman to the kingship might lead to civil war.

Second-wave feminism had made a difference in these books, however. Now biographers had to explain—at least briefly—things the 1950s had taken for granted: that a husband would expect to rule his wife, and that the idea of a woman's ruling a nation "by herself, without a strong husband, was unheard of" (Lace 1995, 14), "almost unthinkable" (Frost 1989, 4) or "unnatural" (Bush 1988, 15):

> Women were considered to be inferior to men and they were brought up to believe that when they became wives, they should obey their husbands. . . . The English people expected that their young Queen would soon marry a suitable man who could take over the affairs of state and leave her to become a royal wife and mother (Zamoyska 1981, 25).

Bush quoted John Knox, who offended Elizabeth by his pamphlet attacking the rule of women (although it was directed against Catholic queens; Elizabeth, as a Protestant, was the exception). Greene (1990, 5), writing for the very youngest readers, simplified: "Henry thought a boy could be king after him. A girl couldn't."

"English society was still largely sexist," Green (1997, 27) explained. Others elaborated. Twenty-six references to women were indexed in *Behind the Mask* (Thomas, 1998), most under the subheading "attitudes toward and legal position of." Two of the social histories included separate chapters on women. There was an occasional mention of what they *could* do, such as inherit and run businesses: "In actuality, some women did wield a great deal of power," noted Price-Goff (2001, 64). But she also noted that most "had no rights whatsoever," and their disenfranchisement was the more common theme. Deary and Tonge (1993) listed "ten terrible ways" a woman's life was hard, including early marriage, lack of education, the hard labor of housewives, and punishments for nagging. Hodges explained that the ceaseless work required of ladies affected their status:

> That 'a woman's place is in the home' was a teaching easier to accept in
> days when women had little time or opportunity to be anywhere else.
> From that it was only a short step to thinking that it was actually not
> *natural* for women to be elsewhere, or to want to be. . . .
>   It was in the time of the Tudors that women at last began to come
> out from the shadow of all that ancient nonsense (Hodges 1980, 60-62).

Much as Trease had dismissed religious warfare, Hodges implied that
sexism belonged to the less enlightened past. As evidence that women in
Elizabeth's day were emerging from the shadows, he pointed to five
women monarchs or regents. But widows and daughters had inherited the
roles of dead leaders for centuries without ending "that ancient nonsense."
Price-Goff came closer to the mark when she commented that Elizabeth
was an exception. There is no evidence that Elizabeth considered her own
success an argument for respecting the potential of women or bettering
their lot. She was a special case, an anointed monarch ruling by divine
right, and the usual rules did not apply.

She did, however, manipulate the themes and symbols of femininity
for political advantage. By the 1980s, several traits that earlier children's
books had held up as weaknesses began to appear as strengths. Some
writers continued to emphasize her vanity; Turner (1987, 22) said she
"loved fine clothes and jewels and endlessly fussed over her appearance."
But others noted the practical importance of appearances: "ostentatious
clothing . . . was necessary to Elizabeth's position" (Thomas 1998, 79);
she "dressed gorgeously to impress people" (Hazell 1996, 36); dress was
part of her expertise in "regality as a profession" (Bush 1988, 62-63).
Zamoyska, Thomas, and others found practicality even in her
encouragement of a chivalric "myth" or "cult" of the Virgin Queen:
Elizabeth "had to keep the [almost entirely male] Court in order and
maintain [a] spotless reputation" while at the same time attracting
"important men" to her service (Zamoyska 1981, 28-32).

Other traits formerly perceived as weaknesses were equally valuable.
Elizabeth drove Cecil and her councilors to distraction by what they saw
as feminine irrationality: she delayed, she stalled for time, she made
excuses; when forced to make statements, she hedged them in ambiguity
and reinterpreted them later. Earlier generations of children's writers had
displayed her shiftiness as a bad example, glossed over it, or justified it.
The tone of most newer books implied that it was acceptable for a woman
to have power ("she was the boss"; White-Thomson 1984, 11) and to
retain it by whatever political strategies she needed:

> Elizabeth used these tactics not only with foreign countries, but also
> with her own councilors. She rarely met with them as a group, since they

might unite to overwhelm her. She talked with them separately and sometimes played on their feelings of rivalry to divide them. She didn't mind throwing a temper tantrum now and again if that would gain time, change the subject, or win her point. Once she had heard the opinions of her advisors, she made her own decisions, and she expected to be obeyed (Stanley and Vennema 1990, n.p.).

Thomas, who compared Elizabeth's political strategies to Machiavelli's, noted more than once that her survival depended on her retention of power; a deposed princess could never be safe. Hodges (1979, 133) said that Elizabeth was like her grandfather, who had "dressed up" his kingship with the cultivation of poetic symbols like the Tudor rose and King Arthur, but behind the scenes "had been shrewd, steady-handed and managerial." Like him, she was "a professional," and treated her task as "a skilled job."

Old stereotypes persisted. Deary and Tonge, always quick to please their audience by subverting piety, collected lively quotes and anecdotes to document Elizabeth's vanity, her double-dealing hypocrisy, and her fearsome temper. The stereotypes were not without basis in fact, and most of the biographies were objective. Thomas (1998, 129) provided background for both individual outbursts and the generalized public response to them: "People don't like to suppose that great leaders . . . behave badly, as all humans do. . . . Elizabeth's failings raised a constant undercurrent of disapproval. . . ."

Where earlier writers might have glossed over Elizabeth's deviations from traditional feminine virtue or proposed psychological excuses for them, there was now a tendency to explain them in social and political context. The emphasis was less on her function as a role model and more on her role as a unique figure in history. This shift paralleled trends in the production and expected use of nonfiction books for children. Format, organization, illustration, and rhetoric increasingly seemed designed to support school assignments that asked students to search a book with specific questions and take discrete pieces of information from it, rather than to immerse themselves in a narrative flow or identify with a protagonist.

Format and Organization

Juvenile biographies of Elizabeth looked dramatically different by the early 1980s. Taller and wider, they had on average fewer pages and broader margins. In the 1950s and 1960s, Nolan's profusely illustrated account for younger readers (36 pages long) and Cammiade's documentary text for older ones (79 pages) were exceptions; the other books discussed ranged from 138 to 191 pages. By the 1980s, brevity was the rule. Of the ten biographies discussed in this section, seven had fewer than 70 pages, Bush and Price-Goff had 112 each, and only Thomas's *Behind the Mask* was longer, with 196 pages. The five histories ranged from 60 to 144 pages. Books for the younger grades proliferated; Greene, for Children's "Rookie Biography" series, squeezed Elizabeth's life into a scant twelve hundred words, not counting captions.

In addition to tables of contents, chapter headings, and indices, longer books often had subheadings to help readers follow their organization or locate specific information within chapters. Most of the books offered sustained narratives, but in some cases the flow was broken by sidebars and in almost all cases by captions—often quite substantive—to numerous illustrations. Quotations from Elizabeth's contemporaries might be worked into the text, but they might equally appear in boxes (Lace) or in the page margins (Bush). Thus readers in many cases had to choose between continuity and elaboration; possibly to avoid this, Greenblatt's life-and-times book separated Elizabeth's life, the everyday lives of her people, and a collage of quotations into three sections.

But sidebars and other textual interruptions seemed to invite a busy interactivity. Set apart by shaded backgrounds, carefully designed borders, or distinctive typefaces, they enticed the reader to explore a multidimensional topic but did not constrain the order of exploration. The format implied that writers had assembled the facts, but readers were responsible for putting them together and interpreting them; moving freely between text and graphics, children could be active learners, collating information and constructing their own understandings of it.

This interactive trend was pushed to amusing limits by a British team, Deary and Tonge (1993, 7-8), whose conceit was that history can be "*horribly boring*" because teachers tend to stick to "the bits about the kings and the queens and the battles and the endless lists of dates," but knowing more than your teacher about the gross conditions of daily life could be "*horribly interesting*." Conservatives have suspected that what Diggins (1996) called "the new social history" has a subversive agenda; Deary and Tonge made subversion explicit with sly, collusive humor at the expense of authorities. Readers were urged to imagine themselves tripping up their teachers with little known facts, or practicing Shakespearean insults on parents, policemen, and priests (what could be more desirable than studying Shakespeare?). After a list of reasons to suspect that Shakespeare might not have written his own plays, and a quick outline of the Marlowe murder, readers were invited to form their own theories:

Possible? What do you think? Remember, history is not always simple or straightforward. In cases like this historians make up their own minds from the facts that they have. So, you can be an historical "police officer". In cases like this, what *you* think is as good as what another historian might think (Deary and Tonge 1993).

This approach did not advance the idea that a good historian's conclusion is worth more than an uninformed guess, but at least it implied that children could be active investigators (and debunkers) of history, rather than passive recipients of its moral lessons. Martin Brown's small black-and-white cartoons punctuated the text with silly puns, but textual sidebars interrupted the narrative more insistently. Deary and Tonge provided a hyperkinetic array of lists (six "filthy facts" that help explain why only one person in ten lived to the age of forty), quizzes (match ten illnesses with their Tudor cures, one of which might actually work; or guess why the judge decided not to execute the thief), rules for Tudor games, recipes ("to make pies that the birds may be alive in them and fly out when it is cut up," but also one or two things you might want to eat), a glossary of thieves' cant, and more.

The dispersal of text among captions, sidebars, and marginalia was not always combined with such open irreverence. Bush's 1988 entry in the Chelsea House World Leaders Past & Present series, for instance, invited a slightly less frenetic interactivity—no quizzes, but plenty of opportunities to move back and forth between the main text and supporting materials. Lace's 1995 contribution to Lucent's World History series had a similar design.

Most of the books examined here were series entries, and in some, predetermined formats appeared to dictate the space allocated to topics. Frost (1989) and White-Thomson (1985) confined each chapter or major section of their books to one colorfully illustrated doublespread. After a first chapter summarizing Elizabeth's life in three doublespreads ("Early life," "The young queen," and "The later years"), White-Thomson placed sections on government, internal threats (Mary, Queen of Scots, and the Earl of Essex), threats from abroad (Spain), religion, everyday life, and voyages of discovery. Few previous books had presented so much information about Elizabethan poverty, education, law, and health for such young readers, but the value of this one was undermined by an organization that obscured many logical connections. Drake's piratical voyage came at the end of the book, long after a discussion of piracy as a contributing cause of the Spanish Armada; Henry's divorce came after Elizabeth's last speech to Parliament.

White-Thomson was writing social history, not biography, and the abandonment of chronological order was common in the genre, which could be organized naturally along thematic lines. Even so, chronology sometimes improved the organization. Hodges (1979) began his graceful account of Tudor life with two revivals of the Arthur legend in 1485: Caxton's printing of Malory's *Morte d'Artur*, and the founding of the Tudor dynasty by Elizabeth's grandfather, Henry VII, who named his first son Arthur in hopes of a new golden age. Through chapters on practically everything from the economic effects of new styles in agriculture and the slow improvement of housing arrangements to the status of women and the attractions of London, Hodges laced the stories of the Tudors themselves and two Warwickshire families exemplifying common life, upward mobility, and cultural progress: the Ardens, whose daughter Mary was the mother of William Shakespeare, and their neighbors the Fields, whose son Richard became his printer. The resulting balance of narrative and exposition was unusually supple.

While Hodges wove biographies into his social history, others wove social history into their biographies. Sabin (1990) used Elizabeth and her family with imperfect success to illustrate the conditions of sixteenth-century life; her text flowed smoothly, but it was oversimplified and misleading—perhaps inevitable when so much is attempted in forty-eight pages. Given a longer text and the expectation of more sophisticated readers, Thomas (1998) accomplished a satisfying balance that was in some ways the inverse of Hodges: where his exposition was enlivened and held together by narrative threads, her narrative was illuminated by much careful exposition, and easily incorporated material on English bedtimes and silverware, attitudes to children and inheritance laws, the rise of the middle class and relations with France.

Illustrations and Design

The graphics in books for younger readers sometimes occupied more space than the text; even in books for middle school they drew the eye not only by their size and quantity, but also by their varied layout. Especially gorgeous were Diane Stanley's paintings for her 1990 picture-book biography, carefully reflecting Tudor styles in their intricate patterns and deep, rich colors. Children could see for themselves the splendor of Elizabeth's attire and the press of courtiers or councilmen or soldiers around her; or the English fireships gliding into the midst of a moonlit Spanish Armada; or the draping of a snowy sheet over a fat actor in a laundry basket.

The best thing about such distinctive illustrations is their appeal to the imagination; but Stanley's were also filled with evidence of careful research, not all of it mentioned in the text. She copied clothes and ornaments, for instance, directly from contemporary portraits. The first known portrait of Elizabeth, at fourteen, shows her in a low-cut, wide-sleeved red dress; but would she have worn it for a lesson with her tutor, who was all bundled up in a coat with a fur collar, on a snowy winter day? And wasn't she wearing white velvet, not blue, when she rallied the troops at Tilbury? Such quibbles are trivial, and yet they remind us that illustration is interpretation. Stanley visually quotes a 1554 painting by Hans Eworth. In the original, Philip stood apart from Mary, looking as if he had indeed "married [her] for duty, hardly able to conceal his distaste for her" (Thomas 1998, 68); in Stanley's illustration he held her right hand with his and rested his left arm on the back of her chair, looking as affectionate as she could have wished. The mullioned window, with its lower pane open, stood behind Philip's right shoulder instead of between the couple.

The vivid interpretation of character and relationships in illustration could outweigh text. Illustrator Martin Salisbury, for instance, drew Elizabeth with hands on hips and a shrewish expression on her middle-aged face, glaring at a bemused Leicester. Turner's caption said, "Elizabeth was a strong-willed, self-reliant woman" (Turner 1987, 25), but Leicester's open-handed stance, eloquent of misunderstood innocence, gave the words a negative connotation. Stanley's portrayal of a vehement Elizabeth getting her own way was an attractive contrast to Salisbury's harridan: the queen rose in her seat, clenched her right fist and leaned toward a councilor—probably Cecil—who listened, respectful but unalarmed, still evidently hoping to make his point.

Like sidebars, illustrations and their captions broke the text, sometimes with redundant or contradictory information. In Frost's opening doublespread, the main text ran between a sidebar on the Tudor succession and a full-page picture of Anne slumped in bed, looking depressed, as Henry scowled down at his unwanted daughter and anxious courtiers studied his reaction. A caption beneath the sidebar explained:

> Anne was tired after the long birth, but happy. The future seemed bright for the beautiful young Queen. But Henry found it hard to hide his disappointment that the baby was not a son (Frost 1989, 4).

Separated by a column of text from the illustration it explained, the caption denied Anne's dejection but reinforced information on subsequent pages: her belief that "there was plenty of time for a son to be born" (6) and Henry's angry absence from the christening. An active reader, attempting to construct a coherent understanding of Elizabeth's family, would have to reconcile the visual and verbal contradictions.

Fictionalization, in the form of imagined conversations and scenes, had largely disappeared from the texts of these books. The illustrations, however, occasionally represented legends or episodes that we know never took place. Bush, Greene, and Deary and Tonge all included pictures of Raleigh spreading his cloak at Elizabeth's feet. Deary and Tonge said the story was invented by seventeenth-century historian Thomas Fuller; Bush (1988, 93) called it "a popular legend"; and Greene (1990, 31) said "The story is told that Sir Walter Raleigh . . . once spread his cloak over a mud puddle so Queen Elizabeth would not get her shoes dirty," leaving readers to decide the truth of the matter for themselves.

Similarly, a dramatic illustration in Bush's text represented a confrontation between Elizabeth and Mary Queen of Scots. In fact, the two cousins never met, but here a furious Mary, barely restrained by a lady-in-waiting, raised a threatening hand; Elizabeth reared back in indignation, one fist protectively against her breast and the other clenching a rose bush. Two male courtiers behind her looked aside, as if embarrassed by such a display of female emotion. The caption was technically accurate, quoting Elizabeth's letters to Mary, but with the illustration it helped create a false impression that they met face to face:

> Mary and Elizabeth exchange harsh words in 1568. Although Elizabeth addressed Mary as "ma chère soeur" (my beloved sister) and "my dear cousin," she was contemptuous of Mary's political and personal judgment (Bush 1988, 57).

One could argue that the depiction of imaginary scenes does children no harm. The enmity between the two queens was real, and the illustration, although factually inaccurate, might be true in spirit. In older books, writers used fictionalization to streamline their narratives; in newer ones, graphic representation served similar purposes, condensing information and highlighting the essential, often at the expense of less important detail. In either case, the information offered to a child was introductory and impressionistic. Young readers needed only to construct a general historical frame of reference; the fine details would come later. But the frame of reference would be constructed on a foundation of visual anachronisms.

There were minor anachronisms of detail in both text and pictures. Vance (1954, 122) had Mary Tudor in love with a "photograph" of Philip. Gorsline's illustrations for Malkus (1953) showed a coach rumbling past a thatched cottage with a smoking chimney, although early Tudor roads were not good enough for coaches (Elizabeth traveled by sedan chair) and common village homes were unlikely to have chimneys at the time. White-Thomson (1984) devoted one doublespread to witchcraft, emphasizing the superstition and need for scapegoats that kept people from realizing "there were no such things as witches"; but his judicious tone was undercut by Wood's two snaggle-toothed hags, their eyes as scarlet as those of the bright green fiend looming incandescently above them. The picture was lurid and implausible even on economic grounds; what raggedy peasants could have afforded that bronze cauldron, ornately sculpted with diabolical faces? The visual conventions seemed to owe as much to horror movies as to sixteenth-century belief.

A more subtle form of anachronism evolved in the use of documentary illustrations. Between 1962 and 1981, books by Cammiade, Hodges, and Zamoyska used reproductions of Tudor art and photographs of Tudor artifacts. In picture credits or acknowledgments they listed museums, libraries, archives and other sources, but in their captions they usually gave more historical context, explaining who created the pictures and when. A photograph showed "a reconstruction of Drake's ship," not the original (Hodges 1980, 95); a castle was shown "in an early 17th-century painting," slightly after Elizabeth's time (Zamoyska 1981, 33); a sketch of the execution of Mary Stuart was "made by Robert Beale, Clerk to the Council of Elizabeth, who read out the death warrant" and must have been an eyewitness (Cammiade 1962, 51). Such comments gave readers some basis for assessing the accuracy of pictures.

In more recent books, archival sources were still meticulously acknowledged—usually in small-print lists of picture credits on the back of the title page—but little was said about the real origins of the pictures. At the same time, reproductions of art and artifacts created by Elizabeth's contemporaries were mingled with more modern art. If an individual book illustrator was named on the title page, the continuous style of the new art contrasted with the reproductions. But increasingly, book designers used a combination of archived Tudor reproductions and archived nineteenth- and twentieth-century historical illustrations; examples of this approach can be found in books by Bush, Greene, Lace, and Green. For a child with little knowledge of art history, it could be almost impossible to distinguish between portrait and imaginative reconstruction.

Like fictionalized texts that failed to distinguish between the recorded words of Elizabeth's contemporaries and invented conversation, undated illustrations introduced an element of confusion. The visual recreation of history, like its verbal narrative, is always vulnerable to presentism. Richly imagined illustrations are richly interpretive, and the interpretations say as much about the artists' own times as about their subjects. Dating illustrations would provide a useful tool for constructing a historical frame of reference, without complicating the text, and it seems unfortunate that it is done so seldom.

Quotation

Perhaps the prevailing sketchiness in citing pictures reflected a sense that they were merely ancillary, and words were the true raw materials for readers' construction of historical understanding. Certainly citation of textual sources was more detailed than in the past. Cammiade's was the only one of the thirteen books published from 1951 to 1969 to have a bibliography; of the fifteen published from 1979 to 2002, eleven had at least one. Some had separate lists of additional readings for children and scholarly sources. Lace's annotated bibliographies took five pages, his notes three, and his index another five.

Frequent quotations from Elizabeth's contemporaries further heightened the impression of authenticity. Quotes were nothing new. In the 1950s, no children's biography seemed complete without a passage from Lady Bryan's letter requesting clothes for the neglected child who was no longer a princess. Winwar (1954), because it was "such a quaint letter," devoted a full page to it, carefully glossing words like "bodystitchels" and "biggins." The letter remained a popular reference, but newer books gave it less space; Bush, who merely noted the fact that Lady Bryan had been driven to write it, was typical.

After 1980, quotations were generally shorter, but more numerous and representative of more viewpoints. The older books, with continuous third-person narration, allowed a reader to identify with Elizabeth; the newer ones, glancing at her from a number of different angles, tended to encourage a more critical stance. Now the reader's task was to construct a collage from available pieces of evidence.

Many of the quotations were culled from secondary sources, a reasonable but slightly risky procedure. (Lace, in 1995, illustrated the richness of Elizabethan language with twenty-seven lines of Shakespeare's *Richard II*—misidentified as *Henry VI, Part 2*—taken from the *Horizon Book of the Elizabethan World*.) Nevertheless, this liberal use of quotation hinted at the processes of historical research. Writers like Hodges, Zamoyska, Bush, and Deary and Tonge gave at least partial descriptions of sources in their texts. Four books, published in and after 1995, used endnotes, sometimes giving the exact source of each quote and sometimes more general sources for each chapter. From both textual references and notes, an alert child might begin to understand how historical evidence is pulled from letters, judicial proceedings, diplomatic communiqués, and sermons.

As much as historical research, however, the quotations suggested journalism. Where Tappan had relied on fictionalized conversations among courtiers and merchants, a new generation of biographers used the documented voices of Elizabeth's contemporaries for man-in-the-street color. Zamoyska (1981) exemplified the technique: maintaining a lively pace, she worked in the viewpoints of "an anonymous Spaniard" who witnessed Anne Boleyn's death (6); Elizabeth's tutor Ascham, who described her academic progress in an enthusiastic letter "to a friend" (11); and her cofferer, Parry, who after "a week of questioning, . . . told all that is now known about Elizabeth's relations with Seymour and his interest in her property" (17). Hodges (1980, 81), for vivid pictures of Christmas revelry and Sunday football, referred to the sermons of "Philip Stubbes in his shocked, pulpit manner." Bush (1988, 89) quoted Pope Sixtus V, who helped finance the Spanish Armada but afterward exclaimed in admiration, "It is a pity that Elizabeth and I cannot marry; our children would have ruled the whole world."

The words were authentic; contemporaries of Elizabeth actually said them. But they were often sound bites, quoted out of context. Elizabeth once rebuked Leicester, who had overstepped his authority when he threatened to dismiss a member of her household: "God's death, my Lord! I have wished you well, but my favor is not so locked up in you that others shall not participate thereof. . . . I will have here but one mistress, and no master" (Hibbert 1991, 154). The last line of that speech was often quoted to illustrate either her imperious nature or her refusal to marry; the context, which included her exasperated friendship and her care for petitioners other than her favorite, was generally forgotten.

Journalistic Style

With vivid quotes (sometimes out of context), stylish layouts, and arresting illustrations, the new biographies often looked more like glossy magazines than like the old biographies. Like magazines and newspapers, too, they placed a conspicuous emphasis on objective facts. The tendency was especially noticeable in Bush (1988). Captions gave carefully detailed information about their subjects. A picture of Catherine of Aragon pleading with Henry was captioned with dates for Catherine, Henry, Wolsey, Pope Clement VII (an off-stage character), and the church hearing; one of the Spanish Armada numbered its ships (130), sailors (8,350), galley slaves (2,080), soldiers (19,290), cannonballs (123,790), and guns (2,630).

Numerical details found their way into the body of the text, as well. Traditionally, most biographies had begun with a dramatic episode— young Elizabeth throwing a tantrum, or pondering news of her father's death, or hiding her affection for Thomas Seymour—and then filled in the beginning of the story with flashbacks. Sometimes the opening scene was assigned a date, but its salient ingredients were usually strong emotion and elaborate visual scene-setting.

Bush opened, like Vance (1954), with the execution of Anne Boleyn, contrasting the traditional joys of May to the dramatic horror of Anne's fate. But Vance, fictionalizing liberally, devoted leisurely pages to visual description of the weather and the palace where two-year-old Elizabeth's servitors watched over her and exchanged snatches of gossip. Heightening the pathos, the narrator slipped into a nurse's consciousness to watch the innocent child's merry response to the cannon that signaled her mother's death. Bush, too, contrasted joy and despair:

> Staring disconsolately at the gray waters of the Thames River, and quite oblivious to the beauty of the English countryside, Anne Boleyn, queen of England, rode in her royal barge to imprisonment in the Tower. In this grim fortress, for more than 400 years, traitors to the crown had been detained and put to death at the monarch's pleasure.
>
> According to an old English song, the month of May was supposedly a merry one, a time for rejoicing at the coming of spring. But May 2, 1536, was a fateful date for this hapless queen. Her journey that day was to be the last she would ever make. Anne knew that having once entered London's mighty citadel she would never leave alive. On the orders of her husband, King Henry VIII, she was to be executed for treason (Bush 1988).

Here, visual description was held to a minimum and punctuated with objective details. Fictionalization, too, was minimal, although the omniscient narrator did tell slightly more than can be known about Anne's state of mind: was she truly "oblivious to . . . beauty" on that last ride? Vance focused immediately on Elizabeth, a child at the mercy of forces beyond her ken, and used Anne's execution to engage the reader's sympathy; Bush used it to engage the reader's interest in exploring those merciless political forces, establishing the historical context for Elizabeth's life before introducing her as a character.

The opening passages signaled different kinds of reading experience. Vance's text was novelistic; her focus was on Elizabeth's psychological development, and her technique invited readers to see things from Elizabeth's point of view. Where her fictionalizations contradicted the historical record, they often increased Elizabeth's resemblance to an idealized mid-twentieth-century girl. Bush's journalistic approach, juxtaposing short quotes from many contemporaries and exploring the politics of Elizabeth's reign, invited a more distant sympathy.

Conclusion

It is dangerous to generalize trends in juvenile biography from these individual treatments of a single subject. Two books published in the same year—like Trease's, with its balanced political exposition, and Malkus's, with its sanitized fictions—may differ as much as two published decades apart. Certainly not all juvenile biographies in a given year are intended for the same readers, or the same purposes. Most of the older books, however, had a narrative form that invited the reader to identify with Elizabeth as with a fictional protagonist. Euphemism and omission rendered her story appropriate to the innocent eyes of mid-twentieth-century youth, and references to her virtues and the cruelty of her enemies implied that good character was rewarded. In general, the newer books had less fictionalization; more coverage of sensitive facts; shorter texts, with more sidebars, captions, and marginalia; more viewpoints represented, both of literate contemporaries and of her poorer countrymen; and far more graphics. Cumulatively, these changes suggest a shift in the predominant use of juvenile biography, from the provision of inspirational role models to the support of history curricula.

A century ago, Elizabeth was one of the few women whose stories were told and retold to girls. Glamorous, powerful, and not too saintly, she came as a relief from the virtuous nurses and dutiful wives on our biography shelves. Writers had to make conscientious efforts to keep her from being altogether too inspiring. The Victorians displayed her power and her faults and warned us against them: time itself had punished that unfeminine woman who so cruelly ordered the execution of her beautiful cousin. The Cold War generation hid her power behind the glamour of her wardrobe and the excitement of her sea dogs, leaving a hole at the center of her story that was never quite filled by the compassionate inventions they provided for us to admire and emulate. In the 1960s, young adults were given glimpses of an introspective, romantic Elizabeth, who sacrificed her personal fulfillment for the good of her country; Bigland, for example, showed her as uncannily sharp and intuitive (but dependent on Cecil for rational guidance), indomitable but frail, glittering with a magical aura but always lonely.

In more recent biographies, graphics compete with text for attention, and journalistic conventions create an atmosphere of objectivity. Authors continue to summarize Elizabeth's character, often concluding, as Tappan did, that in spite of her "vanity, temper, and deceit" she was "exactly what England needed" (Lace 1995, 112). Assessments of her achievement are sometimes sweeping; she changed England from "a small, insignificant country" (Zamoyska 1981, 66) into a "far-reaching power" (Sabin 1990, 47). Readers are encouraged to see her influence on modern life, in areas as diverse as economics (her Poor Law began "a tradition of state aid to the disadvantaged which has lasted in England to this day"; Bush 1988, 102), exploration (she presided over the chartering of the East India Company), religious tolerance (her settlement contented neither Catholics nor Puritans, but lasted uneasily through her reign), and culture (without her defense of the theaters, "we might never have known the work of William Shakespeare, who wrote the greatest plays in all history"; Stanley and Vennema 1990, n.p.).

Today's final judgment on Elizabeth is rarely harsh, sometimes even inflated. It is often reinforced with some acknowledgment of the profound antifeminism of her society, although even a writer as subtle and sympathetic as Hodges may be unable or reluctant to suggest that modern girls could face similar barriers. But today's judgments differ from those of the Victorians in flavor as much as in content. Narrators do not present themselves as moral authorities, condescending to edify their readers. On the contrary, they present objective facts to readers who are presumably competent to construct their own meanings; Deary and Tonge go so far as to collude with readers against obnoxiously enlightening authorities. Texts are supplemented and sometimes undermined by the graphics that surround them. Assembled collages of facts and opinions, graphics and quotations imply that readers, not authors, have the final responsibility for interpretation, and this implication is reinforced by the journalistic trick of abdicating final judgment; many writers end by agreeing that Elizabeth was "a complex, mysterious figure" (Turner 1987, 23), "the most private of persons" (Lace 1995, 13), impossible to understand or summarize, but always to be remembered as "the remarkable queen who loved her people so dearly and ruled them so well" (Stanley and Vennema 1990, n.p.).

Appearance is not the whole of reality, but it is what we have to work with, these books seem to be saying. Thomas's title, *Behind the Mask*, is an apt comment on the difficulties of knowing Elizabeth, but perhaps also on our changing sense of what it means to be an individual self: not necessarily a consistent, predictable character who can be fully understood, but maybe a set of roles and predispositions, reflecting on each other as the illustrations and sidebars reflect on a continuous text. As we try to understand either individual or book, our attention is drawn back and forth; we must synthesize disparate bits of evidence, and construct meaning for ourselves.

This kind of postmodern interpretation seems especially appropriate to Elizabeth, who was both elusive and a major historical figure. The following chapters will survey juvenile biographies of women published in the United States in three different years: 1946, 1971, and 1996. Each year yielded a more diverse selection; the pool of notable women has grown exponentially. Few of them exercised the kind of power Elizabeth did, in any field—but many, even if they had already tried to tame their own images, had to be filtered and gentled before they could serve as acceptable role models. Their characters, like Elizabeth's, have been variously communicated in fictionalized and more journalistic biographies, shaped by the insights of individual writers and by the needs and tastes of different generations.

Reference List:
Children's and Young Adult Books

Bigland, Eileen. 1965. *Queen Elizabeth I*. New York: Criterion Books. 151 p.

Brooks, E. S. 1891. Elizabeth of Tudor: The girl of Hertford Manor. In *Historical girls: Stories of girls who influenced the history of their times*, 174-191. New York: G. P. Putnam's Sons.

Bush, Catherine. 1988. *Elizabeth I*. New York: Chelsea House. 112 p.

Calcott, Lady. 1884. Chapters 38-46. In *Little Arthur's history of England*, 142-189. New York: Thomas Y. Crowell.

Cammiade, Audrey. 1962. *Elizabeth the First*. New York: Roy. 79 p.

Deary, Terry, and Neil Tonge. 1993. *The Terrible Tudors*. Illus. Martin Brown. London: Scholastic. 127 p.

Edwards, Clayton. 1920. Queen Elizabeth of England. In *A treasury of heroes and heroines*, 137-146. New York: Cupples and Leon.

Farjeon, Eleanor and Herbert Farjeon. 1953. *Kings and queens*. Rev. ed. Philadelphia: Lippincott.

Frost, Abigail. 1989. *Elizabeth I*. Illus. Gwen Green. New York: Marshall Cavendish. 32 p.

Green, Robert. 1997. *Queen Elizabeth I*. New York: Franklin Watts. 64 p.

Greenblatt, Miriam. 2002. *Elizabeth I and Tudor England*. Tarrytown, NY: Marshall Cavendish. 88 p.

Greene, Carol. 1990. *Elizabeth the First, Queen of England*. Chicago: Children's Press. 48 p.

Hanff, Helene. 1969. *Queen of England: The Story of Elizabeth I*. Illus. Ronald Dorfman. New York: Doubleday. 144 p.

Hazell, Rebecca. 1996. Queen Elizabeth I, England, 1533-1603. In *Heroines: Great women through the ages*, 32-37. New York: Abbeville Press.

Hodges, C. Walter. 1980. *The battlement garden: Britain from the Wars of the Roses to the age of Shakespeare*. New York: Houghton Mifflin/Clarion Books. (Published in UK in 1979.) 144 p.

King, Marian. 1940. *Elizabeth: The Tudor princess*. Illus. Elinore Blaisdell. Philadelphia: Lippincott. 190 p.

Lace, William W. 1995. *Elizabethan England*. San Diego, CA: Lucent Books. 128 p.

Linington, Elizabeth. 1961. *Forging an empire: Queen Elizabeth I*. Illus. Robert Boehmer. Chicago: Encyclopaedia Britannica Press. 191 p.

Malkus, Alida Sims. 1953. *The story of Good Queen Bess*. Illus. Douglas Gorsline. New York: Grosset & Dunlap. 177 p.

Marshall, H. E. 1937. *Kings & things: First stories from English history*. London: Thomas Nelson and Sons.

Nolan, Jeannette Covert. 1951. *Queen Elizabeth*. Illus. Marie Lawson. Evanston, IL: Row, Peterson and Company. 36 p.

Plaidy, Jean. 1961. *The young Elizabeth*. Illus. William Randell. New York: Roy. 134 p.

Price-Goff, Claire. 2001. *The importance of Queen Elizabeth I*. San Diego, CA: Lucent Books. 112 p.

Sabin, Francene. 1990. *Young Queen Elizabeth*. Illus. John Lawn. Mahwah, NJ: Troll Associates. 48 p.

Stanley, Diane, and Peter Vennema. 1990. *Good Queen Bess: The story of Elizabeth I of England*. Illus. Diane Stanley. New York: Four Winds. n.p.

Strickland, Agnes. 1852. Elizabeth: Second queen-regnant of England and Ireland. In *The queens of England: A series of portraits of distinguished female sovereigns, drawn and engraved by eminent artists with biographical and historical sketches from Agnes Strickland*, new ed., 271-284. New York: Appleton.

Tappan, Eva March, Ph.D. 1902. *In the days of Queen Elizabeth*. Boston: Lothrop, Lee & Shepard. 294 p.

Thomas, Jane Resh. 1998. *Behind the mask: The life of Queen Elizabeth I*. New York: Clarion. 196 p.

Trease, Geoffrey. 1953. *The seven queens of England*. New York: Vanguard. See esp. chapters on the Tudors: Mary, quite contrary, 39-75, and The first Elizabeth, 76-114.

Turner, Dorothy. 1987. *Queen Elizabeth I*. Illus. Martin Salisbury. New York: Bookwright Press. 32 p.

Vance, Marguerite. 1954. *Elizabeth Tudor: Sovereign lady*. Illus. Nedda Walker. New York: Dutton. 157 p.

White-Thomson, Stephen. 1984. *Elizabeth I and Tudor England*. Illus. Gerry Wood. New York: Bookwright Press. 60 p.

Winwar, Frances. 1954. *Queen Elizabeth and the Spanish Armada*. Illus. C. Walter Hodges. New York: Random House. 184 p.

Zamoyska, Betka. 1981. *Queen Elizabeth I*. New York: McGraw-Hill. 69 p.

Reference List: Background

Austen, Jane. 1993. *The history of England from the reign of Henry the 4th to the death of Charles the 1st.* Chapel Hill, NC: Algonquin Books.

Brooks, E. S. 1891. Preface. In *Historical girls: Stories of girls who influenced the history of their times,* iii-iv. New York: G. P. Putnam's Sons.

Compton comment. 1953. *Horn Book Magazine* 29 (3), 172.

Diggins, John Patrick. 1996. The National History Standards. *The American Scholar* 65 (4), 495-522.

Erickson, Carolly. 1983. *The First Elizabeth.* New York: Summit Books.

Hibbert, Christopher. 1991. *The virgin queen: Elizabeth I, genius of the Golden Age.* Reading, MA: Addison-Wesley.

Lee, Elizabeth. 1922. Agnes Strickland (1796-1874). In *The Dictionary of National Biography,* vol. 19, 48-50. London: Oxford University Press.

Levin, Carole. 1994. *"The heart and stomach of a king": Elizabeth I and the politics of sex and power.* Philadelphia: University of Pennsylvania Press.

Ridley, Jasper. 1987. *Elizabeth I: The shrewdness of virtue.* New York: Viking.

Somerset, Anne. 1991. *Elizabeth I.* New York: Knopf.

Starkey, David. 2000. *Elizabeth: The struggle for the throne.* New York: Perennial.

Strachey, Lytton. 1928. *Elizabeth and Essex: A tragic history.* New York: Harcourt, Brace.

Van Loon, Hendrik Willem. 1942. *Van Loon's Lives.* New York: Simon & Schuster.

West, Mark I. 1988. *Children, culture, and controversy.* Hamden, CT: Archon Books.

White, Hayden. 1987. *The content of the form: Narrative discourse and historical representation.* Baltimore: Johns Hopkins.

Chapter 2

1946: Private Women and the Public Good

In 1946, the children's book world was recovering from World War II. Book production, depressed by wartime rationing of paper, was rising; 877 new children's books and editions appeared, up 27 percent from the previous year's 691, but still less than the 1,041 published in 1938 (American Book Production 1947). Librarians and editors had continued to promote children's reading during the war years, and in 1943, largely to provide an institutional basis for Children's Book Week, the Association of Children's Book Editors was organized (Fish 1946). In July, 1946, R. R. Bowker Company placed an ad in *Library Journal* announcing a new edition of "the most widely used children's book catalog in the field": "The Children's Book Parade is back—for the first time since the war."

I found and examined twelve biographies of individual women published in 1946 and recommended for young readers. (For an annotated list, see appendix A.) Notably, with the sole exception of Edgar Parin d'Aulaire (coauthor with his wife of *Pocahontas*), the women's biographers were women themselves. Most of the books were for girls of about twelve or older; exceptions were the d'Aulaires' *Pocahontas,* a picture storybook, and two entries in the Bobbs-Merrill *Childhood of Famous Americans* series (Seymour's *Pocahontas* and Stevenson's *Clara Barton*), recommended for nine-year-olds, fourth graders, or (in the polite phrase of the day) "retarded readers" (Bechtel 1946; Andrus 1946; Dawson 1946a).

Climate for Children's Book Reviewing
in a Postwar World

Children's book editors, reviewers and librarians evaluated these new books in a professional climate touched with idealism. The war, terrible as it was, had raised fervor for democracy to a high pitch, and some hoped to turn that moral energy to the fight against domestic injustice. At the 1946 conference of the American Library Association, President Ralph Ulveling urged members to lead in fighting the "evils of racial and religious hatred" which persisted, although the Allies had beaten governments that nurtured them. He saw prejudice even in the United States, and called librarians to help overcome "limitations on men's freedom" by using their libraries to advance understanding and tolerance for "the Jew, the Negro, and the foreign-born" and for "all the millions of people who in one way or another follow courses divergent from our own" (Ulveling 1946). In a memoir written for adults, Ruth Smith (1946) reported her decades of teaching in black schools, working on the legal defense of falsely accused black men, and occasionally passing as black "to evade my part of the white world's responsibility" for the evils of racism; reviewing for *The Horn Book Magazine,* Jordan (1946d) urged young people to read it "for its charity and insight."

The founding editor of *The Horn Book Magazine* added an internationalist note to an early postwar editorial when she called for "peacetime resistance": individual resistance to evil, remembrance of the suffering of innocents, "a new sense of world brotherhood—and the will to express it" (Mahony 1946, 6). Not everyone dared believe that books for the young could help achieve this. Children's biographer and illustrator James Daugherty (1940), who found "the approach of the makers and mentors of juvenile literature too stuffy, too Victorian and romantic" (234) had doubts: it worried him that American children could enjoy "a beautiful book about Chinese children" while American bombs dismembered Chinese babies (232). Still, he predicted that "modern juvenile literature today and tomorrow can confidently challenge the Nazi primer, the brutality and dullness of dictator propaganda as well as our own apathy and indifference, and in its own particular field help to realize the fullness and goodness of living that is the American faith" (235). A leading youth librarian saw "a world uneasy in peace, troubled by man's mastery of the atomic bomb, united in hope for security but divided on the means for attaining it"; in such times, she felt, we could expect not "great creative writing" but only books with "immediacy rather than permanence." Yet she, too, held out the hope that books for young people would help "the peoples of the world know one another" (Scoggin 1946, 1416).

Such hope was not limited to the United States. In Germany in 1946, Jella Lepman was arguing with the Allied occupation for permission to establish an International Exhibition of Children's Books: "If the war really is over," she told an American general, "the first messengers of that peace will be these children's books" (Lepman 1969, 34). In France Paul Hazard, writing on children's literature between the wars, had already invoked an international republic of childhood, nourished by books. Mahony had published his *Books, Children and Men* in 1943, and by 1947, when she issued a third edition, it was becoming a classic; his passionately witty advocacy of excellence resonated with the ideals of children's librarians and book editors.

In Hazard's egalitarian republic of childhood, boys and girls were prepared for complementary roles. The wise children's writer "knows that little girls show signs of coquetry, and boys of pugnacity, at an early age" (Hazard 1947, 28), and their reading tastes naturally differ:

> Girls demand books that demonstrate maternal feelings in action. Their sympathy is won by heroines who are kind to the afflicted, charitable to the poor, devoted to the sick; by those who take up bravely the daily tasks of the household so as to provide for the loved ones not only the security of affection, but well-being, material comfort, a happy life: both Martha and Mary. Boys demand books of valor, where cowards make a poor showing, where liars are unmasked and punished, and the vainglorious are derided; stories of generous rivalries, where the best man wins; adventures and vicissitudes which exalt the human and increase his strength. Boys and girls want books where truth and justice triumph in the end (Hazard 1947, 168).

These differences between boys and girls were presented as self-evident, and Hazard's American audience, consisting largely of working women, apparently accepted without indignation this view of boys and girls working toward common goals in different ways but with mutual respect.

American Women in 1946

American girls who read new biographies of women in 1946 were the daughters and granddaughters of women who had agitated for the right to vote. The girls had seen women prove they could do men's work; but they had also seen women acquiesce to lower wages for equal work, and to a view of themselves as "an emergency group, a labor reserve for industry, who are called on to fill in when men are not available because they are off to war" (Mezerik 1945, 81). While sociologists spoke of increasing "equality" between boys and girls and erosion of differences between the roles of men and women (Breines 1992), popular culture stressed the undying importance of femininity. So the climate within which new biographies were evaluated was idealistic, but it was also cautious.

The year's biographies reflect the ambiguity of the times. Biographies set before the mid-nineteenth century present young readers with images of strong, cheerful women and girls who perform bravely when occasion demands, but gladly relinquish control to men when the emergency is past. They are charming, and do not demand their own way. Like Caddy Woodlawn or Jo March, they are healthy, intelligent, capable, but willing in the end to be proper ladies. The more recent lives (still firmly rooted in the nineteenth century) show more retiring women—a reclusive poet, two reclusive children's book illustrators, and a Pennsylvania teenager who sacrifices, for the sake of others, her outrageous longing for red silk pantalettes. These are heroines who know how to keep a low profile.

Self-effacement was habitual for women—and it could also be a deliberate strategy. It was an era when African Americans were urged to be nonconfrontational and to rely on education for slow, incremental progress toward social justice; women, too, might hope to achieve more by quiet persistence than by open struggle. Even Mary Beard's 1946 *Woman as Force in History* has passages that breathe a similar atmosphere: tactful, gently humorous, and unthreatening. Beard was a Progressive historian who, with her husband Charles, had written one of the most widely used American history texts. She inspired feminist Gerda Lerner, who calls *Woman as Force in History* the "most important" work on the subject in the early twentieth century, although it "was ridiculed by academic reviewers and otherwise ignored" (Lerner 1993, 271). In it, Beard sought to foster respect between the sexes by "demolishing the long-accepted myth of woman's subjection to man." Advertising recommended it to the female librarian: "it will give you an entirely new view on your sex; you will no longer have to be on the defensive; you will be able to prove that the intellectual, professional woman is not a novelty and that women have always been a powerful factor in the infamies, tyrannies, liberties, and activities that constitute the past" (Macmillan Company 1946). Assuming that the operations of a free economy would naturally favor the exercise of women's competence, Beard challenged fair-minded men only to allow those mechanisms to work without interference or prejudice. Her tone seems pitched to disarm suspicion and allay anxieties about overly spirited women.

In the late 1940s and early 1950s, women's strength worried sociologists. During the war, soldiers left vacancies in the workforce and the wartime defense industry demanded new workers. Older men, teenaged boys, wounded veterans, and the handicapped were not enough to supply this demand, and women filled the gap. Many working-class women moved from service to higher-paying manufacturing jobs for the duration, and many middle-class women now took jobs outside the home. Federal agencies combined both to recruit women and to overcome men's resistance to employing women, working with women, or allowing their own wives to work outside their homes (Colman 1995). At the same time, noncombatant jobs within the military were suddenly open to women in newly formed auxiliary branches of the armed services. To fill a man's job, whether military or civilian, was portrayed as a woman's sacrifice for the war effort. Many women must have felt a heady pride in their individual accomplishment, but in contemporary propaganda and biographies for girls a more corporate pride was salient—a proud solidarity with men in the fight for democracy.

As the war ended, the propaganda changed. Peace would bring "the day when woman may relax and stay in her beloved kitchen," as one optimistic official suggested (Mezerik 1945, 79). Women who had done their patriotic duty by working were now asked to do it by returning home to care for their families. Over three million women had left the workplace by 1946, most of them laid off (Colman 1995). The new "campaign to get women back into the home, to keep them there, emphasized the needs of husbands and children"; the specter of war-strengthened women, "too independent, undomestic, and unfeminine," threatened the security of men (Breines 1992, 33).

Two collections of short biographies published in 1946—Stoddard's *Topflight*, comprised of sketches from wartime issues of *The American Girl* magazine, and Knapp's *New Wings for Women*—introduced career women as inspiring examples to girls seeking vocational guidance. Women had been entering traditionally male occupations in increasing numbers since the nineteenth century, and several of the women profiled in *Topflight* and *New Wings for Women* had been helped and mentored by the pioneers before them. Most were successful before the war, but for many of them, it had opened unexpected opportunities; pilots, businesswomen, and administrators called from established careers to organize and head women's auxiliary forces, all seemed energized by new challenges. Still, in spite of mentors, war work, and their own accomplishments, many of the women spoke of the barriers against girls in their fields and the need to overcome male prejudice, and several felt obligated to warn aspiring girls of difficulties ahead. "It is hard to say just what the opportunities for women pilots will be with so many men now returning from the air forces," admitted test pilot Teddy Kenyon. "Of course, as in many other professions, they will have to be better qualified than men applying for the same job to get it" (Knapp 1946, 16-17). This was not presented as cause for bitterness; it was simply the way things were, for women as well as for racial and religious minorities.

In this climate, prejudice would be fought quietly. Librarians might deplore injustice, but hope to combat it with tact and patience, through education. Open battle for women's issues was not on the professional agenda of the children's book community, where the critics (mostly women), addressing audiences of children's librarians and teachers (almost all women), still used the inclusive male pronoun with magisterial authority in discussions of children's writers (many if not most of them women) and young readers (at least half of them girls).

Critical Standards: Evaluating Biographies for Young Readers

Children's literature experts of the 1940s and 1950s had little doubt that biographies had a role to play in the education and character development of young readers. "These biographies give us new courage and minister to our faith in the essential rightness of the world, the eventual triumph of decency and goodness over the forces of evil," wrote May Hill Arbuthnot (1947, 501) in her influential textbook, *Children and Books*. Lillian Hollowell, recommending the life of George Washington Carver, said "biographies do more than almost any other type of literature to encourage and inspire." At the same time, she commended new biographies for breaking with the dreary, didactic past, when the object of the genre was "to commemorate or instruct, to turn the dead into a fruitful example for the living" (Hollowell 1950, 5). Both in quantity and quality, children's biographies since 1920 excelled their predecessors—a "rare and fine development" which Nesbitt (1953, 392) attributed to "radical change in the conception, teaching, and writing of history for children" after World War I. "The present emphasis," she said, was "almost completely upon the social values of history, upon its economic, cultural, political, and civic aspects," contrasting strongly with the earlier "legendary approach."

Taking her standards for biography from Harold Nicolson's definition of the genre—"the history of the lives of individual men as a branch of literature"—Arbuthnot (1947, 471-478) identified authenticity, objectivity, and a scholarly use of sources as criteria for "biography as history." Discussing "biography as the individual," she pronounced "typed characters unacceptable" and called for depictions of "the whole man," made real by the use of "vivid details." Finally, "biography as literature" required "theme and unity," and "style and pattern." These criteria overlap and occasionally seem to contradict each other. The first few—authenticity, objectivity, scholarly documentation, and portrayal of "the whole man"—are semantic criteria, having to do with the truthfulness or accuracy with which these books depict their subjects. The others—theme, unity, style, pattern, and the use of vivid details— are syntagmatic criteria, having to do with how well the depiction is done, or how effectively the tools of medium and genre are deployed to make a picture that goes beyond mere accuracy. Pragmatic criteria, having to do with the books' use and their effects on young readers, do not fit into Arbuthnot's three-pronged evaluative scheme, but were clearly never far from her mind; her chapter ends with sections on "using biography with children" and "encouraging the reading of biography," and explicit or implicit ideas about the books' use underlie her discussion of all other criteria. In this she was representative.

Choice of Subject

This criterion, which could be considered either semantic (the choice of subject determines which facts are relevant) or pragmatic (the choice of subject is affected by the perceived uses of the genre), was not much emphasized by children's literature critics of the 1940s and 1950s. Arbuthnot (1947, 481) noted that biographies for young children should feature "heroes of action," because "the pre-adolescent child loves action" and "his special heroes . . . are doers." Viguers (1953) commented on publishers' willingness to supply educators' needs for material on "subjects which would help children to understand modern political and social movements and to create racial and religious tolerance"—a "purposeful note in the writing of biography" leading not to literature, but to "a form of didacticism peculiar to this period." Both comments suggest that pragmatic considerations could or should bias the choice of subjects toward those whose stories would appeal to young readers or support curricular needs. They did not make explicit prescriptions, however. Certainly they did not call for more books on specific groups of subjects, although Arbuthnot recommended titles on both "heroines" and "Negroes" under the heading of "Biographies which meet special interests."

Subjects of the 1946 publications include both women of great courage and shy recluses—women who played important public roles in their communities and women who sought private havens. (Often the same women did both.) Reviewers, assessing the subjects almost as often as the books, usually found them worthy. Coincidentally or not, most had played roles in wars: Pocahontas and Madeleine de Verchères in the conflicts between European colonists and Native American peoples, Dolly Madison in the War of 1812, Florence Nightingale in the Crimean War, and Elizabeth Blackwell and Clara Barton in the American Civil War. They had proven their courage and ability in emergencies, and then had gracefully yielded the reins to men, finding outlets for their energies behind the scenes.

Most had lived in the nineteenth century or earlier. The most recent was Beatrix Potter, who had died in 1943; but even she seemed more remote, having produced her famous *Peter Rabbit* before World War I. Perhaps lives and accomplishments that belonged safely to the past made for safer role models. Writers did not disturb the status quo in 1946 when they admitted that women in earlier generations had been unfairly denied the right to education, professional occupation, or the vote. What Elizabeth Blackwell and Florence Nightingale had gained was no more than their just due, and since their efforts had helped reverse the injustices against which they had crusaded, their stories could be used to inspire girl readers to accomplishment without raising questions about the limitations imposed on women in more enlightened modern times.

Reviewers admired at least two subjects for their success in traditionally male activities. The "gallant" de Verchères, with her "magnificent courage, determination, and clever strategy," was "a new and very real heroine for American girls" (Anon. 1946c); and Blackwell, "hewing her way over tradition and prejudice" (Jordan 1946a) had "opened the way for other women" (Anon. 1946a). The more recent subjects, however, were also the more private—and sedentary—as if women's adventuring were a thing of the past. Reviewers were sympathetic toward the three artists: reclusive poet Emily Dickinson, and shy illustrators Potter and Kate Greenaway, caught up in "the creations of her own magical world" (Anon. 1947). Compared to the reformers, the artists posed only modest challenges to society at large; their nonconformity found expression in imaginative creation rather than worldly action. Potter and Greenaway posted their alternate visions in the pages of children's books, and Dickinson, for all her "baffling personality" and "rebellion against the conventions of her time" (Jordan 1946b), kept her poems quietly in drawers. Perhaps even more comfortable to the reviewers were Martha Jane St. Clair, a Pennsylvania girl who cheerfully shared "her mother's cares" (Jordan 1946c) and Dolly Madison, whose "fine personality is a very real inspiration" (Wennerblad 1946). On the whole, reviewers showed a preference for unabrasive heroines with pleasing manners.

Semantic Criteria:
Authenticity, Objectivity, Documentation

Documentation

Documentation, the third of Arbuthnot's semantic criteria, was to some extent a surrogate for the others. Authenticity came from the biographer's thorough familiarity with all relevant sources, and objectivity let those sources speak for themselves, with no distortion or exaggeration for the sake of theme or interpretation. The critics' explanations of all this might be more directly useful to writers than to book selectors, however. In practice, it has always been difficult for children's librarians to know how well new biographies have been researched. Hollowell (1950, 334) observed that biographies for children usually omit notes and bibliographies because they do not "appeal to young readers." Arbuthnot, however, called for more scholarly apparatus:

> Although children may never read footnotes, nevertheless, careful documentation is a guarantee to adults of the authenticity of the material, and it could serve a similar purpose for older children and young people. . . . A continuous acknowledgment of sources is a guarantee to the reader of the historical accuracy and the objectivity of a biography (Arbuthnot 1947, 473).

None of the 1946 biographies had footnotes, but several did indeed include more or less detailed bibliographies or authors' notes. Desmond listed, in no apparent order, twenty "books used for research," ranging from memoirs and letters edited by "Mrs. Madison's grandniece" to biographies of Burr and Madison and a history of Quakers published as recently as 1941; Newcomb listed twenty books "consulted." Two of the most successfully fictionalized books drew on anecdotes which had doubtless been elaborated—Harper built on family reminiscences of Martha Jane Sinclair's romance, and Brill on an account given by Madeleine de Verchères in 1732, forty years after the Mohawk account (Madeleine 2005). Both did extensive research on the backgrounds of their stories, and included two-page bibliographies of sources in regional, local, and social history and genealogy (eighteen of Brill's forty-six entries were in French).

Authenticity and Fictionalization

Biography "should be as accurate and authentic as research can make it," wrote Arbuthnot (1947, 472). Hollowell agreed: "The first test is authenticity: the biography should be truthful and accurate" (1950, 334). In children's biography, however, authenticity was not considered incompatible with a degree of fictionalization. Arbuthnot distinguished between "fictionalized biographies," which were "based on careful research" but cast "known facts into dramatic episodes complete with conversation," and "biographical fiction," which could stray further from the historical record and was perhaps "the finest pattern of biography for young people and children" (Arbuthnot 1947, 479).

Fictionalization was the rule in the 1946 biographies. Lane's scholarly life of Potter was the exception: a twentieth-century life, presented without fictionalization. Brill, Desmond, Gould, Harper, Kerr, Morgan, Newcomb, Nolan, Seymour, and Stevenson all used more or less novelistic strategies to interpret their subjects' personalities and careers. Newcomb (1946) explained that she had "created a character to serve in the place of the 'girl-cousin' briefly mentioned in the definitive life of Kate Greenaway" because, unable to find information about the cousin, she felt it would be "unfair to picture some one about whom I could get no information." She had also "incorporated into the dialogue" material from the letters of Greenaway and John Ruskin. Few writers described their practice so explicitly, but the use of correspondence and other primary sources as a basis for dialogue was common practice and was at least implied by Morgan (1946) in her one-sentence foreword: "When you turn these pages, Dolly Madison's story comes to you from old letters tied with bright ribbons, long treasured diaries, and the happy memories of those who knew Aunt Dolly in the White House."

Not all subjects left letters. Pocahontas is known through the records of the white settlers of Jamestown. Brill (1946) took the story of Madeleine de Verchères and the Iroquois siege from her own account to a later governor of New France, but "Whether she wrote it out herself or one of the Governor's clerks set it down on paper as she told it, we do not know" (Brill 1946, 201-2). The sparse documentation available for such long-dead subjects may have necessitated a certain freedom of invention, but the relationship between fictionalization and authenticity was not simple. Fictional episodes (like Seymour's 1946 interpretation of the "adoption" of John Smith by Pocahontas) often appear to be based on substantial research, even where subsequent scholarship has thrown the old interpretations into doubt.

To determine the factual accuracy of the books is beyond my scope, but it is instructive to see how two biographers select and shape the details of a single life. Morgan and Desmond both embellish the story of Dolly Madison, expanding sketchy material into dramatic episodes. Morgan, in a chapter recalling the Nancy Drew books, has Dolly accidentally trapped in the "dungeon" where a former owner of her family's Virginia home is said to have chained Negroes; the experience prevents her early meeting with James Madison, but teaches her a deeper sympathy for slaves. Desmond's account, more closely based on a traditional anecdote, is no less exciting: British troops occupy the estate while Dolly's father fights in the Continental army, and Dolly hides with her family in the tunnel where the former owner is rumored to have chained his wife.

Although she did not invent it, Desmond's story of underground peril is almost as dubious as Morgan's. Anthony (1949) argues persuasively that Dolly's Quaker father never fought in the Revolution, and that his patriotic record was invented by a nineteenth-century historian. Desmond was faithful to the apocryphal anecdote; Morgan adapted it freely and moved it from Dolly's early childhood to her adolescence, where it highlights the issue of slavery, avoids the issue of spousal abuse, and foreshadows Dolly's love of Madison.

Desmond and Morgan both emphasize the personal aspects of Dolly's life. They do place her in public context. Morgan, presenting Dolly as a responsible and public-spirited woman, often fictionalizes episodes from private life as a way to introduce public issues; thus, taking shelter with a mountain man, the Madisons hear a populist view of federal taxes. The conversation is contrived, but helps explain an authentic political reality, making the Madisons' personal experience serve as a window onto the state of the nation. Desmond focuses on issues in which Dolly was more directly involved, and draws the reader's attention to the private and emotional significance of public events like the treachery of her friend, Aaron Burr. Desmond's account is less fictionalized and better documented, but is it more authentic? Few children's librarians or even reviewers would have the expertise to be sure.

One pragmatic reason for the general acceptance of fictionalized biography was its appeal. Hollowell (1950, 333) believed that fictionalized dialogue "makes the narrative more interesting and more dramatic, especially for young readers," and the practice "is legitimate if not overdone." Perhaps another reason was that a fictionalized episode could cover the omission of an unpalatable fact.

Omissions and Partial Biography

While calling for objective truth in juvenile biographies, critics still expected them to omit "unsavory episodes" (Arbuthnot 1947, 480) or "episodes which are too tragic for young readers or not understandable" (Hollowell 1950, 334). Partial biography was useful for this. Morgan cast her life of Dolly Madison as a rags-to-riches story, beginning with Dolly's midteens and ending with the restoration of the nation's peace and Madison's popularity at the end of his second term. The d'Aulaires ended the story of Pocahontas with her success at court and avoided mentioning her death in England; Seymour, distancing the sorrow, saved it for an impersonal "three hundred years later" epilogue.

The partial biography enables writers not only to avoid "tragic" and "unsavory" episodes, but also to give authentic biographical material the shape of fiction. Brill wrote an adventure story based on only one dramatic episode in the life of Madeleine de Verchères, and Harper wrote a romance by telling only the story of Martha Jane St. Clair's adolescence. By framing a life passage that can be easily adapted to a conventional plot, partial biography facilitates the selection and arrangement of facts and the presentation of a cohesive, plausible character. Omission creates the illusion of completeness.

Historical Placement: Scene-setting and Explanation

Critics expected that writers would omit sensitive material from biographies. At the same time, they expected the addition of historical details and explanatory passages. Assuming that biography could serve as an enticing introduction to history, and that children's store of historical knowledge was less complete than adults', selectors were encouraged to find biographies that recreated "the times and conditions" in which real people lived (Hollowell 1950, 333).

The biographers differed in their attempts to evoke or fill in historical background. Perhaps the most diligent was Laura Kerr, who in *Doctor Elizabeth* repeatedly summarized political events and social conditions. Earl Grey's reform bill and the 1832 riots affected the Blackwells' decision to move from England to the United States, where Mr. Blackwell quickly involved himself in the abolitionist movement. The 1837 depression drove the family's move to Cincinnati. Other events and trends, with less direct personal significance, serve as historical backdrop for Blackwell's life: America's war with Mexico (1848), France's "bitter though bloodless political war" and general European unrest (1849), or the improved New York City water supply and introduction of gas, bananas, and ice cream.

Yet Kerr misses many opportunities to put the events of Blackwell's own life in contexts that now seem relevant. The education of doctors was very different then; Blackwell needed just two years of study at Geneva College, supplemented by private reading and hospital practice, to qualify. Kerr describes the system in bits, as Blackwell grapples with it, but not as a whole. She mentions how much money Blackwell needed to finance her education ($3,000) and how she raised it (giving music lessons, trying to market short stories), but it would also be useful to know things like how much money she earned for a music lesson or a short story. (Was money simply a taboo subject? Norma Johnston in 1991 was far more explicit than Cornelia Meigs in 1933 about the economic conditions of Louisa May Alcott's family.) Kerr says less than she might about the lot of women, too; she is more interested in the contrasts between rich and poor, modern and benighted.

Some of the historical details fit smoothly into the story, as when, describing Blackwell's difficulty in finding a room, Kerr explains that "nice women didn't live alone." At other times the introduction of current events is more contrived. Lodging with people who discuss politics at breakfast, Blackwell says, "When one lives half one's life in England and the other half in America it is difficult to keep up with one's history" (L. Kerr 1946, 129); the polite, self-deprecatory comment is Kerr's pretext for a quick history lesson.

Half a century after their publication, the absence of diversity in these biographies is conspicuous. Blacks are just visible on the periphery of the nineteenth-century lives. Dolly Madison's father, John Payne, was a Quaker who freed his slaves and sold his plantation when Dolly was in her teens. Both Desmond and Morgan give her nurse, "Mammy" or "Mother Amy," an important part in Dolly's early years. She speaks dialect, is always consoling, and in Desmond's account refuses to spend the money she's paid after manumission, saving it all for Dolly. Blackwell, whose father was involved in abolitionist work, is horrified by the treatment of Negroes when she teaches for a time in Kentucky, and Martha Jane St. Clair slips an apple to a chained slave. The young reader is invited to identify with white abolitionists, to whom the very idea of slavery is grounds for indignation; but the issue is not made central, and the portrayal of black characters is stereotyped.

Native Americans are important in three of the biographies, all set in the seventeenth century. Treatments of Pocahontas are discussed in chapter 5; in 1946 she was the only nonwhite subject, with two biographies celebrating her friendship and support of the colonists. Less famous, but also tremendously appealing, was Madeleine de Verchères, whose aristocratic family ran a seigneury, an estate farmed by peasant *habitants* and garrisoned by soldiers, by the St. Lawrence River. Madeleine sees "this dangerous country of New France" as "our own country" (Brill 1946, 2). The "ferocious Mohawks" and other Iroquois are enemies to the French colonists, but Brill does not suggest that the mere process of colonization provokes enmity; rather, France and England are at war, and to "their everlasting shame, both sides [use] their Indian friends against their . . . foes" (48). Fourteen-year-old Madeleine is left in charge when both her parents are called away in 1692. The Mohawks, attacking while the small garrison is hunting and the farmers are at work, capture almost all the men. Madeleine has two cowardly soldiers to protect the women and children in the blockhouse, and an old veteran and two little brothers to help her mount guard above; she defends the settlement for a week, until French soldiers arrive to lift the siege. Throughout the ordeal, she displays courage, strategic intelligence, and a leader's tact, encouraging the best efforts of others.

Her twelve-year-old brother Louis hates "those savages," "those vile Iroquois." Madeleine argues for understanding: "the white man" has not "always been kind or even just to the red man," and she reminds Louis of French violence and betrayal. "Anyone can see why they hate us and want their revenge." Even so, some Indians become Christians and help the French in their campaigns; these are the "good Indians" (Brill 1946, 22-23, 189-190). Madeleine assumes both the French right to colonize and an obligation to judge Indians individually, on a case-by-case basis.

Pocahontas and Madeleine stood at the frontiers where European and North American cultures met. Their stories were told in ways that valorize the colonists' achievements and suppress questions about their costs to Native Americans. From John Smith to Seymour and the d'Aulaires, or from Madeleine de Verchères to Brill, there was a cultural continuity; biographers of European descent shared with European colonists some of the interests and assumptions that shaped their interpretations of events.

Between the biographers and another group of subjects, the working middle- and upper-class women of the nineteenth and early twentieth centuries, there was a greater commonality. Women like Elizabeth Blackwell stood at the frontiers that separated home from the public worlds of work, reform, and volunteer service. Their achievements enlarged the opportunities of women who came after them. In their biographies, too, questions about what their accomplishments could have cost others are elided—as are questions about any remaining gender bias in society.

Breines (1992) reports that sociologists in the 1950s worried about the cost to middle-class families of women's advancement: some believed that working wives threatened men's self-esteem as wage earners, and working mothers fostered juvenile delinquency. The 1946 biographies do not address such concerns directly, but most portray their subjects in ways that disarm anxiety. By omitting any discussion of ongoing prejudices against Native Americans, African Americans, or women, they give the impression that such evils are confined to the past and that modern young readers inherit a world of tolerance and enlightened brotherhood. (Girls, of course, are included in the brotherhood.)

Objectivity, Theme, and Characterization

Arbuthnot (1947, 472) made objectivity her second criterion for biography: "A biographer is not free to give his own opinions or to present an interpretation for which he has no evidence." Her fellow critics agreed. "Romantic bias is no guide to the seeker after truth," said biographer Jeannette Eaton (1942, 122). Yet, biography was also literature, and although as a historian the biographer could not impose his opinion on the facts, as a writer he had an obligation to impose order on them. "There must be no juggling with the historical facts of the case—or at least no more than is needed to cast [the] story into the form of art. And there's the difficulty," mused C. W. Hodges (1940, 332).

Arbuthnot's solution was theme. The biographer must discover it gradually, she said, while sifting through all the sources. To select a theme prematurely and impose it on the evidence would result in a "biased, subjective biography," but without a theme there could be only "a chronological record which may lack wholeness and charm." Theme should guide the selection and organization of facts "so that they not only reveal the man as [the biographer] has come to see him, but . . . also give unity to that life and to the book" (Arbuthnot 1947, 475). In practice, then, the theme appears almost indistinguishable from the biographer's interpretation of the subject's character or the significance of his life. Noting that titles often reveal theme, Arbuthnot gave as one example the role of destiny in the life of Jeanette Eaton's *Washington, Leader by Destiny*.

Objecting to the "older biographies which presented a man as a type—Washington the ever truthful, Lincoln the sad, and Benjamin Franklin the thrifty," Arbuthnot (1947, 473) called for rounded characterization as both more accurate and more appealing to readers. Again, the two biographies of Dolly Madison offer an interesting contrast, differing profoundly in their interpretations of Dolly's character, and especially her feelings for Madison. Dolly accepted Madison's proposal after some hesitation, and even on her wedding day expressed her ambivalence in a letter to a friend: "Evening—Dolly Madison! Alas!" (Anthony 1949, 89). Morgan shows her deeply in love with Madison, and regretful only because the marriage cuts her off from the Quaker community. Desmond shows her enthralled by the charming but unreliable Aaron Burr, and growing into a deeper love for the faithful Madison only with years of marriage. The evidence, according to Anthony, could support either interpretation.

Morgan's Dolly is a loving daughter and wife, a woman who ably supports her husband's career but longs to retire to his Virginia estate. Genuinely sociable, she assumes the role of a political hostess with graceful verve, but at the expense of her own privacy and comfort. Her loyalty to Madison never wavers. Desmond's Dolly is a conflicted woman who risks sacrificing the public interest and Madison's reputation to her own desire for society, status, and political favors to her family and friends (including Burr). In this account, she does not forfeit her privacy to political duty, but uses political influence for private goals, pushing Madison to continue as president because the excitement of the capital suits her better than his beloved farm. Overcoming his deep reluctance, he declares war in 1812 to assure her "of another four years as First Lady" (Desmond 1946, 186). Yet it was this Dolly, rather than Morgan's sunnily virtuous one, that a *Library Journal* reviewer singled out as an "inspiration" (Wennerblad 1946).

Perhaps the reviewer considered her life inspiring because she weathered hardships—always a popular theme. Desmond's whole-life narrative follows her subject past the triumphant years. In her long widowhood, she suffered from poverty and the impositions of her idle spendthrift son, but "in a shabby, high-waisted gown" continued to be "the most popular hostess in Washington" (Desmond 1946, 258). The *Booklist* reviewer found Desmond's book "superior in every way" to Morgan's (Anon. 1946b). As a piece of literature it is unified by Desmond's focus on Dolly's passion for Burr and slower appreciation of Madison. Could this unconsummated extramarital romance have endeared the book to reviewers by making Dolly believably imperfect?

Maybe not; or maybe a woman's faults, to be attractive, had to be feminine. Accuracy required that juvenile biography should present "the whole man" (Arbuthnot 1947). At the same time, the genre was supposed to inspire young readers to emulate its subjects. It was one thing for girls to read about women who overcame common domestic flaws in their characters, and quite another thing to read about women who succeeded in life by acting altogether too masculine.

Reviewers praised Nolan's *Florence Nightingale*, but noted that the subject is portrayed as not "an altogether likable person" (Anon. 1947) or "an entirely lovable character" (Scoggin 1947). The popular image of Nightingale—the Lady with the Lamp, soothing the wounded in a barracks hospital; the young aristocrat who sacrificed her personal ease for the good of others—might inspire girl readers to fine endeavors; it had a romantic resonance. But Nightingale's contributions did not end with the Crimean War, and neither did Nolan's biography. Behind the inspiring image lay a steely character who, in the decades after the Crimean, spearheaded the reform of British military hospitals; published instructive pamphlets on nursing and hospitals which "were in reality the basis for all methods of modern treatment of the sick"; lobbied successfully for sanitation in India; and helped to found a training school for nurses, to reform the workhouses and infirmaries, and to enact new Poor Laws (Nolan 1946, 181, 187-189). She managed most of this from her sickbed, with the help of loyal friends like cabinet minister Sidney Herbert and John Sutherland, whom she drove unmercifully. Nolan's portrayal of Nightingale's adult life closely parallels Strachey's in *Eminent Victorians* (1918), a famous debunking of cultural icons.

Strachey, a master of the ironic, must have relished the fact that his "debunking" of Nightingale consisted largely of establishing that she was more accomplished, more effective, and even more valuable than people thought.

Syntagmatic Criteria:
The Rhetoric of Fictionalized Biography

Arbuthnot placed her syntagmatic criteria (including theme and unity, style and pattern, and the use of vivid details) well after authenticity and objectivity: first the truth told should be true, and then it should be well presented. Yet presentation influences content. The choice of theme may be governed by the facts, as she said, but it governs in turn the selection and arrangement of facts. It is embodied in style and pattern—rhetorical choices that color the reader's experience of a book's truth.

Style

"Biographies often read aloud well," wrote Anne Thaxter Eaton (1940, 221), and she praised an autobiography that "reads like an adventure story" (223). Contemporary discussions of style in biography emphasized its effects: the sound of the language, and the text's ability to hold a reader's interest. Arbuthnot (1947) quoted an unnamed expert: "style is 'the auditory effect of prose.'" Hollowell's suggestions for the evaluation of style also point to its effects:

> Some points to be considered are these: Is the biography so well written and so well organized that it reads like a novel? Has it humor, vitality, and vivid details? (Hollowell 1950, 334).

For better or for worse, most girls' biographies published in 1946 do indeed "read like novels." The critics, discussing fictionalization, usually meant the invention of dramatic conversations and the inclusion of subjects' thoughts. The biographies also resembled fiction in narrative strategy. Third-person narration, either by an omniscient narrator or restricted to the subject's viewpoint, was the rule. Voices ranged from the d'Aulaires' folkloric evocation of Powhatan's woods to Lane's scholarly restraint.

The introductions set the tone for these books. They serve both to secure the reader's sympathy and to help reconstruct the historical setting. For example, we meet the future Dolly Madison as a March wind blows about the old plantation and the clock strikes eight:

> Dolly Payne tilted her head to listen while she tied the threads of a square of linen just taken from her loom. Folding the cloth, she sang,
> "'All in the merry month of May
> The green buds they were swelling.'"
> Her song was interrupted by someone calling, "Dolly, I'm ready to give thee the house keys." A trace of sadness tinged the Irish lilt of the voice.
> "I'm coming, mother." Dolly blew out the candle on the stand and threw the cloth on its pile in the drawer of the cherry bureau, then lifting her gray skirt from the floor with both hands, she sped down the stairs so fast that her cheeks became as pink as the arbutus in the woodland near by (Morgan 1946, 11).

As literature, this is somewhat handicapped by its weight of information. Morgan has introduced a handicraft, a folk song, an ethnic heritage, a piece of furniture, the family's religious adherence to Quaker gray, and a local wildflower, all in her first page of text. She has implied that a girl of fourteen would be weaving by candlelight. Perhaps, although she hasn't documented it with a bibliography or notes, Morgan has done almost too much research. But the details of Dolly's life are there for the reader to experience, not to study; the major effect of the passage is to establish Dolly as a cheerful and energetic character, quickly obedient to her mother, and to raise a question: why is Dolly's mother sad? This is the rhetoric of fiction, not nonfiction, with its combination of scene-setting, character description, and narrative hook.

In another introductory scene, young Florence Nightingale checks the arrangements for her family's annual charity banquet. All is in order: "'And a good thing!' thought Florence, who, at thirteen, had no patience with plans which failed" (Nolan 1946, 3). Nolan's early chapters, like Morgan's, embed traditional anecdotes in a fictionalized account of her subject's youth: Nightingale, with her "strange knack of understanding strange people" (5), comforts the needy and nurses sick dolls and pets. Readers learn quickly that she is hard-working, well organized, and eager to right wrongs, but also "a little stubborn . . . in a polite and sweet-tempered way, of course; which, as everybody knows, is the most wearisome sort of stubbornness to combat and overcome" (16). The gentle humor is one of the book's minor pleasures, simultaneously flattering and enlarging young readers' developing insight into human nature.

As the book continues, however, gentle humor sharpens into an irony that distances Nightingale from the reader. The shift in tone must owe something to the availability of more factual (and critical) sources for the subject's later life; Nolan's later chapters echo his ironic tone, as well as his content. This tends to undermine sympathy for Nightingale, even when the irony is used to express her own impatience with others. For instance, at the barracks hospital in the Crimean, hidebound officers who resented her reforms called her "the Bird":

> Oh, yes, a thoroughly objectionable female, the Bird. Perhaps the most unpardonable, really maddening of her habits was that of always being right. . . . Of course, such a woman must not be countenanced. Whisper about her, harass her—ridicule her! (Nolan 1946, 115-116).

This is meant to be turned back against the officers. It has a triumphant undercurrent, rather like the quiet "we showed them" attitude of the aviators in *New Wings for Women* (Knapp 1946): Nightingale's clear vision, hard work, and dedication prevail, and rightly so. Yet Nolan turns the same kind of indirect discourse against Nightingale herself. She argued against the marriage of nurses at Scutari, but they

> went on and got married, just the same—as she had supposed they would. In such circumstances, her hands were tied, her superior insight of no avail; she could do nothing to prevent their folly (Nolan 1946, 135).

One could read this as affectionate exasperation, ventriloquizing Nightingale's own exasperation with the nurses, but there is an implied distance between the narrator's attitude and Nightingale's that encourages greater skepticism. Is she arrogant, crediting herself with "superior insight"? Is she trying to hold onto power? The style prompts readers to question, rather than embrace, the heroine.

Pattern

Rather than defining pattern, Arbuthnot gave examples: Carl Sandburg's evocation of wild crab-apple trees and stars in the experience of Nancy Hanks, and Elizabeth Janet Gray's foreshadowing of "scattered lives" that would be intertwined with that of the newly born William Penn. "These examples show how biography, although as scrupulously documented as history, may become in the act of composition a branch of literature" (Arbuthnot 1947, 478). The underlying assumption seems to be that a literary work is defined by its unity; what makes a biography literature is the use of rhetorical devices to give it consistency, to make the life seem coherent and unified.

Several of the 1946 biographies seemed to take their patterns from juvenile fiction. Not all used the same genre. The d'Aulaires shaped the story of Pocahontas into a kind of fairy tale, while Seymour made it more of a girl's adventure story, with an episodic structure and domestic interests. Morgan used some of the same conventions to tell Dolly Madison's story. The themes that most effectively unified these books were common to fiction, as well. There was desire—for love, for achievement, or for the meaning of life—and there was the quest for character development and self-mastery, which often meant the denial of desire. Desmond's Dolly Madison gained nobility as she overcame her longing for Aaron Burr, and Harper's Martha Jane Sinclair, much as she longed for red silk pantalettes, habitually put the needs of others first. Harper, although she started from family history, had more leeway than most for fictionalization; Martha's dream of red silk, threading through her mostly homespun existence, becomes a powerful metaphor for the way an imaginative, quirky nineteenth-century girl fits herself into an outwardly humdrum community.

The one unfictionalized biography in the 1946 sample was just as patterned. Lane's tactful life of Beatrix Potter, an adult book reviewed for young readers, used metaphor to achieve a subtle unity in the account of Potter's long and varied life. The child of wealthy middle-class parents who expected her neither to work nor to marry, Potter spent her childhood and youth in mothballs, making polite but determined efforts to get out. Unable to establish herself as a scientific illustrator—mainly, it seems, for lack of opportunity rather than ability—she achieved both financial independence and a first romance with *The Story of Peter Rabbit*. Her fiancé, publisher Norman Warne, died before they could be married, but at the age of forty-seven she defied her parents to marry a lawyer, William Heelis; she became a successful farmer and the first woman to chair the Herdwick Breeders' Association.

Lane did not rake up the decently buried details of Potter family quarrels, but she created a current of dramatic tension by a metaphoric use of the mundane. Striped woolen stockings evoke the prickly stuffiness of a too-protected childhood. Whole chapters are named for houses: Bolton Gardens, in which Beatrix was isolated as a dependent for so long; Bedford Square, where in the Warnes' home "she had her first experience of what happy human family life could be"; and Hill Top Farm, where she invested not only the proceeds of her unexpected commercial success but her life and happiness. There were, as well, the many nests and burrows of her small animal householders; Lane makes it tempting to see them as Potter's imaginative shelters for her spirit, no longer needed once she had established a happy home of her own. Without resorting to imagined episodes or conversations, Lane used metaphor and narrative effectively to create sympathy for a character who is shown as complex, but deeply integrated and complete.

Pragmatic Criteria

Behind all the considerations of accuracy and quality were the critics' beliefs about how juvenile biographies were to be used. Anne Thaxter Eaton (1940) regretted the unpopularity of the genre, but Arbuthnot (1947) and Viguers (1953) both reported that children had discovered biographies and they were no longer languishing unread. Hollowell (1950, 334) expressed concern about age appropriateness, saying that a "common weakness of biographies for children has been their use of a vocabulary too mature for children's comprehension." The consensus, however, was that juvenile biographies were better than ever: less didactic, better researched, and more popular.

Biography served children's intellectual growth, giving them "the easiest and most natural bridge from fanciful and imaginative literature to realistic and factual" (Hollowell 1950, 333). It introduced them to history, and could boost patriotism, giving "to American boys and girls a fine flavor of their own country" (A. Eaton 1940, 225). It could be correlated with school subjects, giving added interest to teaching units (Arbuthnot 1947).

More important still, however, was its role in moral development: it provided heroes to emulate. Fiction of the time was praised when the protagonists were basically good people, with only slight character flaws (Andrews 1946). Other characters might be evil, cowardly, or weak, but the writer made it clear which traits were admirable and which were not. This approach would help prepare young readers for life, Andrews argued, by showing them how to recognize evil and respond to it. Similar rationales were applied to biographies, in which good people with slight character flaws triumphed over hardship and evil: "to live with heroes for a time is to know beyond doubt and terror how strong is goodness. . . . To watch those who have walked ahead is to know that we ourselves need not falter" (J. Eaton 1942, 125).

Heroines: Shy Women with Missions

Who were the proper role models for girls to emulate? Arbuthnot, demonstrating that books on heroines really did exist, recommended titles on Joan of Arc, Clara Barton, Louisa May Alcott, Julia Ward Howe, the English queens Elizabeth and Victoria, Madame Curie, the Soong sisters, and Anna Pavlova. Few girl readers would be expected to grow up as saints or queens, physicists or ballerinas. More would follow Barton and Nightingale into nursing, but what could be emulated in most subjects' lives would be their characters and moral decisions, as portrayed by the biographers.

The very achievements that made a woman famous enough to merit a biography could also make her less appropriate as a model for girls, and might be downplayed to make her life story reflect the ideal of contemporary womanhood. Oddly, this practice may have been more confining in some ways in 1946 than in the Victorian era. Vicinus analyzed girls' books on Nightingale (not including Nolan's) from the 1880s to the 1950s, and found the nineteenth-century biographies likelier to inspire girl readers to engage in public work:

> Until the 1950s girls' biographies based their plots upon the opposition between the benighted public and the far-sighted heroine. Authors avoided introducing their young readers to sexual conflict. But the post-World War II era saw the growth of the "feminine mystique," with its emphasis upon romance, the nuclear family and the subordination of women to men. This is obviously reflected in stories for girls (Vicinus 1990, 102).

Most of the 1946 biographies foreshadow the 1950s trend Vicinus describes. Authors minimized conflict between parents and children, sisters and brothers, and (above all) men and women; they emphasized instead moral purpose, sacrifice for others, and—even in the case of subjects who had foresworn marriage for work—their heroines' feminine appeal and deferential consultations with men.

The writers of these fictionalized biographies, while advocating freedom of choice for women, emphasized their subjects' femininity; their charm, attractiveness to men and reliance on male support; and their desire for privacy. Few of their subjects were whole-hearted feminists. "Strangely, perhaps, Miss Nightingale was never an advocate of feminism," remarks Nolan; "she did not favor the participation of women in either politics or government." This seems contradictory in a woman who regularly consulted with cabinet ministers and devoted her best energies to reforming a branch of the government, but she was not alone. Kerr reports that Blackwell deplored suffragists as "women fanatics . . . wearing trousers" (L. Kerr 1946), and Blackwell's correspondence supports this, revealing her antagonism toward "bloomerism, abolitionism, woman's rightism" and her sister-in-law, suffragist Lucy Stone (A. Kerr 1992).

One element in subjects' resistance to feminism may have been dislike of publicity, which is depicted as troublesome in several of these books. Andersen (1996, 4) notes that by the first two decades of the twentieth century, women were beginning to inhabit public spaces like streets, parks, and stores more freely and there was a consequent erosion of "the distinctions between 'good,' 'respectable,' 'private' women on the one hand, and 'bad' or 'public' women on the other." Still, press coverage was not considered altogether appropriate for ladies in the 1940s, and readers would not have been surprised that nineteenth-century women shunned it. Smith (1946), in her memoir of the fight against racism, rarely used the first person singular or mentioned living people by name; she shielded her own and her friends' privacy behind a corporate first person plural.

For some, publicity was adverse; Desmond shows Madison surrounded by political controversy and gossip. Almost always it was distasteful. Blackwell, like "all nice young ladies," dreaded notoriety. Newspapers around the nation reported her medical school entrance, and women living near the school ostracized her (L. Kerr 1946, 82-83). Beatrix Potter's "passionate obsession with her own privacy" was legendary (Lane 1946a, 440). Kate Greenaway, "driven to the end of her patience" by prying journalists, wrote to one of them, "You must wait till I am dead; till then I wish to live my life privately—like an English gentlewoman" (Newcomb 1946, 95). Nightingale, by contrast, made ruthless use of her celebrity, threatening publication if a slow-moving cabinet secretary did not move on her reforms: "The last thing he could afford was to find himself pitted against her in a public airing of her cause" (Nolan 1946, 171).

In some of the subjects, ladylike avoidance of public exposure was intensified by shyness. Barton and Greenaway shrank from attention; Gould's Emily Dickinson was occasionally diffident in spite of her popularity. Was there a relationship between avoidance of society and thirst for great achievement? An element in shyness is the uneasy consciousness of one's difference, exposed to critical view; by withdrawing, one escapes ridicule or condemnation before it is voiced. Their very ambition marked women professionals and artists as different in times when women were not supposed to be ambitious for achievement or recognition beyond their own intimate circles.

In some of these books, youthful shyness is portrayed as a mild character defect to be overcome. As faults go, it may have been a desirable one, allied to a virtuous feminine modesty; but on some level it was also recognized as a form of selfishness. Stevenson introduces Clara Barton as an able child handicapped by extreme bashfulness. She is unable to conquer it until she bravely volunteers to help nurse her brother; her family prayed "she would get the strength to fight battles," and in the end "strength was given her to fight battles for others" (Stevenson 1946, 122). For some of these women, shyness may have been a feminine camouflage for unacceptable ambition. It could be cured—as ambition could be excused—by devoting one's life to a noble cause.

Kerr and Gould portrayed Elizabeth Blackwell and Emily Dickinson as heroines devoted to noble causes. Blackwell was the first woman to gain admission to a medical school in the United States, and graduated at the top of her class. Not welcome to practice in American hospitals, she interned in Paris before beginning private practice in New York City. Male physicians did not refer patients to her, but she gave public lectures on hygiene and sanitation, gained the support of philanthropically inclined women, and in 1857 opened the "first hospital for women and children to be staffed by women doctors and nurses"; it became a teaching hospital after the Civil War, with the addition of a college for women doctors. In 1869 Blackwell opened a practice in London, becoming one of the first professors in the London School of Medicine for Women and helping to found the National Health Society. After 1873 she gave up practice because of poor health, but stirred new controversy a few years later with the publication of a book advocating sex education (L. Kerr 1946, 167-196).

Unlike the Nightingales, the Blackwells had suffered economic ruin, and Elizabeth's work contributed to her family's survival; gender, more than class, barred her from work in medicine. Kerr opposes her achievement to the typical domestic responsibilities of women; work and marriage offer mutually exclusive ways to define identity. As a comfortable wife in England, Elizabeth's mother is decorative and does "little of importance" with her days (L. Kerr 1946, 16); as an impoverished widow in Cincinnati, she is "only half a person" (42). Elizabeth tells her mother that although she enjoys men's company, she will never marry: "I think it is that I should hate to lose my individuality" (56). She confides in her brother Harry that "[s]ewing and flirting and learning to cook just don't interest" her; she feels called to do "something big," to "be really useful in the world" (62). She cannot accept the local doctor's advice to "bake a good pound cake, my dear. You will be far happier and so will some young man" (64).

Blackwell has a noble mission, however, so that what might otherwise appear a selfish ambition to retain her own individuality can be seen instead as a sacrificial dedication to helping others. As a child she is outraged by social injustice, and vows to correct it when she grows up. Although she has "a strange feeling that in some way I can better learn to serve mankind" (45), she finds herself "drifting aimlessly" until she realizes that "thinking only of myself and my own pleasure" causes her unhappiness (57-58). When her dying friend Sophie proposes that she should become a doctor, because women "need women doctors," Blackwell is revulsed; she has to overcome a loathing for "anything to do with the human body" before she can consider it (60-61)—a reluctance that makes her work seem more of a sacrifice than Nightingale's. She finds comfort in prayer, and, like Nightingale, validation for her mission in mystical experience.

In her long quest for medical training, Blackwell is helped by a few established physicians who give her access to their books, support her applications to medical schools, and advance her careers. Kerr shows her friendly deference to these mentors; her friendly camaraderie with classmates at Geneva and her brothers Harry and Sam; and friendships verging on romance with Charles Plevin in England and Dr. Blot in France. Although she meets opposition and resentment from young interns with whom she practices in Philadelphia, Kerr passes quickly over it, noting merely that in a typhoid epidemic Blackwell works "side by side with the young men who so recently had hindered her at every turn" (L. Kerr 1946, 92).

Blackwell resembled Nightingale in the nature and scope of her accomplishments. Emily Dickinson resembled her in another way: she became a recluse. As a girl, Dickinson attended Amherst Academy and Mount Holyoke Female Seminary; she was a good student, and Gould emphasizes her popularity with classmates. Her reclusive life and the suggestions of passion, loss, and doubt in her poems have stimulated speculation about some hidden drama in her life, but although much of her voluminous correspondence has survived, even her earliest letters raise as many questions as they answer. Her "Master" remains unidentified—one of several unsolved mysteries.

Dickinson as a girl was not without romantic possibilities. There is a tradition—probably apocryphal (Sewall 1974)—that her father forbade her to marry George Gould; but Gould (1946), in fictionalized dialogue, attributes the rejection of his proposal to Emily herself:

> The way I feel is not enough—it's hard to explain, but—well, if I ever marry, I shall expect to give up my whole heart and soul, to be holding out even as the man, whoever he is, asks for it. To me, marriage must mean complete union of the two who enter it—or else it is valueless, even wicked. . . (Gould 1946, 162).

Like Kerr's Blackwell, Gould's Dickinson cannot imagine reconciling the absolute demands of her mission to the absolute demands of marriage and homemaking; but she appears deferential to men, actively searching for mentors. Gould's account of her girlhood and youth centers on her quest for personal, religious, and poetic truth, and her reliance on a series of men for support and guidance. Most important in her early years is Ben Newton, a fellow seeker who recognizes and encourages her gifts. Most important in the end is the Reverend Charles Wadsworth. She hears him preach in Philadelphia and consults with him in his office; after their interview she has a vision that leaves her permanently reassured, "all doubt gone from her mind." Secure in her faith, she returns to Amherst, where he visits her twice. After his second visit she withdraws from the world to dedicate her life entirely to "the search for truth"; "only alone could the mind soar into unknown worlds and discover unknown thoughts" (Gould 1946, 207-211). Thus her relations with men are asexual, and the explanation for her seclusion is a transcendent dedication to religious and poetic truth.

This interpretation is based on incomplete documentary evidence; Gould could not have had access to the "Master" letters, which were not made public until 1955. According to Sewall (1974, vol. 2, 444-462), Dickinson probably did hear Wadsworth preach in Philadelphia, and may have been attracted to him not by spiritual certainty but by an "undercurrent of unbelief . . . that he was too honest to hide from her completely. . . ." He was probably not the "Master" for whom she felt a passionate and frustrated love. Gould's version passed muster with reviewers, however. *Horn Book*'s Jordan (1946b) pronounced it free of sentimentality, and *Library Journal*'s Dawson (1946b) found it "authentic" in its facts. Both felt it would inspire young readers to explore Dickinson's poetry.

What made reviewers prefer Kerr's Blackwell and Gould's Dickinson to Nolan's Nightingale was probably interpretation. Both Nightingale and Blackwell recorded mystic experiences that strengthened their sense of mission, but Nolan (1946, 38-39) describes Nightingale's "divine call" with irony as well as sympathy: she "was to be an instrument of destiny, divinely appointed. The voice was mysterious, not human; it may have been only the stirring of the wind. . . ." Kerr's account of Blackwell's experience is less skeptical. The future doctor is touched "gently" by a "sort of peace . . . , filling her whole being" (L. Kerr 1946, 70), and what she takes from the moment is comfort, rather than a sense of personal destiny that could border on self-aggrandizement.

Both Nightingale and Dickinson became recluses in their most productive years. Nightingale returned from the Crimean in broken health; in middle age she withdrew into bedridden privacy and admitted only a chosen few to her presence. Veith (1990) points out that invalidism was not uncommon among upper-class American and British women at the time. Although Nightingale (and other invalids) lived to old age, leading some scholars to conclude that their sufferings were psychosomatic or socially constructed, medical knowledge was limited and some—including Nightingale—could well have had undiagnosed chronic illnesses. Nolan favors a more psychological explanation, pointing to the advantages of sickness as a time-management tool: "in a queer way, physical weakness became a protection to Florence, a haven from the interruptions and distractions which fret one who leads a more normal life, an economy measure to conserve time and energy" (Nolan 1946, 178).

Lerner (1993, 181) has suggested, in much the same vein, that Dickinson's retreat from public life was "carefully calculated," and "freed her from unwanted social obligations, from the need to explain her refusal to get married and from many of the domestic obligations expected of young women of her class." This is not inconsistent with Gould's interpretation ("only alone could the mind soar into unknown worlds"), but Gould, relying on Dickinson's nunlike dedication and her continued love of children, presents a romantic image that remains open to sentimental approval. Nolan's portrayal of Nightingale is harsher, and her willingness to use her illness—as she had used her unwanted fame—appears as evidence of an essentially manipulative personality. To the reviewers, self-will made Nightingale a less attractive woman; as Strachey had pointed out, she wanted to be a nurse much more than she wanted the luxury and possible romance she had "sacrificed" for her mission. The more acceptable role models for girls in 1946 were those who really wanted what they sacrificed (Aaron Burr, or marriage) and had to overcome inner reluctance before they could embrace their duty (James Madison, or the practice of medicine).

Yet to dwell on the ways in which these books helped diminish girls' ambitions, encourage self-denial, or channel them into acceptably feminine pursuits would risk overlooking the very real courage and strength they honor. Brill's Madeleine de Verchères exemplifies the valor of women. She protests her brother's stereotyped comments about feminine weakness; she points out that their own mother, who success-fully defended the fort two years ago, was "brave and cool" in that cri-sis (Brill 1946, 26). By the end of the book, Madeleine is justly proud of her own achievement. Resigning her command to the French officer who brings reinforcements, she smiles at the "mere gallantry" of his assumption that it has been in good hands and replies, "Better perhaps than you think, Monsieur" (177). Her self-respect is genuine, but she is far too feminine to threaten male pride. Self-reliant but modest, respon-sible but quick to blush, Madeleine seems remarkably adapted as a role model for the demobilized girls of 1946.

Conclusion

A tension between autonomy and responsibility, personal accomplish-ment and relatedness, runs through many of these books. Girls in 1946 heard mixed messages. On the one hand, women should be proud: they had made great progress as workers and as citizens, they had contrib-uted to the nation's war effort, and it was clear from their achievements that many were as able as men and deserved equal opportunities. Girls could expect to find challenging roles in public life. The biographies honor trailblazing women like Blackwell and Nightingale.

On the other hand, women were not like men, and the wise girl would take pleasure in the femininity that allowed her to find a niche without alarming the men in her life. Diffidence, avoidance of publicity, and renunciation of personal wishes were admirable feminine traits, and the activities of these heroines, however daring, did not seriously threaten either the web of obligations and affinities that related them to their communities or the postwar social order.

We tend to assume that the old fictionalized biographies were mis-leading because they introduced factual errors. Many of them were con-scientiously researched, however, and minor errors of fact are no more inevitable in fictionalized than in "authentic" biography. It is true that interpretations of some heroines' personalities were based on conjec-ture, on informed guesswork. But the greatest fiction inherent in the genre is the portrayal of each individual as a coherent, understandable personality.

The narrative framework that supports an illusion of understanding is both a resource and a danger. It encourages readers to enter into a text sympathetically and identify with the subject. Fictionalized biography is accessible and appealing; as Vicinus (1990, 97) observes, the simplified formula leaves "room for the reader to insert herself." As she imagined herself fighting off Mohawks, test flying a bomber, or nursing wounded soldiers, a girl might well be receptive to the messages of these books: the patriotism, the sense of responsibility, the possibility of solid achievement, and also the desirability of relatedness, participation in family and group enterprises, service to humanity and high ideals. Reviewers expected biographies to inspire readers to emulation and occasionally to further study of a subject. Their literary quality varies, but most books in the sample are well suited to these purposes.

They are less apt to inspire doubts about the status quo. Since the 1970s, it has been impossible to consider the portrayal of women or minorities in children's literature without raising questions about stereotyping. In portraying the relationships between Native Americans and Europeans, or between women and men, the fictionalized biographies in this sample touch only lightly on conflicts that now seem deeply problematic. Readers are encouraged to sympathize with Iroquois indignation at French treachery, but not to question the inevitable rightness of European colonization. Similarly, readers are invited to take pleasure in the way Nightingale and Blackwell confounded preconceptions about women, but not to see any hint that gender bias continued after their time. What is left out of these stories is unlikely to be missed. The omissions are strategically covered, the texts flow smoothly, and there are few obvious holes to trip the understanding.

The novelistic approach taken by most writers in this sample was not the only available model for juvenile biography at the time. One noteworthy alternative was provided by Genevieve Foster, who in *George Washington's World* (1941) used quotes from primary sources to illustrate what was happening in other parts of the world at each stage of Washington's life. The more traditional genre remained popular, however, and its conventions favored the simplicity of personal interpretations; focusing on the subject's individual concerns, it is easy for a biographer to leave broader political questions in the shadows. The girls' biographies of 1946 idealized the achievements of women, but subtly encouraged the feminine behavior that would help girls fit themselves seamlessly into postwar American society. They downplayed any need for confrontation or disruption, and while seeming to offer a realistic platform for contemporary dreamers, they nudged their readers toward conventional private life, where courage and competence—and modesty—would always be useful.

Juvenile Biographies Discussed

Brill, Ethel C. 1946. *Madeleine takes command.* Illus. Bruce Adams. New York: McGraw Hill.

D'Aulaire, Ingri, and Edgar Parin d'Aulaire. 1946. *Pocahontas.* New York: Doubleday.

Desmond, Alice Curtis. 1946. *Glamorous Dolly Madison.* New York: Dodd, Mead.

Gould, Jean. 1946. *Miss Emily.* Illus. Ursula Koering. Boston: Houghton Mifflin.

Harper, Martha Barnhart. 1946. *Red silk pantalettes.* Decorations Betty Morgan Bowen. New York: Longmans, Green.

Kerr, Laura. 1946. *Doctor Elizabeth.* Illus. Alice Carsey. New York: Thomas Nelson & Sons.

Knapp, Sally. 1946. *New wings for women.* New York: Thomas Y. Crowell.

Lane, Margaret. 1946b. *The tale of Beatrix Potter: A biography.* New York: Frederick Warne.

Morgan, Helen L. 1946. *Mistress of the White House: The story of Dolly Madison.* Illus. Phillis Coté. Philadelphia: Westminster Press.

Newcomb, Covelle. 1946. *The secret door: The story of Kate Greenaway.* New York: Dodd, Mead.

Nolan, Jeannette Covert. 1946. *Florence Nightingale.* Illus. George Avison. New York: Julian Messner.

Seymour, Flora Warren. 1946. *Pocahontas: Brave girl.* Illus. Charles V. John. Indianapolis: Bobbs-Merrill.

Stevenson, Augusta. 1946. *Clara Barton, girl nurse.* Illus. Frank Giacoia. Indianapolis: Bobbs-Merrill.

Stoddard, Anne, ed. 1946. *Topflight: Famous American women.* Illus. Bela Dankovszky. New York: Thomas Nelson & Sons.

Other References

American Book Production, 1946. 1947. *Publishers' Weekly* (January 25): 419.

Andersen, Kristi. 1996. *After suffrage: Women in partisan and electoral politics before the New Deal.* Chicago: University of Chicago.

Andrews, Siri. 1946. Florence Crannell Means. *Horn Book* 22 (1): 15-30.

Andrus, Gertrude. 1946. Review of *Pocahontas: Brave girl*, by Flora Warren Seymour. *Library Journal* (November 1): 1546.

Anon. 1946a. Review of *Doctor Elizabeth*, by Laura Kerr. *Booklist* 42: 230.

———. 1946b. Review of *Glamorous Dolly Madison*, by Alice (Curtis) Desmond. *Booklist* 42: 319.

———. 1946c. Review of *Madeleine takes command*, by Ethel Claire Brill. *Booklist* 43: 89.

———. 1947. Review of *Florence Nightingale*, by Jeannette Nolan. *Booklist* 43: 191.

Anthony, Katharine. 1949. *Dolly Madison: Her life and times*. Garden City, New York: Doubleday.

Arbuthnot, May Hill. 1947. Chapter 17, Biography. In *Children and books*, 470-501. Chicago: Scott, Foresman.

Beard, Mary R. 1946. *Woman as force in history: A study in traditions and realities*. New York: Macmillan.

Bechtel, Louise Seaman. 1946. *Books in search of children, 10th R. R. Bowker Memorial Lecture*. New York: New York Public Library.

Breines, Wini. 1992. *Young, white, and miserable: Growing up female in the fifties*. Boston: Beacon Press.

Colman, Penny. 1995. *Rosie the riveter: Women working on the home front in World War II*. New York: Crown Publishers.

Daugherty, James. 1940. Children's books in a democracy. *Horn Book* 16 (4): 231-237.

Dawson, Dorotha. 1946a. Review of *Clara Barton, girl nurse*, by Augusta Stevenson. *Library Journal* (December 1): 1718.

Dawson, Dorotha. 1946b. Review of *Miss Emily*, by Jean Gould. *Library Journal* 71 (May 15): 764.

Eaton, Anne Thaxter. 1940. Chapter 11, Men and manners of the past. In *Reading with children*, 220-226. New York: Viking.

Eaton, Jeanette. 1942. A biographer's perilous joy. *Horn Book* 18 (2): 120-125.

Fish, Helen Dean. 1946. What is this Association of Children's Book Editors? *Library Journal* 71 (April 15): 544-546.

Foster, Genevieve. 1941. *George Washington's World*. New York: Charles Scribner's Sons.

Hazard, Paul. 1947. *Books, children and men*. 3rd ed. Boston: Horn Book.

Hodges, C. Walter. 1940. Adventures with a problem. *Horn Book* 16 (5): 331-333.

Hollowell, Lillian, ed. 1950. *A book of children's literature*. 2nd ed. New York: Rinehart.

Jordan, Alice M. 1946a. Review of *Doctor Elizabeth*, by Laura Kerr. *Horn Book* 22 (3): 212.

Jordan, Alice M. 1946b. Review of *Miss Emily*, by Jean Gould. *Horn Book* 22 (3): 211-212.

Jordan, Alice M. 1946c. Review of *Red silk pantalettes*, by Martha Barnhart Harper. *Horn Book* 22 (6): 468.

Jordan, Alice M. 1946d. Review of *White man's burden*, by Ruth Smith. *Horn Book* 22 (6): 473.

Kerr, Andrea Moore. 1992. *Lucy Stone: Speaking out for equality*. New Brunswick, NJ: Rutgers University Press.

Lane, Margaret. 1946a. On the writing of Beatrix Potter's life story. *Horn Book* 22 (6): 438-445.

Lepman, Jella. 1969. *A bridge of children's books*. Trans. Edith McCormick. Chicago: American Library Association.

Lerner, Gerda. 1993. *The creation of feminist consciousness from the Middle Ages to Eighteen-seventy*. New York: Oxford University Press.

Macmillan Company. 1946. Advertisement for Mary Beard's *Woman as force in history*. *Library Journal* 71 (April 1): 419.

Madeleine Jarret de Verchères. 2005. *L'encyclopédie de l'Agora*. http:// agora.qc.ca/mot.nsf/Dossiers/Madeleine_Jarret_de_Vercheres.

Mahony, Bertha E. 1946. Peacetime resistance. *Horn Book* 22 (1): 6.

Mezerik, A. G. 1945. Getting rid of the women. *Atlantic Monthly* (June): 79.

Nesbitt, Elizabeth. 1953. Events and people: History and biography [1820-1920]. In *A critical history of children's literature*, ed. Cornelia Meigs, 392-398. New York: Macmillan.

R. R. Bowker Company. 1946. The Children's Book Parade is back—for the first time since the war. [Advertisement.] *Library Journal* 71 (July): 940.

Scoggin, Margaret C. 1946. 1946 books for young people. *Library Journal* 71 (October 15): 1416.

Scoggin, Margaret. 1947. Review of *Florence Nightingale*, by Jeannette Nolan. *Library Journal* (January 1): 86.

Sewall, Richard B. 1974. *The life of Emily Dickinson*. New York: Farrar, Straus & Giroux.

Smith, Ruth. 1946. *White man's burden: A personal testament*. New York: Vanguard Press.

Strachey, Lytton. [1918]. *Eminent Victorians*. New York: G. P. Putnam's Sons.

Ulveling, Ralph A. 1946. Our past, a prelude. *Library Journal* 71 (July): 943-944.

Veith, Shirley. 1990. The recluse: A retrospective health history of Florence Nightingale. In *Florence Nightingale and her era: A collection of new scholarship*, ed. Vern Bullough, Bonnie Bullough, and Marietta P. Stanton, 75-89. New York: Garland.

Vicinus, Martha. 1990. What makes a heroine? Girls' biographies of Florence Nightingale. In *Florence Nightingale and her era: A collection of new scholarship*, ed. Vern Bullough, Bonnie Bullough, and Marietta P. Stanton, 90-106. New York: Garland.

Viguers, Ruth Hill. 1953. Roads to follow: Biography [1920-1950]. In *A critical history of children's literature,* ed. Cornelia Meigs, 561-570. New York: Macmillan.

Wennerblad, Sonja. 1946. Review of *Glamorous Dolly Madison*, by Alice C. Desmond. *Library Journal* 71 (June 15): 920.

Chapter 3

1971: Public Work
and Private Loss

In 1946, American Library Association (ALA) president Ulveling had urged librarians to direct their wartime zeal to the fight against racism and hatred at home, and idealistic librarians in 1971 were doing just that. The mood of the country had changed. The Civil Rights movement, the women's movement, and widespread protests against the war in Vietnam all questioned established authority. Even the nation's primers had changed. In 1965, the safe white world of Dick and Jane had expanded to include nice African American neighbors; in 1970, Scott Foresman retired the series (Kismaric and Heiferman 1996).

In the world of children's book editors and librarians, too, there was a sense that taboos were being broken, especially in fiction, and that this was a good thing. Death, divorce, less-than-ideal parents and less-than-happy endings appeared in books like *The Chocolate War*, *The Pigman*, and *Harriet the Spy*, looking revolutionary in contrast to the safe, suburban stories that had dominated the postwar scene. The ALA's Young Adult Services Division was established in 1957, breaking off from the former Association of Young People's Librarians, and young adult literature came into its own as a genre, giving a home to books that seemed too challenging for elementary school students. Yet even children were introduced to some of life's dangers; after all, it was remarked, not all of them lived prosperous lives in serene nuclear families, and most of them watched television. In historical fiction, the patriotic certainty of books published in the World War II era yielded to a more doubting, exploratory tone in the Vietnam years. Even the American Revolution, the sacred cause in 1943's *Johnny Tremain*, was open to question in 1974's *My Brother Sam Is Dead* (Tunnell 1992).

The change was not immediate and complete, but it was real. Denise Wilms (1982, 136) felt that biographies lagged "behind the main body of children's literature" in taboo-breaking, and some of those published in 1971 were conservative enough to have won easy acceptance a generation earlier. Others, however, look remarkably frank even now. I examined twenty-six juvenile biographies of twenty-four women published in the United States in 1971. (See appendix B for an annotated list.) There were two each of Israel's prime minister, Golda Meir, and of the painter Mary Cassatt. The rest ranged from a cheerful summary of the career of Jane Addams for second and third graders to a candid account of the life of anarchist Emma Goldman, "the most dangerous woman in the world" (Shulman 1971), for seventh grade and up. Eleven biographies were reviewed for elementary school (second, third, or fourth grade and up), seven for middle school (fifth grade and up), and eight for junior high school (sixth or seventh grade and up).

Climate for Reviewing Girls' Books: Second-Wave Feminism

In the 1960s, a resurgent women's movement was articulating high aspirations for girls and women. Eleanor Roosevelt chaired the first President's Commission on the Status of Women; the commission's report, like Betty Friedan's *Feminine Mystique*, came out in 1963. In 1964, Title VII of the new Civil Rights Act prohibited discrimination in employment on the basis of sex as well as race, color, religion, and national origin. Older feminists worked within the established system, using the Commission's findings to advocate women's causes and push an Equal Rights Amendment. Younger women reacted against sexual inequality in the Civil Rights movement; their protests and demonstrations often employed the rhetoric and tactics of the New Left. In 1966, Friedan and her associates founded the National Organization for Women (NOW); around 1968, Kathie Sarachild coined the term "consciousness-raising" for the storytelling that took place often (but not exclusively) in small, informal groups. So unstructured as to baffle FBI agents assigned to infiltrate it, the new women's movement seemed more cultural phenomenon than organization (Rosen 2000).

In colleges and universities, "Women's Studies" became a recognizable discipline. Gerda Lerner, applying for admission to Columbia's Ph.D. program in history in 1963, told her interviewers that she wanted to "make the study of women's history legitimate," to "complete the work begun by Mary Beard" (Lerner 1979, xix). Seen as marginal at the time, her specialty quickly gained academic currency. By 1971, the *Saturday Review* was reporting women's efforts to end their "second-class status" in academia, both by reversing discrimination in admissions and employment policies and by insisting on coverage of women's achievements in the disciplines (Trecker 1971).

In literature, Register (1989, 2) has identified "three distinct subdivisions" of feminist criticism in the early 1970s; the first ("analysis of the 'image of women'") and third ("a 'prescriptive' criticism that attempts to set standards for literature that is 'good' from a feminist viewpoint") were already being applied to analyses of children's literature by 1971. Alleen Pace Nilsen, speaking at the Modern Language Association's December, 1970 Workshop on Women in Children's Literature, described a "cult of the apron" in eighty Caldecott Award winning picture books and runners-up; at an age when young readers "are in the process of developing their own sexual identity," she said, females were significantly less likely than males to appear in the illustrations of their books, and were often "pictured looking out at the action." Turning to nonfiction, she found a spate of science, math, and social studies books published in the wake of the 1961 National Defense Education Act, "which specified that federal funds could be used to purchase science books for school libraries." Here, too, women were nearly invisible. The Random House Landmark series, "advertised as 'colorful and dramatic chapters in American history,'" had 165 books in print, but "only five of them about individual American women" (Nilsen 1971). While Nilsen's speech was printed for an academic audience, Florence Howe's "Sexual Stereotypes Start Early," published in the same issue of the *Saturday Review* as Trecker's overview of women in academia, brought similar observations to the general public.

Feminist views were surfacing in library publications as well. *School Library Journal* ran an article on nonsexist children's books by Feminists on Children's Literature (1971), "a collective of women . . . preparing a list of nonsexist children's books." Books about boys had won the Newbery Award about three times as often as books about girls, the Feminists reported, and outnumbered books about girls on the American Library Association's *Notable Books of 1969* by more than two to one. Among the books about girls they found not only blatant "Sexist Books," but disappointing "Cop-Out Books" like *Caddie Woodlawn*, in which a strong girl protagonist ends by agreeing to become a young lady. Whole sections in standard bibliographies, with subtitles like "From Tomboy to Young Woman," or "Especially for Girls," drew the Feminists' criticism.

Calculating how well the protagonists of prize-winning books reflected the demographics of their intended readers was an approach rapidly becoming familiar to librarians. Since 1966, the Council on Interracial Books for Children had published *Interracial Books for Children Bulletin*, with reviews and articles critical of racist, sexist, agist, and elitist biases in children's books. While it did not advocate outright censorship of flawed books, the Council urged the acquisition of books with more positive images of women and minorities. This kind of book evaluation, putting pragmatic considerations before literary excellence, worried many. Newbery medalist Emily Neville, in a 1966 conference paper on social values in children's literature, argued against overt didacticism and "moralizing." Novels dealt successfully with social values such as integration and anti-Semitism, she said, only when "they kept their focus on the individual" (Neville 1967, 48). The liberating call for non-sexist books was also a call for didactic books, and members of the children's book establishment had mixed feelings about it.

In spite of recent taboo-breaking, however, there was still didacticism—both liberal and conservative—in children's books. When thirty-eight children's publishers were polled on their criteria for manuscript selection, the most frequent response (mentioned in some form or other by at least twenty-five of them) was "message" (Lowry 1971). The favored messages varied. Many publishers responded to the call for nonsexist children's books; Stavn (1972), reporting on *School Library Journal*'s search for new titles that showed "women and girls realistically and fairly," noticed a "hack bandwagon" effect. But not everybody was on the bandwagon. In 1970, *New Yorker* cartoonist Whitney Darrow published *I'm Glad I'm a Boy! I'm Glad I'm a Girl!* Its cheerful doublespreads reaffirmed the good old facts of life, from "Boys are policemen. Girls are metermaids," and "Boys fix things. Girls need things fixed," to the happy conclusion, "We need each other." Feminists might critique the old assumption that gender distinctions were both natural and benign, but its influence persisted.

Criteria for Evaluating Biographies: What the Experts Said

Textbook coverage of juvenile biographies changed slowly. Even the rhetoric was conservative: the 1968 edition of Huck and Kuhn's *Children's Literature in the Elementary School* and Margery Fisher's 1972

Matters of Fact used the inclusive male pronoun without self-consciousness. So did the 1972 edition of *Children and Books*, by May Hill Arbuthnot and Zena Sutherland, where the biographical subject was still "the man," or "the hero," and biographers were still urged to portray "the whole man." Yet change had occurred. In the 1964 edition of *Children and Books*, for instance, biographies on "Heroines" and "Negroes" were relegated to a "special interests" section. By the 1972 edition, they were integrated into general listings, and care was taken to provide diversity in selections for each age group.

The textbooks reported that biography was more popular than in the past. Arbuthnot (1964, 518) said it was "flooding the market . . . due in part to the rise of exceptionally successful biography series." She spoke sympathetically of the series, although "one suspects they cannot all be excellent," noting that they "seem to have grown out of our deep feeling and jealous concern for our democratic way of life." Huck and Kuhn (1968, 274) were harsher, suggesting that the "proliferation" of mediocre series entries could make us "lose sight of a single biography of outstanding quality amidst the shelves of mass-produced ones." In other respects, biographies were felt to have improved. Huck and Kuhn detected a trend toward more complete biographical coverage, not limited to "childhood pranks and legends" (275), and Dorothy Broderick (1971, 918) declared that the choice of "eminent writers to produce the new biography" had "resulted in a decided swing away from the all-sweetness-and-light school of writing to a sensible and truthful realism."

The criteria by which teachers and librarians were advised to judge biographies had barely changed in twenty-five years. Semantic criteria, having to do with the text's truthful representation of the "real world," still took pride of place. Syntagmatic criteria, measuring the book's organization, style, and illustrations against others of its type, were also considered important. The pragmatic criteria, having to do with use, were not placed first, but influenced interpretation of the others: fictionalization might be a matter of style and objectivity a matter of truthfulness, but critics' attitudes toward both were swayed by their ideas of what was appropriate and appealing to young readers.

Choice of Biographical Subject

Again, textbooks offered practical advice on subject selection. Age appeal was a consideration; the youngest readers, for instance, were more interested in what people *did* than in moral or intellectual development, and their "sense of history is not fully developed" (Arbuthnot and Sutherland 1972, 545, 549). Not every worthy role model could engage their interest. Moral effect remained a consideration, too. "A few biographies of unsavory characters such as Hitler and Mussolini" might be desirable "for older students," but should be "balanced against those that show mankind's struggle to achieve decency, justice, and peace" (Huck and Kuhn 1968, 275). Overall, however, the most important function of biography now seemed to be as a mirror that would help young readers see and strive toward their own best potential. Positive role models were what the children's book establishment owed our developing youth.

Decisions can't always have been made on such pragmatic, straightforward grounds. Authors' notes occasionally hinted at more complex relationships between individual writers and their subjects. Edna Barth confided that she lived in Amherst, Massachusetts, had a grandmother named Emily, loved poetry, and didn't want young readers to miss Emily Dickinson. Mary Carroll Nelson and her subject, Pablita Velarde, were "members of the same branch of the National League of American Pen Women in Albuquerque." In other cases, external evidence suggests that biographers had special affinities with their subjects. Elfrida Vipont had written prize-winning fiction about a protagonist who resembled George Eliot in early awkwardness and creative aspiration. Frances Mossiker had produced a biography of the Empress Josephine for adults, and Esther Douty one about Charlotte Forten's grandfather for youth. Alix Kates Shulman, a radical feminist herself, must have cared deeply about anarchist and feminist Emma Goldman by the time she finished her 1971 biography, if she hadn't before; she followed it with a 1972 anthology, *Red Emma Speaks*, and in a memoir years later invoked Goldman as an inspiration for middle age (Shulman 1996, 6).

Many of the biographies, however, especially those in series, must have been solicited by or proposed to publishers in response to the civil rights and women's liberation movements. Publishers' notes, more frequent and more explicit than authors' notes, suggest as much. Inside the back cover of Heyn's book on Elizabeth Blackwell, the new Feminist Press announced its interest "in changing the character of children's literature." Established publishers were already addressing this new market, offering not only "hack bandwagon entries" but some "good quality and genuinely nonsexist" books (Stavn 1972, 33). Series entries could be strong and original books—Shulman's life of Goldman was part of Crowell's Women of America series—but in entries for younger readers, especially, the didactic element often prevailed. Lives of Susan

B. Anthony, Nellie Bly, and Phillis Wheatley, included in Garrard's "Americans All" series of "inspiring life stories about people of all races, creeds, and nationalities who have uniquely contributed to the American way of life," had a clear purpose:

> Often despite great odds, these famous people have attained success in their fields through the good use of ability, determination, and hard work. These fast-moving stories of real people will show the way to better understanding of the ingredients necessary for personal success (Peterson 1971, 1).

The overt message was that women could do anything, although their abilities had not been recognized in the past. Earlier women had shone as reformers and occupational pioneers, in spite of the barriers they faced "in those days"; girls in 1971, with fewer obstacles to overcome, could achieve as much.

However they were chosen, the twenty-four subjects in 1971, including six women of color, ran the gamut from safe (or at least traditional) to genuinely radical figures. On the "safe" side, three (Pocahontas, Elizabeth Blackwell, and Emily Dickinson) had also been subjects of juvenile biographies in 1946, and many others fell into familiar categories (wives and daughters of national leaders, writers, and artists). But compared to 1946, fewer of the new biographees were what the Feminists on Children's Literature (1971) would have called "Cop-Out" heroines—capable emergency leaders who would return the reins to their menfolk as soon as they could. More were women who had persisted in challenging authority, pushing causes that were controversial in their own times and sometimes were still controversial in 1971. Abolitionists and suffragists like Lucretia Mott, Susan B. Anthony, and Emmeline Pankhurst were precursors of contemporary civil rights workers and feminists.

Moreover, the most active and powerful women in the 1971 biographies were not always those who had lived longest ago. Women in the quite recent past, like muckraker Ida Tarbell, scientist Marie Curie, and anarchist Emma Goldman, were shown as intelligent and opinionated forces in public life. Four subjects were still living in 1971, and of those, Israeli prime minister Golda Meir and U.S. congresswoman Shirley Chisholm were political leaders in their own right.

In keeping with their function as role models, almost all the subjects were portrayed sympathetically. One exception was Emmeline Pankhurst. Like Nolan, whose portrayal of Florence Nightingale in 1946 had struck reviewers as unlikable, Noble used an ironic tone, recounting events from Emmeline's point of view and slipping in bits of self-justification that could be expected to rouse the skepticism of any critical reader. As in 1946, reviewers were unhappy with a character they could not wholly admire. *Booklist* (Anon. 1972a) complained of an "adulatory tone," while *Bulletin of the Center for Children's Books* (Anon. 1971a) called it "admiring but far from adulatory." Most juvenile biographers chose more likeable subjects, or painted them from more consistently flattering angles. This was especially true of subjects who were still living.

Semantic Criteria

With the selection of living or very recent subjects came a heightened need for factual accuracy. Strict adherence to details that could be verified in the public record, such as dates and exact proper names, made biographies written in the new style *seem* more accurate, and at the same time helped avoid statements that could provoke libel suits. Of course, the textbook writers had always held that juvenile biography "should be as accurate and authentic as research can make it" (Arbuthnot 1947, 472; Arbuthnot 1964, 519; Arbuthnot and Sutherland 1972, 534). Yet there was the perennial suspicion that the genre had not been accurate in the past, and improvements were needed. Librarian Jack Forman (1972, 98) called urgently for "more facts, less fiction" in biographies for children.

The best of them, fictionalized or not, had always been faithful to the known facts. Huck and Kuhn (1968, 278) detailed the research habits of "conscientious authors of well-written children's biography," and held that not only the text but the illustrations should be "accurately researched." Biographer Olivia Coolidge (1974, 146) wrote that facts "are the bricks with which a biographer builds," and "it needs great care to do what sounds quite easy, namely to distinguish a fact from a judgment"; the objectivity and discernment she advocated were what she and other excellent writers had been practicing all along.

As always, juvenile biography was not expected to tell the *whole* truth. Many experts hedged, suggesting accommodations to younger readers' inexperience and tastes. Perhaps "dark shadows in a person's life may be omitted from biographies for children," or the book should end "before tragedy or an unsavory incident occurs" (Huck and Kuhn 1968, 275). Perhaps some fictionalization should be permissible "when writing for children whose historical knowledge and experience of life" are limited (Fisher 1972, 304-305). Objectivity was desirable; even more important than presenting facts "correctly" was "an honest attitude toward all available facts" (308). But interpretation was important, too; the biographer should capture the young readers' interest by a careful selection of facts, finding "the central threads of an individual's life that made him an interesting personality" (Carlsen 1971, 154). Accuracy and authenticity, important as they were, should not be carried to extremes that would interfere with the proper uses of these books.

Documentation and Sources

The textbooks approved of documentation. Arbuthnot (1964, 520) repeated her 1947 observation that "children may never read footnotes," but that documentation serves as a guarantee of authenticity to adults and possibly to "older children and young people" as well. The year's twenty-six biographies did not have footnotes, but ten of them had bibliographies; another five listed at least some of their sources in acknowledgments or brief author's statements. Arbuthnot and Sutherland (1972, 536) suggested that good documentation could also encourage "respect for objective, verifiable reporting" in "any child old enough to read substantial biographies," and the more substantial the biography, the more likely it was in fact to have a bibliography: only one book at the elementary level had one, and only one at the junior high level gave no citations at all. Writers who omitted references, however, occasionally quoted letters, diaries, and other primary sources, suggesting active if undocumented research and giving glimpses of the historian's work even to younger readers. The three Garrard books, exemplifying a practice that would be more common by 1996, had only picture credits.

The biographers' reliance on available sources necessarily affected the scope and treatment of their books. The parts of a subject's life for which good sources existed were naturally best covered. Douty relied on Charlotte Forten's journal (Stevenson 1988), and the resultant biography was almost completely devoted to the adolescent and early adult years covered by the journal; her childhood and maturity were sketched in from family sources. In some cases, opportune sources—like Anne MacVicar Grant's memoir of her childhood adventures in America, which was reprinted in 1970—may have prompted a biographer's decision to write for children.

Overreliance on available but biased sources distorted some juvenile biography. The most plentiful source of information on Nellie Bly was Bly, who liked to present herself as a spunky character, "innocent, unaffected and frank" (Kroeger 1994, 50); her "favorite image of herself" was "young, charming, outspoken, modern and adorably bold"

(145). Graves (1971), like many before him, seems to have taken her at her own valuation in his fictionalized biography. Kroeger's research showed that Bly was an unreliable witness, lying about her age, her education, and her health; the true story of her life was far more complex than a half-century's worth of juvenile books let on. It was those old fictionalized biographies that inspired Kroeger, however. She read one when she was ten: "Bly's story had greater impact on my life than that of any other nonfiction heroine" (Kroeger 1994, xiv). Probably little harm has been done by a romanticized image of Nellie Bly.

In other cases, biographers' uncritical acceptance of biased authority may have done insidious damage. A basic source for the life of Phillis Wheatley is an 1834 memoir by Margaretta Matilda Odell, a relative of the poet's owners (Richmond 1974). Fuller (1971), who included no bibliography, echoed Odell's account: a warm white family rescued a frightened black girl by purchasing her as a slave, she was timidly grateful, and they supported her unusual talent. In the end, "This gentle black poetess elevated her life and spirit above her *heritage* of slavery" (Fuller 1971, 92; my italics). Fuller's description of the slave auction was calculated to arouse indignation, but she smoothed over subsequent injustice. The rescuing Wheatleys did not buy Phillis out of slavery, but continued to own her; Fuller obscured this relationship by calling Phillis a "servant" rather than a "slave" and by not mentioning her belated manumission, allowing readers to assume it came much sooner. Letters first published in 1972 cast doubt on Odell's accuracy, showing that the poet had not been introduced to Lady Huntingdon, as previous biographers believed (Richmond 1974, 33). More recent biographers have mined slavers' records, the public advertisement of her sale, Wheatley's own correspondence with friends, and other primary sources to arrive at a more accurate and objective account of her life (Robinson 1984). That level of original scholarship is not to be expected of juvenile nonfiction, but Fuller's well-meaning biography, with its tone of admiration for individual achievement and interracial friendship, strikes an unfortunate note of paternalistic condescension; it may owe too much to Odell.

Historical Placement

One function of biography was "to make the past live" (Huck and Kuhn 1968, 274). Broderick (1971, 916) argued that "the concrete episodes and the individual human beings" in biographies could "bring the past to life for children" better than most "straight historical accounts." The amount of history given in these books varied, however. Some explanation of historical conditions was needed to make subjects' lives understandable, but books for younger readers tended to skimp on it, concentrating more narrowly on individual lives. Keller described poverty in the neighborhood of Hull House and Addams's pacificism in World War I; Graves noted that Nellie Bly was inspired to break the fictional record set in Jules Verne's *Around the World in Eighty Days*, and that she covered the Pullman strike. Fuller said less about slavery, an institution which violently shaped Phillis Wheatley's life, than about the Revolutionary War, during which her poetry brought her fleetingly to the attention of George Washington. On the other hand, Peterson did an exemplary job of contextualizing Susan B. Anthony's abolitionist and feminist activities, and McKown gave lucid and interesting explanations of Marie Curie's research.

Books for older readers had more room to explore the ways in which their subjects' lives were embedded in time and place. Most of them referred to historical events, from the 1832 Reform Bill in England (George Eliot's father was against it) to the Chicago fire (it burned several of Mary Cassatt's paintings) and the GI Bill (it financed the education of Pablita Velarde's husband after World War II). The amount of historical coverage varied with the women's involvement in public life. The American Civil War was dramatically central in the lives of Lucretia Mott, Susan B. Anthony, Elizabeth Blackwell, Charlotte Forten, and (of course) Julia Grant, but it "had not affected Mary [Cassatt] personally" (Myers 1971, 18) beyond the knitting of mufflers and rolling of bandages for the soldiers (Wilson 1971). It hardly touched Emily Dickinson, until her friend and rather inadequate mentor Higginson wrote to her from an army camp (Barth 1971).

The books contain references not only to political, but to intellectual, social, and economic history. What mattered to Cassatt were developments in art (from the work of war correspondents in the illustrated magazines to the innovations of the Impressionists). Dickinson grew up in a time and place where versification was a social skill, Emerson's Transcendentalism was a great intellectual influence, and life expectancy was limited:

> A cough that lingered could mean tuberculosis, fever the beginning of diphtheria, typhoid or scarlet fever. Penicillin and other modern medicines were unknown. Many people died while they were children or in their teens (Barth 1971, 27).

Economic downturns impinged on lives, and were mentioned in several biographies. The recession of 1837 cut short Anthony's education and sent the Blackwell family from New Jersey to Ohio in search of better opportunities; the panic of 1893 caught Tarbell short of funds in Paris, where she pawned her sealskin coat.

At least two partial biographies for fifth, sixth, and seventh graders function primarily as windows into history, using sympathetic young observers to introduce children to the events of their times. Bobbé (1971) recounts the childhood adventures of Anne MacVicar, who travels to America from Glasgow in 1759, as the four-year-old daughter of a British lieutenant stationed at Fort Duquesne. She learns Dutch and Mohawk from new friends along the way; takes a lively interest in the living arrangements of settlers, Indians, and soldiers trapped too long in boring forts; and meets several key figures in the French and Indian War. The charismatic Margaretta Schuyler, aunt and advisor to General Philip Schuyler, becomes her mentor, and the progress of their friendship is the emotional core of Bobbé's account; Anne, who loves learning, is drawn by Mme. Schuyler's depth of knowledge and humane understanding.

The MacVicars' grant of land in Vermont's Green Mountains was contested, and they returned to Scotland not long before "that disastrous war," the American Revolution, made Anne's old friends into foreigners. Years later, she published her memoirs "of manners and scenery in America, as they existed previous to the Revolution." She warned that "in the dim distance of near forty years, unassisted by written memorials," she could "mistake dates, misplace facts, and omit circumstances" (Grant 1808, 5), but her narrative was lively and plausible. Bobbé lists a dozen other sources in her bibliography, but is by and large faithful to Anne's own version of events. The result is really a kind of late eighteenth century travelogue.

Thomas Jefferson's daughter Martha, known as Patsy, was another well-documented eighteenth-century girl. From 1784 to 1790 she lived in Paris, where her father represented the interests of the new United States. Kelly (1971) describes Patsy's coming of age, as her father lovingly grooms her for marriage; the book is shaped and unified by this private theme. Like Anne MacVicar, however, Patsy Jefferson is an active observer, and the book's real interest is in the famous people she meets, the contrast of American and French ways, and political events leading up to the French Revolution. *School Library Journal*'s reviewer said the account was "interestingly presented against the background of political upheaval in France" (Karmazin 1971); but the *Bulletin of the Center for Children's Books* reviewer disliked the laborious exposition of history in conversations prompted by "Patsy's rapt absorption in French politics" (Anon. 1972d). In reality, Jefferson probably didn't make such a routine of discussing public affairs with Patsy (D. Malone 1971). Even if he did, it is difficult to make fictionalized conversation into a plausible vehicle for exposition; it tends to disrupt the novelistic consistency of character development. Thus two major uses of the juvenile biography, the teaching of history and the introduction of an individual with whom young readers could identify, come into conflict.

If Patsy's life serves Kelly as a pretext for the introduction of historical facts, history serves Mossiker (1971) as a backdrop for the romantic life of Josephine Bonaparte. Marie-Josèphe-Rose de Tascher de la Pagerie, the daughter of a struggling Martinique plantation owner, was caught up in the French Revolution and its aftermath. Her disastrous first marriage ended when her aristocratic husband, Alexandre Beauharnais, was guillotined, and Josephine herself barely escaped—the execution of Robespierre brought the Terror to an end just before her scheduled execution. Left with few assets other than her looks, charm, and sweet disposition, she accepted Napoleon as a father for her two children. The five-part book resembles a series of tableaux, beginning with a slave's prophecy that the island teenager will become "a queen . . . *more* than a queen!"; climaxing with the ceremonial divorce in which Josephine is a willing sacrifice to the glory of France; and ending with the "flicker of a thousand candles burning around the bier" of the former empress. The over-all effect, reinforced by Eagle's heraldically posed figures against disappearing backgrounds, is introspective and static. One learns less about French politics from Mossiker's Josephine, so near the center, than from Kelly's Patsy on the edges. This may be partly because, in adapting Josephine's controversial life for young readers, Mossiker carefully veiled rumors of her sexual misconduct and made her appear more honest than the outwardly "docile, submissive, passive, pliant," but actually manipulative woman portrayed in her adult biography (Mossiker 1964).

Shulman's frank portrayal of Emma Goldman showed her as a politically active idealist, dedicating her life to the fight for universal freedom and the justice she believed it would inevitably bring, and responding in deeply personal ways to news in the national and anarchist press. For Goldman, history was to be not passively endured but actively engaged. A Jewish immigrant to the United States, she had brought socialist ideas with her from Russia, but it was news of the Haymarket Affair that made her an activist. In 1886, when Chicago police moved to break up a reportedly peaceful demonstration in support of the eight-hour workday, somebody threw a bomb into their midst, killing seven policeman and injuring more than sixty others. It was labeled an "anarchist plot," and eight prominent anarchists were convicted, not for throwing the bomb (there was little evidence) but for their opinions. Goldman, convinced the decision was unjust, was stirred to join the anarchists. She had known students, teachers and workers who held radical ideas, but here, she felt, were "*real* revolutionaries, people whose ideas and dreams directed every action of their lives, even to their deaths" (Shulman 1971, 47). She moved to New York City, and became widely known when her lover and comrade, Alexander Berkman, attempted to assassinate Henry Clay Frick of the Carnegie Steel Company.

Shulman contextualized Goldman's life in several ways. She described historical events and conditions that affected Goldman, from pogroms against Jews and political terror in Russia, to America's reaction against anarchists after the McKinley assassination, to the phenomenon of hoboism during the 1908 depression. She explained events and activities in which Goldman was directly involved, from speaking tours to the Spanish Civil War. Notably, since Goldman's activities were always based on ideas, Shulman interrupted the narrative with whole chapters entitled "What Is Anarchism?" and "The Woman Question," offering lucid, sustained exposition of the background and development of her most important positions.

Goldman was not the only politically engaged subject. Biographies of Emmeline Pankhurst and Ida Tarbell were richly informative about the fight for women's suffrage in Britain (Noble 1971) and the role of investigative journalism in exposing John D. Rockefeller's monopolistic practices at Standard Oil Corporation (Fleming 1971b). Biographers of Golda Meir (Mann 1971; Morris 1971) and Shirley Chisholm (Hicks 1971), too, were thorough in linking their subjects' activities to the historical events that concerned them. Meir's original path, from czarist Russia to a politically involved immigrant community in America, was similar to Goldman's a generation earlier; Meir turned to Zionism as Goldman had turned to anarchism, in pursuit of justice. Chisholm was a strong feminist, and Hicks reproduced in its entirety her speech in support of the Equal Rights Amendment, which was passed by Congress in 1970 (but not, in the end, ratified by the required majority of the states). Accounts of these intensely political women necessarily addressed the role of social conditions (including racism, anti-Semitism, and gender expectations) and political events in shaping their characters and motivating their actions.

If Anne MacVicar and Patsy Jefferson were interesting as observers of history, the biographies of committed activists made history itself interesting because of their own fiercely partisan engagement in it. Objectivity has often been advanced as a criterion for children's nonfiction, but these texts were arguably improved by bias. When subjects interpreted their worlds and acted on the basis of passionately held beliefs, the authors' sympathy for those beliefs helped shape dramas that would catch readers' attention and give some of them, at least, appetite for deeper investigation.

Syntagmatic Criteria

Style, organization, illustration, and book design had not changed radically since 1946. All the books in the sample were continuous narratives, and most were at least somewhat fictionalized. But like Lane's 1946 biography of Beatrix Potter, several of the 1971 books for older readers and those on contemporary subjects avoided fictionalization and relied instead on the conventions of scholarly biography or of journalism. Even in books for younger readers, subjects' adult lives are less fictionalized than their childhoods—possibly because the adult careers were better documented, leaving fewer gaps for speculation.

Fisher (1972, 304-305) argued that "story biography" was an appropriate genre for young readers, distinguished from "historical fiction" not only by its style but by its uses: "A biography is overtly didactic in a way that a novel is not," and the biographer could legitimately deploy fictionalized scenes to make points about the interpretation of character or to clarify historical ideas. Some critics objected to fictionalization only when it was poorly done. For instance, Huck and Kuhn (1968, 276) complained of "unbelievably stilted" dialogue that was used to convey information, and created "an impression of wooden characters." The experts called for gracefulness and tact in organization, for vivid and arresting details, for an appropriate match between style and subject, and for a coherently developed theme. All these virtues would add to the book's appeal and help it serve its purpose: "biography must do more" than give children the facts in a well-organized fashion, "it must help them to *know* the person as a living human being" (Huck and Kuhn 1968, 274).

Evaluating Text: Style and Organization

The more fictionalized accounts used many conventions of novels and storybooks, reporting their subjects' thoughts and conversations as a matter of course. Fictionalized conversations were not necessarily invented out of whole cloth. Barth, Bobbé, and Shulman said they based theirs on letters and existing records, and others, including Peterson and

Kelly, apparently followed the same policy without saying so. Even verbatim quotes, however, could be somewhat misleading in fictional contexts. As a minor example: in a letter to her sister, Abigail Adams gave an affectionate description of little Polly Jefferson, who stopped with the Adams family in England on her way to join her father in France (Randolph 1939). Kelly (1971) put Abigail's words of praise into an oral message, relayed to Jefferson by a servant in front of Polly herself. The words are not changed, but their meaning and effects are influenced by context.

Besides conversation, another much-used technique was to open with a vividly imagined set piece as a hook. This was common even in books that made minimal use of fictionalization after their early pages. Thus Noble (1971, 7) begins her book in the Pankhurst parlor, where Emmeline moves gracefully about plumping pillows, brushing crumbs, and patting arms, trying to comfort her gentle and idealistic husband. Frustrated by another defeat for women's suffrage, Dr. Pankhurst suddenly bursts out, "Why don't you [women] *force* us to give you the vote? Why don't you scratch our eyes out!" Noble largely abandons fictionalization later in the book, but repeats Dr. Pankhurst's question at strategic intervals.

Typically in 1946, the fictionalized opening vignette set the tone for a book by capturing its theme or some essential truth about the protagonist's character—along with reader interest, of course. The facts were put off until later, making their delayed appearance in an expository flashback. But in 1971, a variant of the old novelistic gambit was becoming more common: writers signaled their objective accuracy by embedding details in the opening passage itself. For instance, De Leeuw (1971, 7-8) sneaks the facts of the Tallchief sisters' young lives into a typical afternoon excursion to buy ice cream cones:

> The little town of Fairfax, this summer day of 1933, drowsed in the warm Oklahoma sun. It was part of the Indian reservation on which the Osage Indians lived and where, some years before, oil had been discovered. Many of the Tallchiefs' friends had become rich, and their father, Alex, had invested his oil royalties in real estate.

The proper nouns, the date, and the careful tucking of information into a dependent clause all suggest a proper journalistic concern for factual underpinnings.

Alternatively, Vipont, Fleming, Shulman, and Morris used the scholarly convention of opening with the subject's family background. Without the fictional scene to forecast theme, writers might increase textual unity by the repetition of thematic ideas or phrases, strengthening the impression of wholeness and integrity in their subjects' lives. George Eliot (when she was still just Marian Evans) once wished for "a very high attic in a romantic continental town, such as Geneva" (Vipont 1971, 80, 97). Threading this phrase through her book, Vipont traces Eliot's search for literal and metaphorical havens until, "safe in the high attic created for her by George [Lewes]'s love and constancy" (133)—symbolizing "that inward peace which at last enabled her to create a significant world" (137)—she "fulfilled her destiny" (133). Hicks (1971), writing about Shirley Chisholm, makes similar use of repetition. Referring again and again to Chisholm's trademark "unbossed and unbought" speech (12, 64, 74), her fearless "mouth" (11, 78, 111) and her deceptive resemblance to a "nice librarian" or "schoolteacher" (11, 12, 54, 111, 113), Hicks underlines her subject's consistent inner strength.

In accounts of the adult lives of contemporary subjects, a more journalistic approach was emerging. These books did not all list their sources, but seemed to be based largely on interviews and newspaper reports. Mann (1971), describing the emplacement of Russian missile installations in Egypt, outlines Golda Meir's typical "easy" days (when she worked only from 7 a.m. until midnight) and "crisis" days; the material is based on interviews with Meir's aides, Lou Kaddar and Simcha Dinitz. Hicks (1971) shadows Shirley Chisholm through a "typical day" in Washington and one at home in her Brooklyn district; with its mixture of routine (greeting workers on the way into the office, scanning the mail, meeting with Drew University students) and sudden calls to action (filing papers, endorsing a candidate, dealing with the embarrassing discovery that friends are being charged to attend "Shirley Chisholm Day"), the text seems to be based on observation or analysis of press reports.

Whether fictionalized or journalistic, juvenile biographies were shorter than popular adult biographies, and more details had to be omitted. This did not always entail falsification or deliberate skewing, but could facilitate either. Mossiker's two books on Josephine were drawn on the same research and had the same basic plot: Josephine, who married Napoleon for expediency rather than love, became deeply attached to him as his love for her dwindled. In abridging the story for younger readers, however, she veiled both partners' extramarital affairs, and Josephine now appeared as an unjustly suspected innocent. Mossiker denied no established facts to achieve this effect, but relied on omission and redirection. She dropped all mention of Josephine's possible lovers; used words like "light-hearted" and "flirtatious" to describe her behavior; and above all emphasized the venal jealousy of Napoleon's family. Thus, Josephine's second marriage seemed to fail not through any fault of her own, but because of her failure to produce an heir and the malicious plotting of her in-laws.

Omission, not only of controversial material but of players and incidents in a subject's life, enhanced clarity and unity, and perhaps that very unity is the greatest fiction in these books. They portray their subjects as coherent selves, whose trajectories through life have a dramatic inevitability. Elizabeth Blackwell finds her mission in a dying friend's wish for a woman doctor; Emma Goldman, hearing of the Haymarket Affair, suddenly wakes to the possibility of living and dying for what she believes; Mary Cassatt is driven to paint and Golda Meir to serve Israel. Heroines are unswerving in their missions, their lives shaped by consistent dedication. The very form of these books seems to imply that a worthy character makes sense; a worthy adult life lends itself to convincing summary.

Evaluating Graphics: Visual Appeal

Like the narrative form, the format of these books was conservative. They were shorter, on average, than the biographies of 1946, averaging 139 pages instead of 174; nine of the twenty-six were under a hundred pages. Almost all of them ranged from five to six and a half inches wide, and from eight to nine and a half inches tall. (An exception was Heyn's biography of Elizabeth Blackwell, published by the new Feminist Press as a paperback, eleven inches wide, eight and a half inches tall, with a doublespread layout.)

Illustrations were more numerous than in 1946, but not so integral to the books as they would become by 1996. Their amount and form varied with the age of intended readers. All the books reviewed for elementary school were illustrated: ten with drawings, one with photographs and reproductions, and four with both. Six of the illustrators had been allowed to accent their drawings with washes in one or at most two colors. Color was expensive, requiring a separate run for each ink used; frugal publishers used it sparingly. Thus, every doublespread of Keller's book on Addams sported drawings by Aloise, but only alternate doublespreads were enlivened with pink and orange wash. There was nothing to compete with the d'Aulaires' 1946 *Pocahontas*, or with the lavish picture book biographies of 1996. Those few photographs and reproductions were the strongest indicators of future trends.

All but three of the books for fifth grade and up were also illustrated: eight with photographs and reproductions, and four with drawings. Books for junior high readers might have only a frontispiece (like Morris's biography of Meir), or might have photographs and reproductions segregated in eight-page sections of plates (like Vipont's book on Eliot, or Shulman's on Goldman). Even Myers' book on Mary Cassatt featured only one photograph and five reproduced artworks, hard to appreciate in black and white

In 1946, at least one biography was published with notable attention to book design: Addison Burbank's illustrations and decorative capitals for *The Secret Door* were taken from subject Kate Greenaway's own work. In 1971, much of the illustration was purely functional. Victor Mays brought his usual precise draftsmanship and sense of historical detail to the books on Bly and Wheatley. Hoover's illustrations for *Lucretia Mott* were disappointing: faces were emotionally expressive, but characters were not drawn consistently from one illustration to the next, and little girls could be told from older women only by size. Where the text specified that Quakers "wore plain gray or brown clothing" (Faber 1971, 12), blue and gold washes brightened them up at the expense of historical accuracy. Still, *Booklist*'s reviewer spoke approvingly of the "many colored illustrations" (Anon. 1972b). Illustrations, if mentioned at all in the reviews, were usually appreciated, although Hoover's drawings for *Maria Tallchief* were called "balletically incorrect" (Stanton 1971). In these books for younger readers, Mays, Hoover, and others continued a robust tradition of historical line drawings in which protagonists moved against fully realized crowd scenes, ships, or interiors.

By contrast, in the few artist's illustrations in books for older children, backgrounds shaded into nothing. Richard Cuffari drew a pensive Emily Dickinson gazing out a window in a barely suggested wall. Eagle's illustrations of Josephine Bonaparte, Lebenson's of Julia Grant, and Allen's of Patsy Jefferson focused on the protagonist's face and upper body much as some of the narratives themselves focused on her emotions, creating an introspective effect—perhaps the visual equivalent of that inwardness Vicinus (1990) saw in juvenile biographies of Florence Nightingale from the 1950s on.

Pragmatic Criteria: Conflict and Ambivalence

The pensive, introspective look of those illustrations was perhaps better suited to Dickinson and Bonaparte than to the outgoing Grant and Jefferson, but girls coming of age at this time had good reason for introspection. The old certainties about women's roles in American life were being questioned. Of course, this had happened before; but the biographies of 1946 had managed to imply a comfortable consensus. By taking the protective coloring of femininity for granted, they had suggested that women could indeed achieve anything with tact and persistence—but that most women would prefer to operate within the private sphere, and that any emergence into public view would be for the public good. This impression was reinforced by the 1946 publication of books about Blackwell and Nightingale, who deprecated the women's suffrage movement, but not about Anthony, Mott, Stanton, Stone, or any of its other movers and shakers.

Social developments affected the way pragmatic criteria were applied, but not necessarily the way they were formulated. Children's literature textbooks continued to emphasize the role of biography in transmitting values and introducing heroes to emulate. Huck and Kuhn (1968, 274) described the natural uses of "hero worship"; Broderick (1971, 918) claimed that the encounter with "heroes and heroines" would give children "more knowledge of themselves, a deepened sensitivity to the needs and struggles of other people, and the realization that achievement, even with its accompanying risks and hardships, is gloriously worth while." Biography developed character, and traditionally the character it developed was outward looking, responsive to the needs of others, and eager to participate constructively in the maintenance and development of public values.

But by the 1970s, emphasis was shifting inward, from the child's future social contribution to society's present influence on the child. The case was made that each child's development of individual potential is affected by the internalization of environmental messages; books that reserve "active mastery skills" like "creativity, ingenuity, adventurousness, curiosity, perseverance, bravery, autonomy" (Register 1989, 20) for white male characters are giving only white boys permission to excel. Mavis Wormley Davis (1973, 75) stated, "It is widely acknowledged that the child's self-image is created in the early or formative years, and that it is partly through books that this image is formed." The Feminists on Children's Literature (1971, 19) called for the book that "would offer the girl reader a positive image of woman's physical, emotional, and intellectual potential—one that would encourage her to reach her own full personhood, free of traditionally imposed limitations."

In the 1850s, ridicule of attempted dress reform betrayed anxiety: if women wore the trousers, could men still be men? (Fischer 1997). Now similar anxieties emerged around the new women's rights movement. If women insisted on equality with men, who would take care of the children? Individual biographies in 1971 encoded a variety of responses to the question. They celebrated women's achievements, they encouraged women's political engagement—and they counted the cost in family strife and isolation. Within the texts, the most important relationships were to family and to work. The subjects' characters were shown to emerge in the context of (and sometimes in opposition to) their families of origin, and their missions were pursued with the help (or opposition) of their parents, husbands, and children.

For a woman to pursue a career could be seen as selfish; this concern lay closer to the surface than in 1946, and was likelier to be put into words. To maintain the sympathetic tone expected in juvenile biographies, writers stressed both the public good resulting from women's careers and the element of sacrifice. In general, if these biographees diverted resources of time and energy from their own families they did so in service of the wider human family, and their dedication was not to be seen as self-serving.

Competing Claims: Parents and Vocation

Their mothers were seen to live in passive obscurity, personifying the common lot of women in their times. There were exceptions: Lucretia Mott's mother opened a store; Golda Meir's mother, left with her children in Russia while her husband tried to make a home for them in America, made strong independent decisions; and Maria Tallchief's mother—the most recent, and the one not motivated by sheer economic necessity—worked to put her daughters on the stage. More often, mothers appeared self-effacing, protective of their husbands' peace, as when Heyn showed Elizabeth Blackwell's reluctant mother consenting to leave England for America because her husband appeared run down and the change might do him good. Mothers taught daughters their place in the social order. Bly's mother, for instance, warned her against expecting to succeed in journalism: "Most editors believe that only men can write the news" (Graves 1971, 11). Where girls were expected to excel was in making themselves and their homes beautiful, and George Eliot, who "was plain, untidy, unpredictable, and supremely unsure of herself" (Vipont 1971, 3), never seemed able to win her mother's love and approval.

In several of the books, mothers were virtually invisible. Noble never mentioned the mother of Emmeline Pankhurst, and Wilson usually referred to Mary Cassatt's mother only in joint references to her parents. Seven of the biographees lost their mothers in childhood, and cherished vague, idealized memories of them, like Marie Curie's impressions of her mother's "beauty and . . . sweet disposition" (McKown 1971, 9). The longest passages about mothers who survived into their daughters' adult years were often about their final illnesses and deaths. The relationship between Mary Cassatt and her mother "grew even closer and more tender as Mrs. Cassatt became ill and helpless" (Wilson 1971, 165); and Emily Dickinson, who had seen her mother as "a mere shadow" of Squire Dickinson (Barth 1971, 41-42), learned sympathy by nursing her for seven years.

Many passages about the mothers sounded like obituaries, perhaps because obituaries were the best records their daughters' biographers could obtain. Yet this cannot always be the full explanation. Ida Tarbell's 1939 autobiography described her mother's career before marriage, fortitude in nursing a burn victim, and feminist sympathies, but Fleming (1971b) portrayed her only as a wife and mother, making her a less complex person. According to Myers (1971, 18), Mary Cassatt's mother discouraged her from even reading newspapers, telling her "she would not find them interesting. What did a girl need to know about politics and business?" Cassatt's painting of her mother engrossed in *Le Figaro* suggests another story. Perhaps some of the mothers have been tamed. In books with few other female characters, the mothers stand in for contemporary women. Against the backdrop of their conformity, their daughters' accomplishments seem all the more singular.

At first blush, fathers in these books seemed more supportive of their daughters' ambitions, lending credence to the popular idea that powerful women were their fathers' favorite children and took strength and inspiration from that relationship. Jane Addams at six was proud to be seen with "her tall, handsome father," and by fifteen had read all his books; years later, casting about for a mission in life, she remembered his saying that each "person should have a chance to improve himself" (Keller 1971, 1, 16). Bly's father taught her to read and write; Pocahontas, Julia Grant, and Emmeline Pankhurst were all said to be their father's favorites; George Eliot's father "would call her his 'little wench' and stand up for her when she was being scolded" by her unloving mother (Vipont 1971, 4). In a fictionalized debate between Elizabeth Blackwell's parents, it was her progressive father who argued on the basis of human equality that his daughters deserved as good an education as his sons. Her mother argued on the basis of practical experience that it would do them no good: "Certainly Latin and arithmetic won't help her to be a better wife and mother" (Heyn 1971, 4-5).

In most cases, the reality must have been more complex than its representation in these short lives. A scholarly biographer, rescuing

Susan B. Anthony's childhood from cliché, is at pains to say that she "was not the firstborn of her family; she was not particularly her father's favorite, nor did she become a tomboy or hate being a girl" (Barry 1988, 11). Peterson (1971), without contradicting this, implied that Anthony's relationship with her father was exceptionally warm, and that he encouraged her independence and involvement in women's rights issues. In a juvenile biography, the popular generalization about fathers and favorite daughters may have been easier to communicate than a more individual truth.

In any case, fathers who indulged their little tomboys and bluestockings often turned out to be disappointingly repressive and overprotective later; like mothers, they enforced society's restrictions on ambitious adolescents. Addams "wanted to go far away to college," but her father sent her to nearby Rockford (Keller 1971, 11). Cassatt's father originally opposed her desire to be an artist—"I would almost rather see you dead," he told her (Wilson 1971, 8)—and especially to study in Paris. He made sure that she was well-chaperoned, summoned her home to avoid the Franco-Prussian War, and in the end moved to Paris himself, with her mother and ailing sister. This arrangement provided her with some traditional Philadelphian respectability and at the same time ensured that she did not escape any of her duties as an able-bodied unmarried daughter. Wilson, more than Myers, muted any criticism of Mr. Cassatt's demands on Mary, but the strain was clear. Mary often "had to choose between her family and her painting," and family needs came first (Wilson 1971, 126).

Robert Cassatt did at last accept his daughter's career and take pride in it. Eliot's father quarreled bitterly with his "little wench" when she lost her faith and refused to attend church, and Pankhurst's father closed his house to her after "her first public speech at an open-air demonstration to demand that civic leaders give jobs to men out of work" (Noble 1971, 13). They were never reconciled.

For women to speak in public was unthinkable to the early audiences of Lucretia Mott, Susan B. Anthony, and their contemporaries; they could be attacked, not just for the content of their speeches, but for speaking at all. It remained controversial in the late nineteenth and early twentieth centuries. A generation after Emmeline's rift with her father, Moshe Mabovitch forbade his twelve-year-old daughter to make a Socialist Party speech on a Milwaukee corner:

> Women, he thundered at Golda, did not *do* such things! His daughter, to stand on a soap box exhorting people in the street! "If you dare go

ahead with that speech," he threatened, "I'll come down there and pull you off home by your braids!" (Mann 1971, 52).

He was converted, however, when he heard his daughter speak, and took real pride in her unaccountable talent. Still later, Shirley Chisholm's father helped finance her early political career by making her the sole beneficiary of his life insurance policy; on the last morning of his life, he told her that he had "always believed in" her because she had "spirit and light" and was "socially minded" (Hicks 1971, 53). Scattered across decades and population groups, these anecdotes hinted at a slow shift in public opinion.

Families in these books acted in their daughters' best interests. When they disagreed about what those interests were, it was usually because the daughters violated traditions and social expectations that the parents had not questioned. Such transgressions could threaten a young woman's future, making her unmarriageable and leaving her without a natural protector after her father's death. George Eliot's brother, Isaac, was perhaps even more upset than their father by her failure to attend church:

> Why did she think her father was indulging in the unnecessary expense of their establishment at Foleshill? Simply to give her a good position in society and the chance to find a suitable husband. And how did she think she was going to find a husband if she persisted in such ridiculous folly? (Vipont 1971, 60).

That she needed to find a husband was a given; otherwise, her brother would have inherited responsibility for her, as Austin Dickinson (with better grace) took on the support of his sisters Emily and Vinnie. To see their daughters well married was the first responsibility of parents, because to be married was a woman's only acceptable lot in life. In parts of the world parentally arranged marriages are still the norm, and two of the biographees—Emma Goldman and Golda Meir—ran from their parents' homes to their sisters' to escape such unions when they were still in their midteens.

Competing Claims: Marriage and Vocation

Juvenile biographies in 1971 afforded glimpses of widely different marriages and decisions about marriage. Six of the subjects never married. Biographies of Charlotte Forten (Grimké), Anne MacVicar (Grant), and Martha Jefferson (Randolph) concentrated on their girlhood years—which could, however, be devoted to moral and practical preparations for marriage, as in *Miss Jefferson in Paris*. Lucretia Mott,

Marie Curie, and Shirley Chisholm were happily married, to men who supported their careers, and Julia Grant to a man whose career she supported; Emmeline Pankhurst adored her husband and, like Curie, carried on his work in her long widowhood. Radicals Emma Goldman and Sylvia Pankhurst worked companionably with their lovers, a circumstance which would surely have disqualified them from juvenile biographies in an earlier generation.

Writers for elementary school readers tended to draw a discreet veil over unhappiness in marriage. Fuller (1971), honest about the economic hardships that faced Phillis Wheatley and her husband, John Peters, as free African Americans in the aftermath of the Revolutionary War, portrayed Phillis as patiently ministering to her embittered man. Graves skimmed lightly over the end of Nellie Bly's life, including her brief marriage to a much older man. John Macy married and then "left" Helen Keller's tutor, Annie Sullivan; Malone (1971) said little about the marriage. De Leeuw (1971), writing for slightly older girls, passed quickly over Tallchief's divorce from Balanchine; she mentioned Tanaquil LeClercq first as Tallchief's fellow dancer and next as Balanchine's wife. The hints were there, but the details were skipped.

In books for young adults, unhappy or irregular matches got more coverage. Pablita Velarde, Josephine Bonaparte, Emma Goldman and Golda Meir were all divorced. George Eliot lived in sin with George Lewes because, having chivalrously claimed his wife's child by a friend, he was subsequently barred from seeking a divorce. Emmeline Pankhurst's socialist daughter Sylvia lived happily with Silvio Corio, but refused to marry him, even after the birth of their son, because she "thought the marriage ceremony an instrument of subjection to both men and women" (Noble 1971, 181). Goldman, married and divorced in her teens, believed that it "was wrong to tie people together for life, wrong to try to force love" (Shulman 1971, 72). For the rest of her life she followed a policy of giving herself to those she loved "without being bound by the rabbi or the law," and leaving "without permission" when love died; her late marriage to "an old anarchist miner" was one of convenience, giving her British citizenship, "free speech and a valid passport" (216).

By contrast, the stories of Patsy Jefferson and Julia Grant were advertisements for traditional marriage. Thomas Jefferson emerges as a protective but enlightened father preparing his daughter for her role in life. Patsy, his chief comforter in the days after her mother's death, accompanies him to France. A "little mollusk," clinging to "the warm shelter of his love for her," she cries, "I never want to leave you, Papa" (Kelly 1971, 24). Jefferson teasingly warns that someone will steal her from him in three or four years. Her eyes "blurred with tears," she gracefully accepts his decision to board her at a convent school. Later, discovering her wish to become a nun, he removes her from the school. She accepts that with equal grace, realizing that her conversion might affect his political career, but also that he is better able than she to recognize her lack of a true vocation. Jefferson shepherds her away from nuns and charming Frenchmen and toward her cousin, Tom Randolph: "Her father had been right, thought Patsy, as she drew closer in Tom's warm, protective arm" (153). The book ends joyously with their wedding. In reality, the Randolph marriage was not happy (D. Malone 1971; Varon 1999), but the troubles came later. By writing only a partial biography, Kelly could idealize Jefferson's role in planning his daughter's life, his enlightened paternalism. This was not a forced marriage, but the parentally approved beginning of what should have been a successful partnership, and Kelly allowed readers to believe in that success.

In *General's Lady*, Julia Grant's marriage is genuinely happy in spite of her father's efforts to prevent it. She is the first and favorite daughter of moderately prosperous Frederick Dent, who considers her a great beauty in spite of her crossed eye, and his wife, who says Julia's "common sense and . . . good disposition" matter more than beauty (Fleming 1971a, 10). She grows up a cheerful tomboy, chasing after her older brothers and secure in the love of parents, siblings, slaves, and assorted relatives. Ulysses Grant, the West Point roommate of her brother Fred, waits four years for her father's consent to their marriage. Their first decade together justifies Colonel Dent's fears that Ulysses is too poor to support a wife, but their mutual affection survives poverty and hardship; they create a warm family life for their children, whether at a failing Missouri farm, an Illinois dry-goods store, or an army camp between major battles. After two terms in the White House, a two-year world tour, and a brief financial career in New York, Ulysses again loses everything, but struggles through his last illness to complete his memoir, a surprise bestseller that leaves Julia financially secure.

Unlike Patsy Jefferson Randolph, Julia is portrayed as an adult. She emerges from her father's shadow, no longer accepting his "opinions without question." Instead, she begins listening to her suitor, Lieutenant Grant, and decides he makes sense (Fleming 1971a, 26). In spite of her loyalty, she becomes Grant's independent companion rather than a submissive shadow. Discovering that he's bet somebody a dollar she wouldn't go down a mine-hole, she tells him, "That was a wicked thing to do. . . . You deserved to lose" (144-145). This appealing portrait of a genuinely happy marriage takes Julia's commitment to husband and children as the norm; there is no conflict.

By contrast, when women did not marry, biographers sometimes went out of their way to demonstrate that their subjects were attractive to men. Susan B. Anthony had received proposals. At college, Ida Tarbell had flirted with fraternity brothers and enraged them by wearing four pins at once. These women might choose to sacrifice marriage to nobler ends, but there was nothing wrong with them. Heyn was unusually frank in her suggestion that sexual ambivalence played a role in Blackwell's decision:

> Elizabeth had deep feelings of affection toward George, yet she refused his proposal. She doubted that he would share her interests. And she was also confused by her own sexual feelings, desiring to be close and intimate with her boyfriend and yet feeling shy and withdrawn (Heyn 1971, 25-26).

Barth (1971) was less direct in describing Dickinson's reclusiveness, which "Emily could not explain . . . even to herself" (53), but gave an understated account of her father's "stern attitude toward his daughters' suitors" (53), the unobtainable men who became her "teachers," the "Master" poems, and the late courtship of her father's friend, Judge Lord. Without consciously probing between the lines, a reader might sense that Dickinson could live "in fear of losing Otis Lord" (88), but would never have brought herself to marry him.

In many cases, however, biographers presented refusal to marry as a rational policy. For most of the women who did marry, there were disadvantages as well as rewards. Lucretia Mott and Marie Curie, united with their husbands in dedication to high goals, were exceptions; Shirley Chisholm—whose husband said "he decided very early in their marriage that there would be only one star, and his wife would be it" (Hicks 1971, 51)—was another. More conventional husbands were troubled by their wives' commitments outside the home. After her divorce from Balanchine, Tallchief married a Chicago businessman who would have preferred her to dance less, although he supported her ongoing career. Herbert Hardin, the Anglo husband of Tewa artist Pablita Velarde, had mixed feelings about her painting. Although he was proud of her success at first and remembered her help in getting him through college, he "did not really like the attention she was getting or the time Pablita spent on her art" (Nelson 1971, 45); the strain broke their marriage.

Even prenuptial agreements might have little force against a husband's traditional expectations. Golda Mabovitch fell in love with

Moshe (Morris) Myerson when she was sixteen, but refused to marry him until he agreed to move with her to Palestine. Not a Zionist himself, he was miserable on the kibbutz and unwilling to have children born or raised there. He was happiest when they lived in Jerusalem, where he "was the breadwinner" and she "was the housewife," who "went shopping every day" and "looked after the child": "This was his world as he wanted it" (Mann 1971, 71). In the end, out of "the deep respect and affection they felt for each other" (90), the two separated. Mann explained that the marriage was impossible because they were different personality types, Moshe an introvert, Golda an extrovert; but Morris (1971, 60), describing Moshe's pleas for Golda to "return to Jerusalem and live a normal life," suggested more openly that the problem lay in Golda's need for a life beyond the family, which Moshe may have found easier to accept in principle than in practice.

Most of the subjects who avoided marriage, then, were seen to have done so to avoid the burdens it customarily placed on women. If she married, Anthony told herself, she "would only become a household drudge, . . . or maybe a doll" (Peterson 1971, 18). Bly, investigating a marriage bureau, told a prospective match, "You don't want a wife. . . . You want a slave" (Graves 1971, 58). For Ida Tarbell, as for Blackwell, Nightingale, and other occupational pioneers, marriage was an individual choice: women could have "either husbands or careers, but not both," and she was committed to her career.

> In addition, a desire for freedom was firmly rooted in her heart. She wanted to live where she pleased, work at what she liked, and come and go at will. It was hardly the type of life that went with running a home and raising a family (Fleming 1971b, 41-42).

Emma Goldman thought of the choice as a societal "injustice to women" that "went much deeper than the matters of birth control or discriminatory laws":

> Girls, she noted, are told from infancy "that marriage is the ultimate goal." They are raised to serve others, not themselves. Thousands of women, she observed, have "sacrificed their own talents and ambitions for the sake of the man. But few men have done so for women" (Shulman 1971, 171-172).

Marriage loomed as an obstacle to women's achievement, and to some men, at least, that seemed to be one of its advantages. Anthony's "good friend" Senator Blair suggested that she stop "fussing around" about women's issues: "I wish you would go . . . off and get married!" (Peterson 1971, 83). Once married, he cheerfully implied, she would be the responsibility of a man who could keep her out of the hair of other men.

Several writers glanced at the tension between marriage and independence; few analyzed it in depth. According to Myers (1971, 65), Cassatt, the daughter of a comfortable Philadelphia family, enjoyed the company of men but didn't expect to marry. She was "much more independent than most women of her time," and although she "liked the company of men," she "wanted to be treated by them as their equal"— an attitude "not likely to attract a husband." This was as direct a comment on sexism as Myers made. She reproduced the affectionate joshing of Cassatt's father (who, when she first announced her intention to paint, suggested "violets on china" as suitable) and other men, but made no open comment about how such teasing might serve to keep a woman in her place. What she emphasized more was the issue of "pretense" or artificiality, in connection with social and gender issues as well as with art; Cassatt "had disliked pretense as a young girl, and she disliked it even more as a woman" (65). She was open to marriage, Myers implied, if it did not involve pretense; she wanted to be seen as her real self, not a fragile treasure.

Spinsterhood allowed the women who chose it a freedom to invent and reinvent themselves that they could not have had in marriage, but it came at a cost. An unmarried woman's ideas (especially about the rights of women) or her desire to work at a traditionally all-male occupation could be discounted on the assumption that she was an unattractive malcontent, unable to catch and hold a man of her own, and therefore unfit to represent other women. Anthony, in later life, may have exaggerated her early romances to give herself more credibility as a woman and as a feminist (Barry 1988). When hecklers accused Emmeline Pankhurst of being an "unnatural female," she was quick to say that she "had been a beloved wife, she was the mother of four children, she held the home together for them and she had nothing but praise for wifehood or motherhood" (Noble 1971, 31). Anthony did not have that protection.

Moreover, the spinster missed the fulfillment of motherhood. Wilson (1971) attributed Cassatt's singleness to love for her impossible friend, Degas. The evidence for this seems sparse—Wilson explained that Cassatt burned "all her treasured letters from Degas" (170)—and scholarly biographers do not usually go so far (Sweet 1966; Pollock 1998). The idea of an unrealized romance, however, fit with Wilson's portrayal of Cassatt as a woman who had given up too much for her art, and who "might have felt a pang of envy" for Morisot: "To be an artist, to be married, and to have your own child to love and to paint—surely a woman couldn't ask for more than that!" (Wilson 1971, 97). When her eyes failed, Wilson's Cassatt regretted her life's choices, thinking bitterly "how wrong she had been not to marry and have children. Wasn't that the only sure way to have a future?" (191). The book's ending was softened with the thought that "her picture children are everywhere," and her château had become a home for small boys (194).

Blackwell, another hard-working single woman, adopted a daughter. Motherhood has traditionally been an important part of a woman's identity, and in these biographies the images of mothers ranged from Julia Grant with her brood in the White House to Phillis Wheatley dead in the cold with her frozen baby in her arms. Most of the working mothers in the year's biographies were shown as loving and attentive to their children. McKown (1971) admitted that little Irène Curie resented her mother's visiting students and cried, "Pay attention to me"; but she carefully detailed the young widow's active care of her daughters. Faber (1971, 49-50) pointed out that when Lucretia Mott attended a conference in England, her "children were all old enough so she could safely leave them with relatives for a few months" and her "husband was going with her"; Mott was not neglecting family responsibilities.

Biographers of at least two women, however, were critical of their subjects as mothers. Emmeline Pankhurst loved her children, but Christabel was her favorite; she failed Sylvia and Harry because "she had no understanding of shy and reserved natures" (Noble 1971, 22). She denied Harry's need for glasses and persisted in believing, until his early death, that a strenuous outdoor life would strengthen him. Noble implied that Pankhurst was too bound up in her own emotions and her admiration for Christabel to be sensitive to her other children.

Golda Meir was acutely aware of her children's needs, but often torn between family and political responsibilities. Once, called to her daughter Sara's sickbed, she found her eight-year-old son there ahead of her; he "looked at his mother with large accusing eyes and said nothing at all" (Mann 1971, 78). As an adult, however, Menachem had "perspective on his mother's constant meetings and traveling":

> "If we really needed her," he said, "she was always there." Then he added, "The last thing you would call my mother is a career woman. She did these things because she felt it was her duty" (Mann 1971, 163).

The implication was that "a career woman" might be motivated by selfishness; Meir's actions were altruistic and therefore deserved her children's understanding. Sara, asked by a reporter "whether she felt neglected as a child," answered "Yes, . . . but for such a mother, it was worthwhile" (Morris 1971, 90-91).

Women Working in Public Arenas: Muted Conflicts

Biographers still sometimes described gender-based divisions of labor and social function without comment; Bulla (1971) seemed to take them for granted, and Heyn (1971, 18), in spite of her conscious feminism, reported neutrally that "the Blackwell women spent many hours sewing for anti-slavery fairs." This might imply that the boundaries had changed very little, and readers, familiar with them in everyday life, would hardly need to have them spelled out. In other passages, however, biographers wrote as if disparities in the status of men and women were long forgotten, and needed to be explained carefully; the boundaries, if still recognizable, were at least contested. Even some of the shortest, simplest texts made room for comment on limitations placed on women "in those days." Keller, for instance, told how Addams, in response to her neighbors' concerns about uncollected garbage, applied for "the job as chief garbage collector in her area":

> Some laughed to see a young woman telling garbage men what to do. Most people thought that only men could run things. But not Jane Addams. She believed that women could do just as well as men at most jobs (Keller 1971, 31).

Vipont (1971, 53), describing the frustration of the young George Eliot, paraphrased Eliot's own words from *Daniel Deronda*: "Nobody . . . could imagine what it felt like to have a man's force of genius and yet to suffer the slavery of being a girl."

Modern girl readers were understood to inhabit a more enlightened world, a world that recognized their natural ability to "do just as well as men at most jobs." They had vastly better educational opportunities than the girls of "those days." In 1837, "the only college in the country that would admit women was Oberlin, but there were boarding schools where girls could take some advanced courses" (Peterson 1971, 14). Tarbell, as a freshman at Allegheny in 1876, "was the lone girl among forty not very friendly boys" (Fleming 1971b, 27); college was unusual for girls, because "parents believed that too much education would endanger their daughters' health and, equally frightening, ruin their chances for marriage" (25).

The girls of 1971 had a wider selection of possible work, thanks in good part to the struggles of occupational pioneers. In portraying their lives, writers tended to smooth out the controversies, on the one hand belittling opposition to women's achievement as "prejudice," and on the other hand presenting individual women in ways that contradicted prejudicial stereotypes. The subjects were not "career women," working for their own satisfaction. They responded to a sense of calling; reformers, artists, and politicians alike were pure in their motives, and those who needed paid work to support themselves found work that promoted ideals they could believe in. They worked hard, proving that they had not taken paid jobs simply from laziness, to escape the burdensome domestic duties of wives and daughters; if they succeeded, their dedication merited success. With mastery their work became more strongly individual: Pankhurst's demonstrations and Goldman's activism are as recognizably their own as Dickinson's poems and Cassatt's paintings. They developed and asserted their identities through work, but at the same time discreetly lost themselves in it, serving purposes that went beyond their individual interests.

Elizabeth Blackwell, for instance, was not selfish in undertaking the study of medicine; she had to overcome a squeamish dislike of the idea, and was moved to it by a dying friend who said, "Had I been treated by a lady doctor, I would not have suffered so terribly" (Heyn 1971, 26). Having overcome her own resistance, she overcame the prejudice of medical school professors by her hard work and decorum. She recognized that winning a prize would not open the same doors for her as for a male medical student, but rather than protest the injustice she simply resolved to work harder. Once licensed, she did not compete with men for a lucrative practice, but pioneered in public health, disease prevention, and women's medicine among the poor of New York City. Politicians Golda Meir and Shirley Chisholm, a century later, were similarly shown as gifted, hardworking, and altruistic in their dedication to the needs of others.

Even when their vocations were less obviously humanitarian, biographees' dedication had to be portrayed as worthy and disinterested. McKown (1971) emphasized early indications of Marie Curie's intelligence, her hard work, and her idealism. Her willingness to suffer cold and hunger in order to study at the Sorbonne helped establish the pursuit of science as a goal worthy of "enormous sacrifices" (87). Her loving partnership with her husband and continuation of his research after his death gave a further narrative blessing to her career; like Mott and Pankhurst, she was a devoted wife whose husband actively supported her work. This version of her life, carefully promoted by her daughter Ève, balances the abuse she endured in the French press when she had an affair after Pierre's death (Quinn 1995).

In these sympathetic biographies, the effectiveness of famous nineteenth- and twentieth-century women was often muted—excused as altruistic or public spirited, approved by husbands, carefully managed and clothed in pert or ladylike femininity to avoid threat. This was not invention on the part of biographers. Many of the suffragists and occupational pioneers had indeed adapted their images to society's belief in good women as peaceful altruists, willing to subordinate their own interests to those of others. The highly effective Jane Addams, according to Jill Ker Conway, "accepted the romantic view of women as passive and irrational," and emphasized her intuitive empathy for the downtrodden rather than her strong leadership capabilities (Conway 1971).

The belief still carried weight in 1971, and portrayals of the women avoided transgressing the old standards. A review of Fleming's *Ida Tarbell* noted approvingly that "Tarbell did not believe in militancy and felt strongly that persistence plus standards of excellence would provide a better route to acceptance in a man's world" (Canoles 1971b). A month later, assessing Noble's book on the Pankhursts, the same reviewer expressed concern that the "sympathetic" account of "[r]ock throwing, arson, acid in letter boxes, window smashing, etc." might "convince readers that violence is a pretty powerful, useful weapon and lead to the conviction that the end justifies the means" (Canoles 1971a).

It is not surprising, then, that most subjects were portrayed as hardworking and principled, rather than combative; to be "shrill" in their demands opened the pioneers and reformers of the nineteenth century to a ridicule still available for use against twentieth-century feminists. Conflicts between competing political interests were muted in these texts, creating a relatively harmonious, progressive view of the past. There was a felt need at the time for material celebrating the progress and achievements of both women and minorities, and biographies of Lucretia Mott and Susan B. Anthony omitted or quickly passed over the suffragists' disappointment with "antislavery men by whose side women had worked long and hard to free the slaves" but who then refused to support votes for women because it was "the Negro's hour" (Peterson 1971, 50).

The reformers and political activists featured in several of these biographies acted in public arenas, asserting their right to autonomy and contesting, openly or implicitly, men's right to define women's sphere as strictly private. Mott, Anthony, and Pankhurst, fighting to win the vote for women, violated norms when they spoke in public and resorted to confrontational tactics in order to be heard. Occupational pioneers like Blackwell, Tarbell, and Bly, making their ways in the traditionally male fields of medicine and journalism, were sometimes skeptical about the fight for woman's suffrage—not least because it was a fight. Tarbell "detested the suffragettes' militancy. She believed that women should have . . . the vote, but she saw no need to be pushy or overbearing about asserting feminine rights" (Fleming 1971b, 141).

Biographers of the earlier feminists presented them as anything but "pushy or overbearing." Lucretia Mott had a "clear, sweet voice," according to Faber, and "she never shouted at people who did not agree with her. Instead she tried to reason with them" (Faber 1971, 35-37). The feminists and their allies disagreed over strategy. Peterson (1971) was unusual in admitting that male abolitionists refused to support woman suffrage, and that Lucy Stone broke with Anthony and Stanton, founding a rival organization with its own newspaper and driving Anthony's out of business. While recognizing these tensions, Peterson avoided discussing personal animosities and focused instead on Anthony's perseverance. Most writers hid dissension from young readers even more thoroughly.

Noble, however, could not be placatory in her biography of Emmeline Pankhurst, who helped engineer the distastefully militant strategies Tarbell had so disliked. Collaborating with her eldest daughter, Christabel, who conceived of the tightly focused suffragist organization and developed its in-your-face tactics, Emmeline led public demonstrations, courted arrest, staged hunger strikes and destroyed property. Her obituary in the *Daily Mail* pointed to her "superb courage" and "that white-hot enthusiasm which gave to the campaign, with all its hysterical excesses, a kind of wild dignity" (Noble 1971, 179). There was no hiding the controversial violence of the Pankhursts' campaign, and to win reader sympathy Noble instead emphasized the justice of Emmeline's cause, her devotion to her husband, and her fine looks.

Conclusion

The lives and choices of these biographical subjects were of course shaped by different times (although most were born in the nineteenth century) and places (although most were American), but also by the visions and goals of different individuals—from Pocahontas, trapped by the English she had helped, to Shirley Chisholm, fighting to represent blacks and women in Congress. Some shared experiences. In the 1780s the future Josephine Bonaparte, cast off by her first husband, lived for a time at the Penthemont, the same fashionable Paris convent where Patsy Jefferson was sent to school. (Could they have met? What would they have thought of each other?) Susan B. Anthony was inspired by Lucretia Mott, admired by Charlotte Forten, and interviewed by Nellie Bly, who also interviewed Emma Goldman. Goldman and Golda Meir, immigrants from czarist Russia to the United States in two generations, both had girlhood experiences of pogroms, parents who wanted to marry them off as teenagers, and associations with excited groups of transplanted intellectuals and activists in America. The lives of these women crisscrossed and coincided in odd ways, and a girl who read many of them might begin to develop a sense of connectedness across time and space.

More fundamentally, these lives were connected by the individualism and didacticism inherent in juvenile biography as a genre. On the one hand, subjects were exceptional women. They were gifted. Mary Cassatt, rising above the amateurism of women who dabbled in painting for lack of more meaningful work, confounded the expectations of Degas both by her sensibility ("That is real. There is someone who feels as I do. . . . A woman!") and by her skill: "I will not admit that a woman can draw so well," he said (Wilson 1971, 64, 140). Phillis Wheatley's poetic achievements undermined popular beliefs about the incapacity of "savages." Jane Addams and Elizabeth Blackwell looked seriously for the missions that would give their lives meaning; Julia Grant had faith that Ulysses was destined for greatness. They believed in their own exceptionality.

On the other hand, biographical subjects were intended as inspirations and models for the ordinary middle-class girls who read these books. In reviews, the words of praise were often more for the subject than for the text: Pocahontas was "a kindhearted, courageous girl" (Anon. 1971b); Lucretia Mott's "contribution was the patient and courageous dedication of a quiet woman" (Anon. 1972c). Patience, courage, kindness, and devotion, along with dedication and hard work, were the prevailing virtues, and family duty was important; "Emmeline Pankhurst's curious detachment from her offspring," said *School Library Journal* of Noble's book, "amounted to virtual child neglect" (Canoles 1971a).

Yet, whether they were written for elementary or junior high school students, about women of the eighteenth or the twentieth century, these books had in common an expectation of unity based on the development of individual character and the playing out of individual destiny. Books for younger readers, and books about women who had left fewer historical records, tended to rely more on fictionalization, although reviewers seemed critical of the practice: the word "fictionalized" implied a criticism which could be moderated ("palatably fiction-alized") or intensified ("undue amount of fictionalization"). Books for older readers often appeared more factual and even objective, provided bibliographies and source notes, and adopted a rhetoric more typical of journalism than of fiction; but they might still use novelistic devices such as a dramatic opening vignette followed by flashback, foreshad-owing of significant events, and repetition of significant phrases to give unity and meaning to the account of an individual life. The convention of the continuous biographical narrative, with its implication that life can and should be coherent, constituted the most important message of these biographies to their young readers.

Juvenile Biographies Discussed

Barth, Edna. 1971. *I'm nobody! Who are you? The story of Emily Dickinson.* Illus. Richard Cuffari. New York: Seabury Press.

Bobbé, Dorothie. 1971. *The New World journey of Anne MacVicar.* New York: G. P. Putnam's Sons.

Bulla, Clyde Robert. 1971. *Pocahontas and the strangers.* Illus. Peter Bur-chard. New York: Thomas Y. Crowell.

De Leeuw, Adèle. 1971. *Maria Tallchief: American ballerina.* New York: Dell Yearling.

Douty, Esther M. 1971. *Charlotte Forten: Free Black teacher.* Champaign, IL: Garrard Publishing Company.

Faber, Doris. 1971. *Lucretia Mott: Foe of slavery.* Illus. Russell Hoover. Champaign, IL: Garrard Publishing Company.

Fleming, Alice. 1971a. *General's lady: The life of Julia Dent Grant.* Illus. Richard Lebenson. Philadelphia: Lippincott.

Fleming, Alice. 1971b. *Ida Tarbell: First of the muckrakers.* New York: Tho-mas Y. Crowell.

Fuller, Miriam Morris. 1971. *Phillis Wheatley: America's first black poetess.* Illus. Victor Mays. Champaign, IL: Garrard Publishing Company.

Graves, Charles. 1971. *Nellie Bly: Reporter for* The World. Illus. Victor Mays. Champaign, IL: Garrard Publishing Company.

Heyn, Leah Lurie. 1971. *Challenge to become a doctor: The story of Elizabeth Blackwell.* Illus. Greta Handschuh. Long Island, NY: Feminist Press.

Hicks, Nancy. 1971. *The Honorable Shirley Chisholm: Congresswoman from Brooklyn.* New York: Lion Books.

Keller, Gail Faithfull. 1971. *Jane Addams: A Crowell biography.* Illus. Frank Aloise. New York: Thomas Y. Crowell.

Kelly, Regina Z. 1971. *Miss Jefferson in Paris.* Illus. Nena Allen. New York: Coward, McCann & Geoghegan.

McKown, Robin. [1971]. *Marie Curie. A World Pioneer Biography.* Illus. Karl W. Swanson. New York: G. P. Putnam's Sons.

Malone, Mary. 1971. *Annie Sullivan.* Illus. Lydia Rosier. New York: G. P. Putnam's Sons.

Mann, Peggy. 1971. *Golda: The life of Israel's prime minister.* New York: Coward, McCann & Geoghegan.

Morris, Terry. 1971. *Shalom, Golda.* New York: Hawthorn Books.

Mossiker, Frances. 1971. *More than a queen: The story of Josephine Bonaparte.* Illus. Michael Eagle. New York: Knopf.

Myers, Elisabeth P. 1971. *Mary Cassatt: A portrait.* Chicago: Reilly & Lee.

Nelson, Mary Carroll. 1971. *Pablita Velarde.* Minneapolis: Dillon Press.

Noble, Iris. 1971. *Emmeline and her daughters: The Pankhurst suffragettes.* New York: Messner.

Peterson, Helen Stone. 1971. *Susan B. Anthony: Pioneer in woman's rights.* Illus. Paul Frame. Champaign, IL: Garrard Publishing Company.

Shulman, Alix Kates. 1971. *To the Barricades: The Anarchist Life of Emma Goldman.* Illus. with photographs. New York: Thomas Y. Crowell.

Vipont, Elfrida. 1971. *Towards a high attic: The early life of George Eliot, 1819-1880.* New York: Holt, Rinehart & Winston.

Wilson, Ellen. 1971. *American painter in Paris: A life of Mary Cassatt.* New York: Farrar, Straus & Giroux.

Other References

Anon. 1971a. Review of *Emmeline and Her Daughters*, by Iris Noble. *Bulletin of the Center for Children's Books* 25 (December 1971): 63.

———. 1971b. Review of *Pocahontas and the Strangers*, by Clyde Robert Bulla. *Booklist* 68 (December 15): 365.

———. 1972a. Review of *Emmeline and Her Daughters*, by Iris Noble. *Booklist* 68 (January 15): 434.

———. 1972b. Review of *Lucretia Mott*, by Doris Faber. *Booklist* 68 (February 15): 506.

———. 1972c. Review of *Lucretia Mott*, by Doris Faber. *Bulletin of the Center for Children's Books* 25 (January): 73.

———. 1972d. Review of *Miss Jefferson in Paris*, by Regina Z. Kelly. *Bulletin of the Center for Children's Books* 25 (February): 93.

Arbuthnot, May Hill. 1947. Chapter 17, Biography. In *Children and books*, 470-501. Chicago: Scott, Foresman.

Arbuthnot, May Hill. 1964. Chapter 17, Biography. *Children and books*, 3rd ed., 518-562. Chicago: Scott, Foresman.

Arbuthnot, May Hill, and Zena Sutherland. 1972. Chapter 15, Biography. *Children and books*, 4th ed., 534-573. Chicago: Scott, Foresman.

Barry, Kathleen. 1988. *Susan B. Anthony: A biography of a singular feminist.* New York: New York University Press.

Broderick, Dorothy. 1971. Biography, introduction. In *The Arbuthnot anthology of children's literature*, 3rd ed., May Hill Arbuthnot, 916-918. Chicago: Scott, Foresman.

Canoles, Marian L. 1971a. Review of *Emmeline and her daughters*, by Iris Noble. *School Library Journal* 18 (2): 125.

Canoles, Marian L. 1971b. Review of *Ida Tarbell: First of the muckrakers*, by Alice Fleming. *School Library Journal* 18 (2): 120.

Carlsen, G. Robert. 1971. *Books and the teen-age reader: A guide for teachers, librarians and parents*, rev. ed. New York: Harper & Row.

Conway, Jill Ker. 1971. Women reformers and American culture, 1870-1930. *Journal of Social History* 5 (2): 166-177.

Coolidge, Olivia. 1974. My struggle with the facts. *Wilson Library Bulletin* 49 (October): 146-150.

Darrow, Whitney, Jr. 1970. *I'm glad I'm a girl! I'm glad I'm a boy!* New York: Windmill/Simon & Schuster.

Davis, Mavis Wormley. 1973. Black images in children's literature: Revised editions needed. In *Issues in children's book selection: A* School Library Journal *Anthology*. New York: R. R. Bowker Company.

Feminists on Children's Literature. 1971. A feminist look at children's books. *School Library Journal* 17 (5): 19-24.

Fischer, Gayle V. 1997. "Pantalets" and "Turkish trowsers": Designing freedom in the mid-nineteenth-century United States. *Feminist Studies* 23 (Spring): 111-140.

Fisher, Margery. 1972. *Matters of fact: Aspects of non-fiction for children*. Leicester: Brockhampton Press.

Forman, Jack. 1972. Up for discussion: Biographies for children—more facts, less fiction. *School Library Journal* 18 (1): 98-99.

Grant, Anne MacVicar. 1808. *Memoirs of an American lady: With sketches of manners and scenery in America, as they existed previous to the Revolution*. Repr., New York: Research Reprints Inc., 1970.

Howe, Florence. 1971. Sexual stereotypes start early. *Saturday Review* 54 (October 16): 76-82, 92-94.

Huck, Charlotte S., and Doris Young Kuhn. 1968. Chapter 6, Biography and historical fiction. *Children's literature in the elementary school*. 2nd ed., 272-330. New York: Holt, Rinehart and Winston, Inc.

Karmazin, Sharon. 1971. Review of *Miss Jefferson in Paris*, by Regina Z. Kelly. *School Library Journal* 18 (4): 58-59.

Kismaric, Carole, and Marvin Heiferman. 1996. *Growing up with Dick and Jane: Learning and living the American dream*. New York: HarperCollins.

Kroeger, Brooke. 1994. *Nellie Bly: Daredevil, reporter, feminist*. New York: Times Books.

Lerner, Gerda. 1979. *The majority finds its past: Placing women in history*. New York: Oxford University Press.

Lowry, Heath W. 1971. Evaluative criteria to be used as guides by writers of children's literature. *Elementary English* 48 (8): 22-25.

Malone, Dumas. 1971. Randolph, Martha Jefferson (Sept. 27, 1772-Oct. 10, 1836). In *Notable American women 1607-1950*, vol. 3, ed. E. T. James, J. W. James, and P. S. Boyer, 116-117. Cambridge, MA: Belknap Press.

Mossiker, Frances. 1964. *Napoleon and Josephine: The biography of a marriage*. New York: Simon & Schuster.

Neville, Emily. 1967. Social values in children's literature. In *A critical approach to children's literature*, ed. Sara Innis Fenwick, 46-52. Chicago: University of Chicago Press.

Nilsen, Alleen Pace. 1971. Women in children's literature. *College English* 32 (8): 918-926.

Pollock, Griselda. 1998. *Mary Cassatt: Painter of Modern Women*. London: Thames and Hudson.

Quinn, Susan. 1995. *Marie Curie: A life*. New York: Simon & Schuster.

Randolph, Sarah Nicholas. 1939. *The domestic life of Thomas Jefferson: Compiled from family letters and reminiscences by his great-granddaughter*. Cambridge, MA: University Press.

Register, Cheri. 1989. American feminist literary criticism: A bibliographical introduction. In *Feminist literary criticism: Explorations in theory*, 2nd ed., Josephine Donovan, 1-27. Lexington: University Press of Kentucky.

Richmond, M. A. 1974. *Bid the vassal soar: Interpretive essays on the life and poetry of Phillis Wheatley (ca. 1753-1784) and George Moses Horton (ca. 1797-1883)*. Washington, DC: Howard University Press.

Robinson, William H. 1984. *Phillis Wheatley and her writings*. New York: Garland.

Rosen, Ruth. 2000. *The world split open: How the modern women's movement changed America*. New York: Viking.

Shulman, Alix Kates. 1996. *Drinking the rain*. New York: Penguin.

Stanton, Susan. 1971. Review of *Maria Tallchief: American ballerina*, by Adèle De Leeuw. *School Library Journal* 18 (2): 109-110.

Stavn, Diane Gersoni. 1972. Reducing the 'Miss Muffet' syndrome: An annotated bibliography. *School Library Journal* 18 (5): 32-35.

Stevenson, Brenda, Ed. 1988. *The journals of Charlotte Forten Grimké*. New York: Oxford University Press.

Sweet, Frederick A. 1966. *Miss Mary Cassatt: Impressionist from Pennsylvania*. Norman: University of Oklahoma Press.

Tarbell, Ida M. 1939. *All in the day's work: An autobiography*. New York: Macmillan.

Trecker, Janice Law. 1971. Women's place is in the curriculum. *Saturday Review* 54 (October 16): 83-86, 92.

Tunnell, Michael O. 1992. Unmasking the fiction of history: Children's historical fiction begins to come of age. In *The Story of Ourselves: Teaching History through Children's Literature*, ed. Michael O. Tunnell and Richard Ammon, 79-90. Portsmouth, NH: Heinemann.

Varon, Elizabeth R. 1999. Randolph, Martha Jefferson (27 Sept. 1772-10 Oct. 1836). *American National Biography*, v. 18, ed. John A. Garraty and Mark C. Carnes. New York: Oxford University Press, 1999.

Vicinus, Martha. 1990. What makes a heroine? Girls' biographies of Florence Nightingale. In *Florence Nightingale and her era: A collection of new scholarship*, ed. Vern Bullough, Bonnie Bullough, and Marietta P. Stanton, 90-106. New York: Garland.

Wilms, Denise M. 1982. An evaluation of biography. In *Beyond fact: Nonfiction for children and young people*, comp. Jo Carr, 135-140. Chicago: American Library Association.

Chapter 4

1996: Objectivity
and the Culture Wars

If in 1971 the children's book world had enjoyed a sense of liberation
from old taboos, by 1996 taboos seemed a thing of the past. It was now
possible to write about women who drank too much or who experimented with drugs, although these lapses were typically followed by
penalties and reformations. Heroines bore children out of wedlock,
suffered sexual abuse in childhood, or lost or aborted pregnancies. The
new books did not protect children from the world, but presumably
armed them with information they might need to tackle it. Yet many
people still wanted to shield children from premature exposure to the
seamier side of life. The American Library Association's Office for
Intellectual Freedom (2004) recorded over six thousand challenges to
books in the 1990s; many of the offending books were meant for children. Challengers objected to what they saw as "sexually explicit,"
"unsuited to age group," or violent; to "offensive language"; and to
occult, homosexual, or religious themes.

Challengers and defenders alike did a lot of counting, as quantitative research pervaded the discussion of educational policy and other
child welfare issues. Much of the writing about children's books was as
idealistic as ever, even if the idealists were in fierce disagreement about
what best served their children; but the language of scholarly discourse
in the field had changed. In the 1940s, it was appreciative, inspirational: "'Give us books,' say the children; 'Give us wings'" (Hazard
1947). This vein of commentary continued in publications for youth
librarians, but from the 1970s on, scholars in English departments were
increasingly successful in distancing themselves from it; journals like
Phaedra (1973-1988), *The Children's Literature Association Quarterly*
(1976-), and *The Lion and the Unicorn* (1977-) provided a forum for

the application of modern and postmodern literary theories to children's books. At the same time, scholars with training in the social sciences performed content analyses, field studies, and other forms of quantitative research on the books and their readers—especially on textbooks, where political commentators decried the over- or underrepresentation of minorities and women.

While scholars read more children's literature, there was widespread concern that children were reading less. The National Center for Education Statistics reported "a decline in the number of reading materials in the home between 1971 and 1996," with fewer students having home access to all four types of reading material checked in the survey (newspapers, magazines, books, and encyclopedias). The amount of time nine- and thirteen-year-olds spent reading for fun had not declined between 1984 and 1996, and neither had the likelihood that they would engage in reading-related activities like telling friends about good books, taking books out of the library, or spending their own money to buy books; but where 65 percent of seventeen-year-olds read for fun in 1984, only 55 percent did so in 1996 (Campbell, Voelkl, and Donahue 2000). Lynch-Brown and Tomlinson (1998) reported decreased sales of young adult literature during the mid-1990s; they suspected that fewer adolescents "read books of much length and complexity, as our society has become increasingly more visually oriented."

In spite of occasional dips, the children's book industry had grown. In 1996, the total number of new juvenile hardback and trade paperback titles published was 5,353 (Ink 1998), well over twice the 1971 total. The market for these books had also grown. In 1971, libraries and schools bought the great majority of juvenile books published. Now the institutional market was being eclipsed. The Children's Book Council (2002) reported "an increasing trend for teachers and parents to purchase educational materials at mass market outlets"; institutional markets accounted for as little as 20 percent of some publishers' sales. Publishers stepped up direct marketing to children themselves.

These trends diminished the influence of library selection criteria on publishing—to the detriment of quality, some claimed. Even if children were still reading, it was feared that their books had been "dumbed down" to be more like television, with bright colors, short sections, and frequent interruptions, a literature for hyperactive readers with impaired attention spans. According to Lynch-Brown and Tomlinson, much of the growth occurred in picture books and "heavily illustrated works of nonfiction," categories with "more immediate appeal to adult buyers in bookstores."

Like children's books in general, juvenile biographies of women were more numerous, shorter, and more profusely illustrated than ever. In 1971, young adult books were becoming a more distinct category. The newly important genre in 1996 was the picture-book biography, straddling a contested boundary between fiction and nonfiction. Fictionalized biographies for older children, however, were more consistently classed as fiction; since they were reviewed in different columns or sections, few were analyzed for this chapter. Combing through nonfiction reviews in 1996 and 1997 issues of *Booklist, The Horn Book Magazine, School Library Journal,* and *Voice of Youth Advocates,* and excluding autobiographies, documentaries, and books about Biblical, mythical or legendary women, I identified a group of fifty-one biographies that were published in 1996 and reviewed for young readers: six for primary school (kindergarten or first grade and up); twenty-three for elementary school (second, third, or fourth grade and up); six for middle school (fifth grade and up); and sixteen for junior high school (sixth, seventh, or eighth grade and up). See appendix C for a list.

Reviewing Climate: The Culture Wars

In 1996, the achievements of liberal feminism were widely taken for granted, even while the word "feminist," like the word "liberal," was used in some circles as an insult. There were more women than ever before in Congress and in corporate management. Women's History Month, the 1987 expansion of National Women's History Week, was celebrated every March, creating an annual demand for more biographies of women in school library media centers. Still, many felt that girls had not escaped their traditional inferior status. The questing protagonist of a contemporary novel, writing home to her baffled husband, said she had been reading "a magazine article about how girls get gypped in school":

> I am so happy this kind of thing is finally being recognized. They also talked about twelve being the age when things start to change for girls, the time when they start to lose their powers, and I think they're right (Berg 1996, 119).

Such magazine articles popularized the insights of feminist scholarship. Gilligan (1982) observed that developmental models of morality based on the study of white males had been widely accepted as normative for all populations, and differences in women's moral vision had been interpreted as incomplete development, or inferiority. Her corrective study inspired others. Belenky, Clinchy, Goldberger, and Tarule (1986) interviewed a heterogeneous sample of women at colleges and family clinics, and found that women's cognitive development, like their moral development, paralleled but differed from men's. They identified class differences as well: poorer women, with less support, were more likely to remain silently trapped in early developmental stages. In 1994, Orenstein's *Schoolgirls* articulated the view that Berg's heroine found in her magazine: girls, as active and confident by nature as their brothers, are socialized into self-doubt and fall silent as they enter adolescence. That same year, Pipher's *Reviving Ophelia: Saving the Selves of Adolescent Girls*, telling clinical stories of the victims of our "girl-poisoning" culture, was a *New York Times* bestseller.

These studies of girls' development tended to be qualitative, based on in-depth interviews and observations of individuals or small groups. To study the books girls were reading, however, many researchers used quantitative methods. Content analysis—a strategy for identifying pattern and meaning in texts by counting the frequency of specified variables—had already been used in 1971 (Nilsen 1971; Feminists 1971). By 1996, there was a significant body of research, with most reports referring "back to a paradigmatic study by Lenore Weitzman and her co-authors" in 1972 (Clark 2002). Ernst (1995), reviewing studies from the 1980s and early 1990s, reported that females were still outnumbered by males in easy books, Newbery and Caldecott Medal winners, and other sampled children's books. There was also an imbalance in how characters were portrayed: males were more likely to be "active problem solvers," while females were "passive" and "dependent."

A quantitative approach could be used on whole library collections as well as on individual texts. Harvey-Slager (1992) determined that representation of women and minorities in the biography collections of four Texas elementary school libraries was not balanced "in proportion to the population," and the collections were therefore "not adequate to serve the role model needs" of students. Referring to studies of girls' "alarmingly low self-image," she argued that "school is a strong link in the female self-esteem chain" and should help prevent its loss by providing more biographies of potential role models.

Debates over the content of school texts also had implications for trade books and library collections. In 1977, to help selectors recognize stereotypes of African Americans, Asian Americans, Chicanos, Native Americans, Puerto Ricans, and women, the Council on Interracial Books for Children issued a manual with checklists for content analysis. Items on each list were graded from +2 for "Full Information" to –2 for "Incorrect Information," and ranged from factual statements like "The 1848 Seneca Falls Convention signified the historic start of the suffrage movement" to more sweeping propositions like "Women's labor has often been recruited, abused and discarded by business interests." An evaluator could systematically grade a text on how well its coverage conformed to the list. The Council's political approach called attention to power imbalances between dominant and marginalized groups, and its emphasis on careful documentation was tailor-made to support legal and political advocacy.

Liberals continued to refine this approach. In *Failing at Fairness: How America's Schools Cheat Girls*, Myra and David Sadker (1994) assumed for textbooks what Harvey-Slager had assumed for library collections: representation of women and ethnic minorities should reflect their share of the population. What they found was far from ideal by this standard: one "upper-elementary history textbook had four times as many males pictured as females," while a 631-page world history devoted "only seven pages . . . to women, either as famous individuals or as a general group" (Sadker and Sadker 1994, 72). They warned, "When girls do not see themselves in the pages of textbooks, when teachers do not point out or confront the omissions, our daughters learn that to be female is to be an absent partner in the development of our nation" (8).

Underlying such reports was a sense that historic wrongs had been perpetuated by the uncritical portrayal of unjust reality in children's books, and that content analysis, by providing evidence of this practice, could be used to effect change. The assumption was that children cannot become what they cannot imagine becoming, and that reading helps form the imagination. As Ernst (1995, 76) put it, literature does more than "simply reflect society"; it also influences society, and "reflection reinforces the status quo." Gender identity is not biologically determined, in this view, but socially and imaginatively constructed in a process to which children's books and classroom experiences contribute. By assuring better representation of girls and women in books, libraries, and especially the schoolbooks that children must read, reformers could help children imagine and create a better future for themselves and their societies.

Naturally, not everybody agreed. Conservatives, too, were using content analysis—to show how textbooks undermined family values. DelFattore summarized some of their concerns about feminist-influenced texts: "Pictures of little girls engaging in activities traditionally associated with boys, such as playing with toy cars or petting worms, threaten American family life because girls might grow up craving male roles." Feminism was seen as one threat to American tradition among many; in *Mozert v. Hawkins County Public Schools*, Tennessee parents objected to Holt readers because they were "full of minorities, foreigners, environmentalists, women in nontraditional roles, and open-ended value judgments without clear right and wrong answers" (DelFattore 1992, 6, 14).

Like feminists and multiculturalists, conservatives appealed to statistical evidence. In a book subtitled "why our culture and our country have stopped making sense," Lynne Cheney (1995) quoted a study showing that 99 percent of women and only 71 percent of men portrayed in textbooks were shown positively. While liberals deplored children's inability to list ten legitimately famous women (Sadker and Sadker 1994, 71), conservatives lamented a 1989 study showing that more American seventeen-year-olds knew who Harriet Tubman was than "that George Washington was the commander of the American army during the Revolutionary War" (Cheney 1995, 33) or "that Abraham Lincoln issued the Emancipation Proclamation" (Sommers 1995, 61). The wrong things were being emphasized, they said, and historical fact was being manipulated to advance new political agendas. In reality, women should be less prominent than men in history books because they had been disenfranchised and unable to take prominent roles in the making of history. Even if the exclusion was unjust, there was "simply no honest way of writing women back into the historical narrative." To give them "30 percent would be too much, and giving women *half* the space in a conventional History would blatantly falsify the narrative" (Sommers 1995, 57).

Controlling the representation of history in textbooks is one way to control children's learning. Another approach is to set educational standards, and in the mid-1990s the debate over the *National Standards for History in the Schools* raised many of the same issues as content analysis of children's books. The National History Standards Project was launched in 1992, in a climate of bipartisan support for better public education. It was initially funded by grants from the National Endowment for the Humanities, at that time headed by Lynne Cheney, and from the Department of Education. But history may be, as project codirectors Crabtree and Nash (1996) called it, the "most contentious field of the curriculum." Designed for voluntary use in schools with varying curricula, the *Standards* were published in 1994 and promptly met with opposition; they were condemned by Cheney, by presidential candidates Bill Clinton and Bob Dole, and in January 1995 by a ninety-nine to one vote in the U.S. Senate (Fonte and Lerner 1997). Revised and reissued in 1996, they continued to attract vehement criticism.

The *Standards* began with a plea for the significance of their subject: "knowledge of history is the precondition of political intelligence." They argued for the importance not only of historical knowledge, a society's "common memory of where it has been, what its core values are, or what decisions of the past account for present circumstances," but also of historical thinking skills. Their frequent references to inquiry and decision-making indicated that history was not a static body of knowledge for students to accept with unquestioning reverence, but a dynamic resource with flexible applications to unforeseen problems. They claimed it as a resource for "nurturing the private individual" as well as for responsible citizenship: "Historical memory is the key to self-identity, to seeing one's place in the stream of time, and one's connectedness with all of humankind" (Crabtree and Nash 1996).

The *Standards* set out to be inclusive both in content (referring to the diversity of the United States, "exemplified by race, ethnicity, social and economic status, gender, region, politics, and religion") and in method (attempting to integrate social, political, economic, and cultural history, and the history of science and technology). Opponents questioned both kinds of inclusiveness. They perceived an anti-Western bias in the inclusion of early American and African cultures at the expense of "some major ideas of Western history," with undue emphasis on the achievements of non-Western cultures and the faults of the West (Fonte and Lerner 1997; London 1997). Cheney herself accused the *Standards* of "gloomy, politically driven revisionism":

> They took the important principle of inclusion to such an extreme that a new kind of exclusion resulted. Harriet Tubman, who helped slaves escape from the South, is mentioned six times in the standards, while two of her male contemporaries, Ulysses S. Grant and Robert E. Lee, are cited one and zero times . . . (Cheney 1995, 114).

The selection of historical facts to be taught was dictated not by accuracy alone, but by educational objectives. Diggins (1996), arguing that the proper object of history in the schools is not therapy and the support of self-esteem but rather the preparation of informed citizens, saw the *Standards* as an inconsistent attempt to "teach the values of freedom and at the same time insist that history is the sole locus of one's identity." Political history, he suggested, was the proper vehicle for teaching young people to participate in a democracy, because it dealt with free individuals wielding power. What he referred to as "the new social history" was less effective because of its concentration on "the life of ordinary people at the bottom or at the margins, specifically workers and their struggles and women and their spheres" (Diggins 1997). Although children might identify with the disenfranchised, they could learn the uses of freedom better from those who shaped events rather than merely enduring them: "Without knowledge of power, can there be knowledge of freedom?" Sommers (1995), while arguing that "both political and social history are important," made a similar point: the activities of women (and of others unnamed in standard political histories) assume greater importance in social history, but this should at most supplement, not replace, political history.

The *Standards* debate, with its heated rhetoric pitting citizenship against identity formation and multiculturalism against patriotism, was one highlight of what some called the "culture wars." This phrase did not have the same currency in the library world that it did elsewhere, but the conflicting goals of the two sides did affect library collections, influencing both the supply of trade books and the climate of opinion within which selectors worked. Multiculturalist and feminist ideals were to a large degree absorbed into general selection criteria; non-stereotyped portrayals were held to be more accurate, and many librarians saw the challenge of books for offensive stereotypes not as censorship, but rather as a call for improved selection. On the other hand, religious and cultural conservatism were more often perceived as threats to intellectual freedom. School library media specialists, in particular, felt driven to avoid collecting materials that might offend by their language or content. Selectors inherited from the 1970s an open commitment to intellectual freedom, even for children; but in the 1990s some exercised it uneasily, increasingly aware of opposition.

Books and Reviews:
Old Criteria, New Applications

Between 1971 and 1996, critics continued to fault children's biography for the same old defects: hero-worship, didacticism, oversimplification, and, as Carr (1982) put it, "sentimentality, unwarranted fictionalization, lack of solid documentation, and distortion of history." As usual, these flaws were imputed to the past: "Children's biographies have come a long way from the old days" (Freedman 1988). Children's literature textbooks agreed that newer biographies were more diverse in their choice of subjects, less adulatory, and better documented (Sutherland and Arbuthnot 1991), and that there was a welcome trend away from fictionalization and toward authenticity. Huck et al. (1997) concluded that in spite of some persistent mediocrity, "the number of high-quality books" in the genre had grown. Writers Jean Fritz and Russell Freedman won critical praise for their lively prose and meticulous research. Russell (1991) held up Freedman's *Lincoln: A Photobiography*, winner of the 1988 Newbery Medal, as "a model for all future biographers for young people" because of its "careful research, including extraordinary illustration with photographs from the period; refusal to condescend to children in either vocabulary or selection of hard facts; honest and unsentimental portrayal of one of the great figures of American history; and avoidance of both debunking and deifying its subject."

Choice of Biographical Subject

A good biographee could represent "a historically important person, a worthy role model, or an attainable career choice" (England and Fasick 1987, 134). The fifty-one biographies published in 1996 ran the gamut, with forty-five subjects ranging from Cleopatra (who died in 30 BC) to Oksana Baiul (who was not yet even twenty in 1996). They included political leaders, victims of injustice, reformers, pioneers who opened new careers to women, entertainers, and sports celebrities. They were international and multicultural. According to Hopkins and Tastad (1997), fewer than 10 percent of American children's books published annually were "multicultural in nature," but for biography the percentage was much higher. Fifteen books (30 percent) were about women from outside the United States (five from Britain, seven from other European countries, and one each from Mexico, Guatemala, and ancient Egypt); seventeen (33 percent) were about African, Asian, Hispanic, and Native Americans; and nineteen (37 percent) were about white, non-Hispanic American women.

Thirty-nine of the books—more than three in four—belonged to twenty-four different series, several of which explicitly addressed the need for realistic multicultural role models: there were four entries in Enslow's African-American Biographies series, one in its Hispanic Biographies series, and two in Lodestar's Rainbow Biographies. Other markets were accommodated as well. There were series designed to promote civic virtues (Rosen's Character Building Books), spiritual commitment and activism (Eerdmans' Women of Spirit), and innovation in everything from women's rights to ornithology (Carolrhoda's Creative Minds). There were series explicitly adapted to curricular needs: a foreword in Lucent's The Importance Of series explained how the books' features would support student research. Others, like the sports biographies and Henry Holt's W5 series (in which two French satirists took a subversively postmodern look at Queen Victoria) may have been intended for more recreational use. (Or maybe not. "Warning: May Be Habit-Forming," reads a notice on the back of *Victoria and Her Times.* "Laboratory tests have shown that prolonged exposure to books in the W5 series can cause the reader to develop increased awareness and an uncontrollable enthusiasm for the subject matter.") There was one representative of the Childhood of Famous Americans series—by coincidence, a new book about Pocahontas, superseding Flora Seymour's 1946 version.

The series books varied in their cultural content, formats, reading levels, and intended uses, and some were extremely effective in layout and illustration. The twelve non-series books were even more diverse. Half were picture-book biographies—three about African American heroines Bessie Coleman, Wilma Rudolph, and Harriet Tubman, the others about Nellie Bly, Eleanor Roosevelt, and Elizabeth Cady Stanton. Distinguished and appealing illustrations dominated these books; the wistful formality of Barbara Cooney's Eleanor, the expressive warmth of Jerry Pinkney's Harriet, and the stylized grace of David Diaz's Wilma necessarily colored readers' experience of the accompanying texts. For older readers, the balance between text and graphics ranged widely. Gloria Kamen's ten distinctive ink and wash drawings, scattered through her book on Fanny Mendelssohn, resembled the illustrations of 1971; most emphasized faces and upper bodies, as her text emphasized the Mendelssohns' psychology. At the other end of the spectrum, Hugh Brewster's gorgeously designed book on the Grand Duchess Anastasia was inspired by her own photograph albums and letters in the State Archives in Moscow; the graphics, carefully selected and dramatically arranged, dominated the supporting text.

Semantic Criteria

Accuracy and authenticity were still commonly listed as the top criteria, by both critics and leading authors. "As a writer of nonfiction, I have a pact with the reader to stick to the facts, to be as factually accurate as human frailty will allow," wrote Freedman (1994), and Fritz (1988) stated, "I do not invent." To help selectors evaluate material outside their areas of expertise, the familiar surrogates, documentation and credentials, were still suggested as indicators of reliability. The reputations of publishers were thought less helpful; because a series could include "pedestrian" books along with others "of major importance," Sutherland and Arbuthnot (1991) warned, it was "best to judge each book individually and to watch for authoritative reviews." The presence of notes, bibliographies, and information about authors, however, was considered important and routinely noted in reviews. Most juvenile biographies now included some or all of these elements.

Authors' credentials

Children's literature textbooks urged selectors to weigh credentials skeptically. The author's "education and current position . . . may suggest no unique qualification for the task at hand," observed England and Fasick (1987). Forty of the biographies (78 percent) included notes on their jacket flaps, covers, or back pages, but they were brief, and book selectors had to read between the lines. Thirty-nine mentioned the authors' writing experience, often describing them as "professional," "freelance," or "full-time" writers; some listed popular, recent, or award-winning titles. Was a veteran freelancer who had "written about 125 books for both children and adults" likely to give more than superficial coverage to yet another sports star? Was a doctoral candidate writing "her first biography for young readers" likely to overwhelm them with scholarly detail? Some of the authors' previous work suggested relevant expertise: Robert Green had written biographies of three ancient rulers before Cleopatra, and Leslie Gourse, who had written about many jazz greats and won an ASCAP award, seemed a natural choice to write *Mahalia Jackson*. But Leslie Gourse also wrote *Pocahontas* (with no author's note), and the biographer of nineteenth-century writer Mary Shelley had previously written about twentieth-century Russian leader Boris Yeltsin and tennis star Pete Sampras.

Eighteen of the blurbs mentioned the authors' educational credentials and/or teaching experience. At least two, Jerry Stanley and Bárbara Cruz, were university professors, and between them William R. Sanford and Carl R. Green, authors of *Calamity Jane: Frontier Original*, had over sixty years of teaching experience. A teaching background hints at something more than expertise: the ability to make things accessible and interesting to young readers. Other typically featured author experiences were editing, proofreading, and research, and nineteen notes mentioned family—a husband, a wife, children; a two-year-old, a teenager, grown children, grandchildren. While saying little that could intrude on a writer's privacy (the author lived "in Seattle with her husband and two young sons" or "on the East Coast with her family"; occasionally she enjoyed "travel" or "gardening"), these notes implied stability, respectability, and family values.

One thing author notes rarely addressed was special affinity between authors and subjects. Considering how many of the books were series entries, many writers (though surely not all) may simply have accepted assignments. Blurbs said that one author had "long wanted to write a biography of the type of woman she admired as a child—one who was independent, adventurous, and successful" (Keller 1996, 128) and another was a "great admirer of Frida Kahlo's work" who had "visited Mexico many times" (Cruz 1996, back cover). Philip Hart, whose introduction was unusually autobiographical, described how his family's stories about a pilot uncle back in the 1920s sparked his interest in the forgotten history of African American aviation and Bessie Coleman (Hart 1996). Other writers, too, may well have had personal interest in their subjects, but silence about these affinities added to the general impression of professional objectivity.

Never mentioned in the author notes were race and gender. Judging by names, thirteen of the books—one in four—were written by men; in 1946, when women often wrote juvenile biographies of men, only one about a woman was even coauthored by a man. Ethnicity was harder to guess, although four biographies included photographs of their authors. Mary E. Lyons, a southern biographer of Irish descent, has said that she's flattered when readers take her for African American "because it means I'm an effective writer" (Holtze 1996). Should gender be considered a qualification for writing about a woman, or race a qualification for writing about a woman of color? Such questions triggered hot debate in the 1970s, when it was argued that white authors, as members of a dominant culture, lacked the cultural sensitivity and inside knowledge to produce authentic portrayals of minority figures. Some regarded this as an insuperable difficulty; others felt it could be overcome by a writer who was a diligent and empathetic researcher.

The discussion usually focused on fiction, and one might imagine that the trend away from fictionalization in juvenile biography would alleviate the problem. Most of the books in 1996 had a detached, dispassionate tone that seemed to make the authors' own identities and affinities less relevant. Still, outsider accounts of minorities continued to draw criticism, and still do; Oyate, a "Native organization working to see that our lives and histories are portrayed honestly," includes careful reviews of "books to avoid" because they misrepresent American Indians (Oyate 2005). Extensive research and a professional style seem to promise objectivity, but may not always be enough. Would more information about author identity help young readers assess potential bias, or would it foster shallow, mechanical judgments?

Documentation

Documentation was considered a stronger indicator of accuracy, and critics reported that new biographies were better documented than ever. "Whether children read the footnotes or are impressed by the author's qualifications is not important," said Sutherland and Arbuthnot (1991). "What matters is that these changes reflect an increased concern on the part of authors and publishers to give young readers the best biographies possible." Russell (1991) called for documentation both as "evidence of careful research" and as a model for "children in the middle and upper elementary grades . . . to learn the uses of supplementary information." Lechner (1997) felt that fine bibliographies did more than "provide . . . additional sources": they explained "the methods . . . biographers have used in researching their subjects." Reviewers were sometimes harsh about lack of scholarly apparatus; Donelson and Nilsen (1997) reported that nonfiction writer Brent Ashabranner had been influenced by critical reviews to be "more careful with his bibliographies" and "let readers know where he has gotten his information."

Forty of these books—all but one of those reviewed for readers above fourth grade—included bibliographies, notes, or authors' comments on sources. Their purposes varied. Twenty-nine had at least one bibliography each, more often geared toward helping young readers find additional resources than documenting the author's research. Some had separate lists for "Primary Works and Sources Consulted" and "Further Reading." Lives of singers might offer selected discographies, and lives of writers usually listed their major works. Robert Green's sources "For Further Information" about Cleopatra included seven Internet sites, guiding young researchers to reputable subject directories and museum pages. (The Internet is notoriously changeable, and by October, 2000, five of the seven URLs had altered; but Green's sites were well chosen for stability, and all could still be found in January, 2004.) Eighteen of the books had endnotes, which substituted for or supplemented bibliographies, including references to magazines, newspapers, or other sources not in "Further Reading" lists.

Other forms of documentation, such as acknowledgments, authors' notes, and internal references, were even more varied. Mary Lyons provided discursive endnotes for *Painting Dreams: Minnie Evans, Visionary Artist*, citing a documentary, a symposium, personal papers, and numerous telephone interviews—most of them unavailable to young readers, but confirming her own diligence in research. Jerry Stanley documented *Big Annie of Calumet* with a two-page bibliographic essay. The reviewer for *Horn Book* found this arrangement "unfortunate," since it wouldn't help a reader trace provocative quotes (Vasilakis 1996). Indeed, Stanley edited some quotations for readability, and anyone who used his documentation to search for the originals would have a daunting array of sources, not all of them published, to locate and read. Although frustrating for a fact-checker, his essay fulfilled two purposes of the documentation criterion better than most: it indicated the depth of his own scholarship and modeled for readers the way historians work.

Illustrations, too, were documented—not so much to assist young researchers as to acknowledge intellectual property. Thirty-six of the books carried picture credits, usually listed in small print on the copyright page or with the book's end matter, but occasionally at the ends of individual captions. Typically acknowledged were the institutions that provided photographs, prints, and other graphic materials: libraries, museums, newspapers, historical societies, and archives. Of the remaining fifteen biographies, thirteen were illustrated by individual artists; it was rare for the immediate source of any book's graphics to go unacknowledged. In beautifully designed books like Krull's *Wilma Unlimited* and Brewster's *Anastasia's Album*, the acknowledgments evolved into lists reminiscent of movie credits: "Color separations by Bright Arts, Ltd., Singapore"; "Production supervision by Warren Wallerstein and Ginger Boyer" (Krull 1996); "*Research and Translation*: Alla Savranskaia"; "*Printing and Binding*: Butler & Tanner Limited" (Brewster 1996).

It was relatively easy to find out who had given permission for the use of historical illustrations and photographs, but harder to know where they had originated. When biographical subjects lived before the invention of photography, or grew up in families unable to afford it, the visual record was often supplemented in these books by thematically related materials. Occasionally this practice was made clear by text or captions. Thus, when Lisandrelli (1996) illustrated Maya Angelou's childhood with a "scene from the television adaptation of Angelou's autobiography," the relationship between life and reenactment was explicitly noted in the caption.

In other cases the relationship was neither clear nor close. In *Learning about Fairness from the Life of Susan B. Anthony*, for instance, a doublespread entitled "Growing Up" was illustrated by a photograph of elderly women, most of them wearing pastel slacks, in what was evidently a Quaker meeting house. The caption said, "Susan grew up following the Quaker belief that men and women are equal" (Mosher 1996c, 7). Credits showed that this picture was copyrighted by

AP/World Wide Photos, but not where it had been taken or when; there was nothing to tell children that elderly women in Anthony's childhood did not wear pastel slacks. The pressure to include such pictures, when series format calls for illustration and a subject's youth predates photography, is understandable.

Admittedly, contemporary pictures could also mislead. Weintraub (1987) described how David Wilkie's painting of the young Victoria's first meeting with her cabinet changed her simple black mourning dress to white (probably to emphasize her "virgin queen" aspect) and left out many of the ninety-seven councilors (to relieve clutter; but some of those left in the picture were more importunate than important). The painting was reproduced in *The Importance of Queen Victoria* (Netzley 1996), with a caption saying merely, "Composed and confident, Victoria sits at the head of her first Privy Council, held at Kensington Palace in 1837."

Admittedly, too, a few books at least raised the question of how some of these images were related to the history they evoked. In Green's *Cleopatra*, with illustrations that ranged from photographs of ancient statues to a 1963 movie still of Liz Taylor as Cleopatra, one doublespread showed three different prints of the lighthouse on Pharos. The caption read:

> As these three pictures demonstrate, artists have had different conceptions of what the lighthouse looked like. Estimates of its height range from 200 to 600 feet (60 to 180 meters). Descriptions and stories of the ancient world have often been exaggerated in retellings. Many times they reflect the tastes of the era in which the story or painting was produced rather than the authentic historic event (R. Green 1996, 13).

But when and where were the prints created? The caption challenged readers to critical thinking, but withheld useful data. Most children would doubtless ignore notes on the origins of historical illustrations, but the curious might begin to notice how visual styles evolve. Authenticity could be enhanced by holding visual material to at least as high a standard of documentation as text.

Use of Sources: Facts, Omissions, and Visual Fictions

As evidence of accuracy, not all documentation was equal, and the mere presence of notes and bibliographies should not have satisfied reviewers. A bibliography intended for young readers would not necessarily list all the author's sources, and even when an impressive array of sources was listed, the bibliography alone did not communicate the author's level of scholarship. Biased and inadequate sources were a perennial problem, and the author's cultural allegiances, the thoroughness of research, and the public's perceived sensitivities could all influence interpretation in biographies for adults. Biographies for young readers, where extensive original scholarship was not the rule (Witucke 1985), sometimes showed signs of reliance on skewed records.

In some cases, the bias started with primary sources. Cleopatra, for instance, fought Octavius, whose propaganda showed her as the seductive ensnarer of noble Romans, a cruel and extravagant woman. With victory, Octavius controlled much of the historical record (Grant 1972), and his version of Cleopatra made for a good story. Green, in the sixty-four-page format of the Franklin Watts First Book series, managed to give enough historical context to make his narrative meaningful, and perhaps one should not fault him for adding zest by repeating a few sensational yarns. He used careful phrasing: "historians told," or "she is said to have enjoyed. . . ." One caption stated:

> This painting depicts the legendary account of Cleopatra dissolving one of her largest and most lustrous pearls into a glass of vinegar, which she then drank, to the astonishment of her guests. The incident reflects not only her interest in cosmetics (the mixture was supposed to be good for the complexion), but also her tendency to flaunt her wealth (R. Green 1996, 38).

By calling this a "legendary account," Green kept his own text scrupulously accurate; but he did not mention reasonable doubts that have been raised about the story (Grant 1972, 176), and his analysis of the picture's significance gives it credence.

Cleopatra's story was told by her enemies, but accounts could be just as slanted by friendly sources. In 1996, juvenile writers sometimes discussed the handling of biased sources. The first biography of Elizabeth Cary, a seventeenth-century English viscountess who wrote plays, became a Catholic, was placed under house arrest, and grew eccentric and forgetful with age, was written by her daughter. Noting that the daughter may have represented her "in a more positive way than an uninvolved, or objective, biographer would," Brackett (1996, 86) told junior high school readers about the process of verifying an unreliable record with clues like book dedications and passages in obscure contemporary writings.

The subjects themselves were not always reliable witnesses. Mother Jones exaggerated her age for effect, while Nellie Bly, Bessie Coleman, and Frida Kahlo shaved years off theirs. Margaret Bourke-

White, a media celebrity from the 1920s through the 1940s, worked hard at both photojournalism and her own image. She hyphenated her middle name and surname; dropped two years, a first husband, and almost all her early photographs from her resumé; burned her diaries; and wrote two autobiographies. Her calculated self-presentation affected the sources available to any biographer (Goldberg 1986), and a history of her emotional life could only be pieced together from fragmentary evidence.

Juvenile writers in 1996 sometimes described or speculated about events that had been suppressed—but did not dwell on them, unless they were relevant to the subjects' work. For instance, Marie Curie's daughter published her famous biography because she was "afraid that someone else would do it first and not get it right." Ève Curie portrayed her mother "as a woman of great nobility, . . . who often didn't get the credit she deserved":

> She tells the story so well that it is not immediately obvious that the biography is serving as a defense of her mother. And yet lurking beneath the surface and motivating the undertaking is an event which had had a devastating effect on Marie Curie: her public exposure and vilification because of an affair she had with a fellow scientist, Paul Langevin (Quinn 1995, 14).

Naomi Pasachoff, whose *Marie Curie* was reviewed for junior and senior high school readers, was sympathetic but frank in her discussion of the Langevin affair. In the 1940s, if such a romance had been mentioned at all, it might have been explored and justified at length; Desmond (1946) had organized a novel-like biography around the idea that Dolly Madison suffered an unconsummated passion for Aaron Burr. Pasachoff's approach in 1996 was different: she mentioned old scandals and rumors, discussed the evidence briefly, and moved on.

But respect for subjects' privacy, coupled with reluctance to raise troubling issues or to sensationalize material, could still lead children's biographers to the traditional omissions. Emily Keller (1996), for instance, glossed over the fact that Erskine Caldwell and Jerry Papurt were both married to other women when Bourke-White's romances with them began. Where a biographer in 1946 might have substituted fictional material to give the illusion of completeness, Keller in 1996 stuck to the facts, simply emphasizing her subject's work over personal life. The result impressed *School Library Journal*'s reviewer favorably: "Information about all aspects of this extraordinary woman's life is presented in a well-balanced, insightful, and sensitive manner" (Schene 1996). The *Bulletin of the Center for Children's Books* reviewer, on the other hand, found the book "surprisingly unexciting," although "Even presented as a chronological series of episodes, Bourke-White's life is fascinating" (Del Negro 1996).

The degree to which biographies should reveal a subject's personal life has always been controversial. Wagner-Martin (1994, 6) claimed that a standard man's biography "has usually been a relatively uncomplicated presentation of the persona, shaped in the pattern of the personal success story," but that a woman's life, being a "tightly woven mesh of public and private events," did not fit the template. If so, the emphasis on work and publicly verifiable facts in these books brought them closer to male biographies. It may also have simplified the handling of details which could be troublesome to living subjects or the families of the recently deceased. In a haunting portrait of African American Minnie Evans, who began life as an "outside child" unclaimed by her father and ended it as an "outsider" artist scorned by many professionals, Mary Lyons (1996) described the dreams and visions that inspired Evans' art—and led even her family to wonder if she were crazy. Was she, if not mad, plagued by some neurological condition that triggered the visions? Lyons did not explore the question; to do so might well have been painful to the friends and family members whose cooperation made the book possible.

Seventeen of the books—one in three—were about living subjects, and this was probably a factor in bringing them closer to the publicly oriented tradition of men's biographies. Biographers of living subjects had access to a wealth of research sources, from interviews to journalism; but that very abundance sometimes veiled inconvenient truths, and, as Sutherland and Arbuthnot (1991) observed, some records were not available to researchers until well after a subject's death. Weinberg (1992) described the increasing difficulty of publishing unauthorized biographies that could be the targets of lawsuits: "These days," he said, "sensible investigative reporters write only about persons long dead" (201). Adherence to the facts might be at least a partial defense against libel suits or charges of cultural bias, but there was no guarantee that a selection of accurate facts would add up to a coherent portrayal of an individual.

Documentary graphics, even more difficult to muster than verbal facts, could have a strong influence on the reader's mental image of the subject. Here, too, the effect was often to emphasize work and public life over private life—a natural bias, given the supply of images available through libraries, museums, and archives. Enslow's African-American Biographies series, for instance, was illustrated with black and white photographs; most were publicity stills of the subjects, but a few were of places (e.g., an aerial view of Howard University, where Toni Morrison studied and taught; B. Kramer 1996b), and people (e.g., Hurston's famous teacher, anthropologist Franz Boaz, and sometime friend, poet Langston Hughes; Yannuzzi 1996). In *Aretha Franklin: Motown Superstar*, all sixteen pictures showed Franklin herself, often in performance, but only two showed members of her family, both at public occasions (Sheafer 1996). Other celebrities, trophies, and microphones were more prominent in this visual record than her nearest and dearest. By contrast, Franklin's family and friends appeared, with her or without her, in most of the private snapshots that illustrated her own memoir (Franklin and Ritz 1999), contributing to a less glitzy, more rooted impression of the star.

Without access to family scrapbooks, the most obvious way to illustrate the childhoods and private lives of subjects was with artists' illustrations. The drawings and paintings in picture-book biographies and a few "chapter biographies" were the visual equivalent of fictionalizing—and, like the old fictionalized narratives, they were often based on research, showing scenes that the illustrators knew about from anecdotes or could reconstruct as part of daily life. Thus Pinkney (1996) acknowledged help from the National Park Service and the Banneker-Douglass Museum in his search for "authentic details regarding backgrounds, dress, food, and living conditions" shown Schroeder's *Minty*, a story about the early childhood of Harriet Tubman.

Few illustrations were documented, however, and selectors had to rely on personal knowledge or fact-checking to gauge their accuracy. Pamela Paparone's engaging acrylics for Reeve Lindbergh's picture-book biography of the pioneering black pilot Bessie Coleman were obviously not intended as literal representation. They stretched the laws of perspective, letting houses lean crazily out of the way and viewers wave from remote windows as Bessie does loop-de-loops over a town. Did she really swoop so low over city streets, or did the crowds watch her "over airports or fields barely plowed," as Lindbergh's text has it? Did the all-black school at Waxahachie really have a bulletin board displaying the children's crayon drawings on manila paper? Did Bessie, often kept out of school to care for her younger siblings (Hart 1996), really have red ribbons for her hair and a toy airplane on her desk?

Paparone had clearly researched the book; wingtip shoes, a wickerwork baby carriage, coats, and cars evoked the period. *School Library Journal*'s reviewer noticed "accurate visual details of the Texas cotton fields" and the subtlety of "Bessie's picture of white clouds against a blue, blue sky" on that bulletin board. "She had already imagined her future, 'flying free, flying truc'" (Flack 1996). But was this an accurate detail, or an imaginative truth? The picture-book biographies, like the old fictionalized biographies, could sometimes be true in ways beyond the completely factual; but they could also mislead.

Historical Placement: Diversity and the New Social History

Good biographies needed to be accurate in drawing not only individual subjects, but also their backgrounds. Some critics regarded historical context as necessary to an understanding of the individuals, while for others, the individuals offered windows on their times:

> It is important that as much as possible be included about the period, showing historical events the person participated in and giving some idea of other famous people whose lives may have been linked with the person who is the subject of the biography. In this way, it is possible for a biography to function as a means of helping readers to see the interrelationships among outstanding events and people in history (Purves and Monson 1984, 63).

Either way, the biographies of 1996 opened new vistas. Multicultural diversity had joined the lists of familiar criteria in some children's literature textbooks; for instance, Lynch-Brown and Tomlinson (1993) called for avoidance of stereotyping. The word "stereotype," which in the older textbooks was likely to be associated with words like "stuffy" and to carry implications of oversimplification and whitewash, now more often connoted racism or sexism.

The word "diversity," by contrast, suggested respect for a broad range of human differences, and critics felt that publishers of juvenile biographies were producing books on subjects who were more diverse in several ways. England and Fasick (1987) noted more "women, minorities, and 'just plain' folk"; Huck et al. (1997) observed sports and entertainment celebrities reflecting "the influence of the mass media." Sutherland and Arbuthnot (1991) commented that greater openness about the facts of life had widened the field of subjects to include the victims of child abuse and the champions of controversial causes. Diversity in the biography shelves, by allowing young readers to glimpse a broader sample of humanity, arguably offers them a more accurate view of the world. For biographers, however, the choice of diverse subjects can add to the challenge of accurate portrayal, both because the primary resources available for biographic research are often more limited and because the biographer must take great care to interpret facts with cultural sensitivity.

The techniques of social history are useful here. Diggins, critiquing the *National History Standards*, spoke of "the new social history" in 1996; but social history was not so new. In 1929, French scholars Lucien Febvre and Mark Bloch, launching their influential *Annales d'histoire économique et sociale*, had called for a new history of social and economic life (Cantor 1991). By the 1970s, when a "third generation" of *Annales* researchers added "an emphasis on the mental structures or *mentalités* of past societies" to their interests, their influence was widespread in English-speaking countries as well (Green and Troup 1999). Fitzpatrick (2002) traced precedents for the practice of social, economic, and intellectual history in the United States as early as the 1880s. Although the work of the Progressive historians did not have the same theoretical underpinnings as the *Annales* school, she argued that the objective "consensus history" practiced before the "new history" of the 1960s was more a "straw man" than a reality.

Attention to the history of daily life was not new even in children's books, and two of the best-documented biographies in 1946, *Madeleine Takes Command* and *Red Silk Pantalettes*, made extensive and imaginative use of local and economic history to flesh out the partial lives of little known girls. In 1971, the partial life of Anne MacVicar gave readers a girl's-eye view of the American colonies just before the Revolution; Anne was an engaging observer and minor participant rather than a major shaper of events. The biggest difference was not in the choice of subject or research strategies, but in the presentation, as the old novelistic style of juvenile biographies gradually gave way to more documentary approaches.

To research and shape the story of less-documented lives, some biographers resorted to the strategies of social history, placing the known facts about an individual in broader contexts. Bessie Coleman, whose moving struggle to become the first African American woman licensed as a pilot inspired two 1996 children's books, left "virtually no personal memorabilia" or letters; biographers had to rely primarily on black weekly newspapers, many available only in microfilm, and on interviews with elderly contemporaries (Rich 1993). Hart (1996), as the nephew of another pioneering black aviator, could draw on oral history for contextual material that had largely been omitted from standard aviation history; his full-life biography of Coleman tempered appreciation for her significant achievement with empathy for her flawed and embattled character.

Annie Clemenc, protagonist of *Big Annie of Calumet*, was more obscure than Coleman, and Jerry Stanley made her less the subject of a partial biography than the focus of a social and economic history.

Clemenc, a young miner's wife who became the symbol of a 1913-1914 Michigan strike, was the strong daughter of Croatian immigrants, over six feet tall. Day after day during the strike she hoisted a giant American flag and carried it for miles, leading parades of as many as two thousand miners and their families. Subtitled *A True Story of the Industrial Revolution*, Stanley's book introduces her life and significance in the first two pages, and then devotes two and a half chapters to the history of mining on the Keweenaw Peninsula, the balance of power between the company and the ethnically diverse miners, and the introduction of an economical but dangerous one-man drill called the "widow-maker." Annie reenters the story a quarter of the way through the book. Her words, captured in the media, echo dramatically. Asked if the flag wasn't too heavy, she said, "I love to carry it." Knocked down in the mud, she taunted soldiers: "If this flag will not protect me, then I will die with it." Arrested, she told a general she wouldn't just stay at home: "My work is here, and nobody can stop me." What we know of her, in the end, is that image of courage. In 1914, divorced from her husband, "Annie moved to Chicago and married Frank Shavs," a reporter who had covered the strike (Stanley 1996). The drama of her life that year must have involved a complex interplay of public and private roles, but we see only the public side.

In many of the biographies (as in those of earlier generations) history of any kind was simply background. Even the shortest sketched in a few historical facts: Oksana Baiul's life had been affected by Ukrainian independence (Rambeck 1996), and Gloria Estefan's family had come to Miami from Cuba to escape Castro's regime (Strazzabosco 1996). Details were sparse (the breakup of the Soviet Union was barely mentioned; Castro was not identified as a communist), but even these minibooks, with fewer than a thousand words each, situated their subjects' lives in history. In the longer books, the historic background ranged from minimal (Cary mentioned that the future children's book writer Jean Craighead George, like many young women during World War II, married just before her husband left for combat duty) to extensive (historical background took up more space than biography in Chiflet and Beaulet's account of Victoria and her times).

Events well covered in traditional history books cropped up frequently: wars (the Napoleonic wars, the Crimean War, the American and the Chinese Civil Wars, World Wars I and II) and disasters (the San Francisco earthquake, the Chicago fire), diseases (smallpox, yellow fever, and polio), and relocations (the Trail of Tears, the Long March) each figured in one or more lives. Lesser known events also figured in the stories. There was the phenomenally cold winter of 1816, during which teenager Mary Wollstonecraft Godwin, who had run away with the married poet Shelley, wrote *Frankenstein* (Miller 1996). There was the burning of a black newspaper building by whites, rioting to celebrate the defeat of North Carolina's black Congressmen in 1898; during this disturbed time, Minnie Evans was sent from Wilmington to live with a Virginia relative for a year (Lyons 1996).

The history of feminist struggle was prominent, with biographies of suffragists (Susan B. Anthony, Lucretia Mott, Elizabeth Cady Stanton, Harriet Tubman) and of women who pioneered fields previously closed to them (Nellie Bly, Bessie Coleman, Wilma Mankiller, Maria Montessori). Writers were more explicit than in the past about what obstacles women had faced and overcome; perhaps this reflected the influence of social history, or perhaps explanation was just more necessary, as old expectations of women's potential receded from children's living memory. Thus, Bessie Coleman was told that women couldn't be aviators (Hart 1996; Lindbergh 1996); Dorothy Day that they "didn't belong in newspaper work" (Kent 1996); Jean George that they "shouldn't be reporters" (Cary 1996); Julie Krone that they weren't "strong enough to be jockeys"(Savage 1996); Wilma Mankiller that the tribe "never had a woman as deputy chief" (Lowery 1996); and Maria Montessori that "women did not become engineers" (Shephard 1996). Women in Lucretia Mott's day were paid less than men and weren't supposed to speak before mixed audiences (Bryant 1996); naturalist Margaret Morse Nice had less access to education and professional resources (Dunlap 1996); girls like Florence Nightingale "were taught that they should be quiet and pretty" (Mosher 1996b). Even the relatively recent past needed some explanation; "In those days, political involvement for women boiled down to carrying out all the tedious chores," wrote Siegel (1996, 43) of Ann Richards' 1957 activities. The seventeenth century was alien territory, and Brackett (1996) had to explain the legal disabilities of a wife who disobeyed her husband to dissent from the state religion. Culture, too, made a difference; as a Chinese woman, Amy Tan's mother "had few rights" (B. Kramer 1996a, 13), and Maya Angelou was told that "No wife of an African leader can go on the stage" (Lisandrelli 1996, 80).

History was much more than background when biographees were deeply engaged in historical events, whether in government (like Cleopatra, Victoria, and Ann Richards) or working for reform (like the nineteenth-century abolitionists and feminists, or Mother Jones and Dorothy Day). Some (like painter Frida Kahlo, and author Zora Neale Hurston) witnessed history through their art. Margaret Bourke-White became more and more socially conscious as her career developed;

while helping to shape the new field of photojournalism, she was shaped by what she observed.

Yet these were biographies, and their focus was on individual rather than general history. One of the most beautiful, *Anastasia's Album* (Brewster 1996)—the only non-picture book in this batch to receive a starred review in *School Library Journal*—was inspired by and based on the imperial Romanov family's photographs and letters in the State Archives in Moscow. It was designed like a scrapbook, and although the text mentioned the poverty of peasant farmers and the miserable city slums, there are no illustrations of these. Instead, the many photographs show impish Anastasia and her loving family at play and work, in candid and formal poses. Anastasia walks on stilts, goes wading, puts in false teeth, and crosses her eyes. The tsarina and her daughters dress in Red Cross uniforms for World War I relief work. Imprisoned in Siberia, the four princesses cheerfully undertake gardening and wood splitting tasks, and pose baldheaded after losing their hair to measles. Interspersed are drawings (by and of the family) and excerpts from diaries and correspondence. The national tragedy is remote background; the individual tragedy is immediate and real.

Syntagmatic Criteria: Signaling Objectivity

Evaluation of accuracy drew on selectors' subject knowledge; evaluation of quality drew on discernment and taste. These, widely considered subjective, could be difficult to articulate and defend in a climate that called for evenhanded accountability and quantitative measures. At least one critic suggested an objective approach to evaluating the quality of biographies: for research purposes, Harvey-Slager (1992) counted the number of reviews for biographies in her database, and categorized as high quality those books with four or more reviews, poor those with two or fewer. This scheme was temptingly simple, and variants had been successfully used in research on selection for adult collections; but as a guide to evaluating juvenile biographies it was imperfect, since even excellent juvenile nonfiction was chronically underreviewed.

Children's literature textbooks still encouraged selectors to evaluate biographies by asking themselves questions about style, organization, and book design. The questions were familiar, but the preferred style now emphasized factual accuracy; the preferred organization lent itself to student research assignments; and the preferred book design, influenced by magazine layouts and benefiting from new technology, featured a collage of brilliant graphics. Schwarcz (1982) observed that the balance between illustration and text affected meaning in picture books: illustration dominates text, he said, when pictures take relatively more space, when they extend beyond their tidy frames, and when they are laid out differently on every page and not in a predictably routine pattern. In 1996, the dominance of graphics surely affected readers' response to biographees.

Style: Journalistic, Not Novelistic

On the surface, criteria for style had not changed. Sutherland and Arbuthnot (1991, 457) still called for a "pleasing style" that was "good to read and . . . appropriate to the subject matter"; Russell (1991, 127) wanted the important facts expressed "with grace and clarity"; Stoodt, Amspaugh, and Hunt (1996, 259) observed that a "lively, interesting style makes the subject of a biography come alive for readers." In fact, the prevailing style had changed, as extensive fictionalization became rare outside picture book biographies. Russell Freedman and Jean Fritz were praised for careful research, but their appealing prose styles had at least as much to do with their success. With lively, individual voices and deftly chosen details, they made nonfiction sound engagingly like storytelling. What most of the new biographies sounded like, however, was journalism.

Van Dijk (1988) has described the studiously neutral style of news as a form of public discourse. It is impersonal, and tends to distance the reader. It emphasizes the factual nature of events by providing evidence from eyewitnesses, authorities, or other reliable sources; by using signals such as numbers, exact dates and times, and proper names to indicate the precision of an account; or by quoting directly from sources. It builds a strong relational structure for facts, embedding them in the context of previous events or in "well-known situation models that make them relatively familiar even when they are new" (Van Dijk 1988, 85). In 1996, juvenile biographies used similar approaches—and, like the news, they tucked their numbers, dates, and other markers of accuracy into complex sentences (see Van Dijk 1988, 77).

The new biographies were shorter, but not necessarily easier to read. Rosen Press's Character Building Books were reviewed for first to fourth grades. Each had nine full-page illustrations, a glossary, an index, and only ten continuous pages of large-print text. Sentences were short; selected words were boldfaced, accompanied by phonetic spellings, and defined in the glossary. Still, most readability formulas placed them above fourth grade level. Most scores for Mosher's biography of Susan B. Anthony, for instance, ranged from fifth to seventh grade level, with only the Spache formula placing it as low as third grade (*Readability Calculations* 2003).

Readability formulas do not agree, and should be taken with a grain of salt. They are based on quantifiable factors. The Fry formula assumes that the more syllables a word has, or the longer a sentence is, the harder it will be to read. The Dale-Chall formula also uses its own graded vocabulary lists to estimate text difficulty (*Readability Calculations* 2003). They do not account for other factors, like reader interest (which makes everything easier) or the familiarity that grows as proper names and polysyllabic words are repeated.

Still, it is notable that, amid concerns about the dumbing down of children's books, the reading levels of biographies had been inching up. The books in my 1946 sample averaged 6.6 on the Dale-Chall and 7.0 on the Fry formula; in 1971, the averages were 6.71 and 7.26 respectively; and in 1996, they were 7.05 and 8.12. Much of the explanation must lie in the increasingly factual style.

It was not only a matter of vocabulary. Sentence structure, too, could be complex, as Van Dijk (1988) had observed. Dependent clauses, parenthetical phrases, passive voice, and precise details combined to give many of these books their objective sound:

> Maya Angelou, born Marguerite Johnson on April 4, 1928, experienced her first significant journey when she was three years old (Lisandrelli 1996, 14).

> Her mother, who was also named Elizabeth, was a demanding and strict woman who made her daughter kneel before speaking to her (Brackett 1996, 15).

These sentences, plucked from two books reviewed for junior high readers, were informative and not too long. They introduced sympathetic characters: a three-year-old making a journey, a dreamy girl with an authoritarian mother. Unlike many of the old fictionalized biographies, however, they did not invite the reader to become absorbed, lost in the experience of reading for its own sake, in what reader response theorist Louise Rosenblatt (1995) would have called an "aesthetic" stance toward the text. Their rhetoric encouraged a more "efferent" stance—the implied reader would be active, conscientious, taking facts and explicit understandings from these books. When short biographies with short sentences seemed harder to read than their more leisurely fictionalized predecessors, it was not just because of long words or complex sentence structure; it was also because their resolute factuality called for objectivity and distance, rather than relaxed enjoyment or unconscious identification with the subject's story.

Good writers used several strategies for overcoming this distance. Some critics still recognized fictionalization as useful or even necessary; at its best, it could be a way to convey truth simply and effectively, rather than a sign of careless scholarship. Girard (1988) praised Jean Fritz's sparing but effective use of fictional techniques, stating that there are times when a biographer can communicate greater truth by modest invention than by slavish adherence to the known facts. Fritz (1988), dismayed to be thought a fictionalizer, wrote a rebuttal; but Girard was not alone in finding the technique useful. Lechner (1997), analyzing sources of error in children's biographies, found that a lightly fictionalized partial biography of Audubon was in many respects more true to its subject than a children's book consisting of edited selections from his journals. The journals may have been primary source material, but they were unreliable to begin with and had been sanitized by Audubon's granddaughter.

At what point do fictional techniques become fictionalization? Freedman (1994) advocated the use of storytelling: "One of the most effective storytelling techniques . . . is to create a vivid, detailed scene that the reader can visualize—like a scene from a movie, if you will." Wilms (1982) had complained of the "artificial novellike opening that's followed or interwoven with straight narrative," but this kind of hook, common when juvenile biographies mimicked novels, was just as common to more journalistic nonfiction. Thus a biography of Maya Angelou opened with a passage in the present tense:

> In a country store in the dusty town of Stamps, Arkansas, a young girl sits near the candy counter. Outside, a sharp wind rustles through the shingles, but inside a potbellied stove warms the small store. Between customers she often writes poetry or reads from her beloved books. These pursuits take her mind off the pain of growing up in the segregated South of the 1930s, where opportunities are denied to her because she is African American. On this day she memorizes the Presidents of the United States in chronological order. . . (Lisandrelli 1996, 5).

This is not fiction, exactly. Lisandrelli had documentation for everything in the passage; she wove details from three different sources into a two-paragraph description of what could have been a typical day. Angelou may not have experienced all those incidents and thoughts at once, but neither were they mere inventions. And there is no invented dialogue—but there is, indirectly, a kind of interior monologue.

Historians recognize the danger of "presentism," interpreting the past too much in the context of the present. Here, the balance of personal awareness and historic consciousness in the passage may subtly misrepresent the young Angelou's experience. She did indeed suffer pains attributable to "growing up in the segregated South of the 1930s," and memorizing the list of presidents may indeed have been a comforting distraction—but was she, on this imagined day in her childhood, likely to have thought about it in just that way? Even the phrase "African American" belongs more to the 1990s than to the 1930s, when "Negro" was still considered a polite term.

Related to presentism in this introduction is the inconsistency of voice. The first two sentences flow in a fairy-tale rhythm, and call up a scene we can easily picture. The diction changes subtly with the third sentence (where "from her beloved books" provides a more explicit clue to Angelou's character than one might expect in a fairy tale) and more definitively with the fourth (where reference to "the segregated South of the 1930s" yanks the reader from timelessness into history). This awkwardness is symptomatic of an uneasy balance between old-fashioned narrative and journalistic exposition. Lisandrelli's introduction consists of two vignettes: the child by the old stove, and the famous poet, reading at President Clinton's 1993 Inauguration. The sharp contrast prepares readers for a book that will explain Angelou's "long and often painful journey to arrive at this shining moment" (Lisandrelli 1996, 13). It will be a book with fully as much exposition as narrative, and it will gain its effects more from the contrast of visual images than from the storytelling voice.

To slip accurate facts into a smooth narrative takes effort and skill. Fritz (1988), uneasy with Girard's praise, insisted that she did not fictionalize:

> Well, I don't make up facts, but at the same time I have no desire to write in a factual style. Nonfiction can be told in a narrative voice and still maintain its integrity. The art of fiction is making up facts; the art of nonfiction is using facts to make up a form.

Logically, there seems no reason that facts cannot be arranged and told reliably as a story. In the eighth edition of *Children and Books* Sutherland and Arbuthnot (1991, 457) repeated verbatim a point made by Arbuthnot (1947, 476) in the first edition: "As one authority has said, style is 'the auditory effect of prose.'" But to write sentences that fell easily on the ear while incorporating precise facts was difficult; writers who handled the new journalistic conventions with brio stood out.

Consistency of tone was easier to achieve in the old fictionalized genre, which survived in some of the picture-book biographies. There were two about Harriet Tubman. In a strictly factual treatment, Mosher (1996a) abstracted known facts of Tubman's ninety-three years, and compressed them into just 818 words, not counting headings, captions, or parenthetical pronunciation aids. She introduced simplified concepts in a way that would rouse children's indignation and sympathy: "Slaves were people who were 'owned' by other people." But Schroeder's fictionalized account had greater emotional impact. It was more concrete, showing a dreamy child ruthlessly punished for playing with a doll, spilling cider, releasing trapped muskrats—essentially for being human in a system that refused to recognize her humanity. Pinkney's illustrations, dramatically capturing a wide range of emotions in facial expressions and posture, revealed the humanity of all involved, even the witchy Mrs. Brodas. At the end of the book, Harriet sat up mourning a lost chance of escape as her exhausted family slept around her. Less bound by fact than Mosher, and no less selective in abstracting a small fraction of a long life, Schroeder and Pinkney let readers feel what it might have been like for a passionate and intelligent child to be a slave.

Organization: Chronology and Theme

Like a good prose style, a familiar structure can make things easier for a reader; it is easier to comprehend what one can predict, and a clear organization helps both novice and experienced readers make sense of new information. Van Dijk (1988, 85) described "strong relational structures" that could help make journalistic accounts plausible and compelling. For instance, events could be embedded in chains of causality, with previous events listed as conditions or future events as likely outcomes of the day's happenings. Facts could be inserted "into well-known situation models that make them relatively familiar even when they are new," and journalists could use "well-known scripts and concepts" or "specific structures," such as narratives.

Narrative had always been the relational structure of choice for juvenile biography, and remained popular, especially in the nonseries picture-book biographies. Here, fictionalization was still common. Blos (1996) followed Nellie Bly's race around the world through the eyes of a monkey. This familiar device, recalling the mouse who gave Benjamin Franklin all his best ideas in Robert Lawson's 1939 *Ben and Me*, allowed the child reader a vantage point within the story while keeping the adult biographical subject at an appropriate remove. McCully

(1996) had an elderly but still feisty Elizabeth Cady Stanton tell the story of her youth to a neighbor child, whose reactions were a model of empathy—and who was inspired by Stanton's example to her own daring show of competence.

Strong narrative cohesion also marked longer biographies, like Kamen's *Hidden Music* (1996), in which Fanny Mendelssohn kept alive a talent that might have matched her famous brother's if she hadn't been actively discouraged at every turn. Kamen fictionalized little, and frequently quoted translations of the many family letters that allowed intimate glimpses into the Mendelssohns' family life. But she arranged the facts into a coming-of-age story, a familiar and engaging narrative pattern. The reader could easily identify with the attractive Fanny, feeling indignation, affection, and pride as she matured into a loving woman in spite of barriers to her creative outlets.

The strongest narratives were shaped by clear themes, like Fanny's lifelong dedication to music. Of course this, too, was traditional. Sutherland and Arbuthnot (1991) still repeated Arbuthnot's 1947 observations about the unifying function of theme and the way a biographer should let it emerge from the evidence, rather than selecting it in advance and making the facts fit it. Themes, like plots, were simplest and most visible in the shortest books: Eleanor Roosevelt grew from an ugly duckling to a magnanimous swan (Cooney 1996); Wilma Rudolph survived a crippling bout of polio to become the world's fastest woman (Krull 1996); Bessie Coleman overcame sexism and racism to become a pilot (Lindbergh 1996). Cooney's *Eleanor* was a partial biography, and both Krull and Lindbergh focused on their subjects' short, triumphant careers; this pairing of strong theme and narrative to make an upbeat story is the "well-known script" of juvenile biography. These biographers adhered to the facts, and the facts of their individual subjects' lives would be new to young readers; but the underlying patterns were familiar and reassuring.

In some of the series biographies, theme and plot dictated the selection of facts to a degree that obscured individuality. The extreme brevity of Rosen's Character Building Books, combined with their whole-life coverage, made abstraction necessary; summarizing the lives of women as different and complex as Gloria Estefan and Florence Nightingale in fewer than a thousand words each, authors had to omit important events, characters, and issues in favor of a radically simplified story line. Sports biographies, with their predictable dedication to achievement, overcoming of tragic obstacles, and glorious rewards, were almost as formulaic. Many of their subjects were not only living but extremely young at the time of writing, and their lives seemed to fit the hopeful formula. Even their brushes with scandal might have didactic value: Savage (1996) quoted jockey Krone's reflection on her marijuana use ("I was young, but that was no excuse for being stupid").

Characterization

Whole-life biographies of women who outlived their successes posed a different set of problems for juvenile writers; they made less plausible fairy tales, because their ever-afters went on too long past the happy bits. Women of color, like visionary artist Minnie Evans and pioneering aviator Bessie Coleman, sometimes achieved distinction without economic security and ended their lives in poverty. So did white women, from the flamboyant Wild West performer Martha Jane Cannary (better known as Calamity Jane) to activist Mother Jones. Sorrow and aging could make identification with older subjects painful. In factual biographies, where an observant child or animal could not be invented as a buffer between the young reader and the aged subject, the objective tone itself could function as a form of distancing.

Ross (1985) found that the typical protagonist of a young adult novel was a "safe survivor"—one who would not only last to the end of the book, but would escape serious physical and moral damage, and with whom it was therefore safe to identify. Calamity Jane was not a safe survivor. Sanford and Green (1996) cast her story as true-life adventure in "a man's world," where a "woman had to be colorful, tough, and sure of herself to share center stage with the legendary male heroes." Orphaned in her teens by drifting and probably alcoholic parents, she made her way in a number of hard, often menial jobs. She was a storyteller and a vivid personality, given to exaggeration. Although she nursed miners through a smallpox epidemic, and was known for a certain gruff kindness, she remained an outsider. She claimed to have been married ten times, but the evidence was against her: "Calamity seldom let the truth interfere with a good story," ran one caption (15). Shunted aside, she relied more on drink as she got older. Sanford and Green showed the gap between her dime-novel image as the glamorous rescuer of Deadwood Dick and the harsh reality of her premature and impoverished old age, but they did not dwell on it as tragedy or analyze it from the perspective of class or gender. Instead, they emphasized the fun both in her wild adventures and in the process of evaluating sources—especially debunking Calamity's own version of the facts. The combination of entertainment and subversion made her more of an object than a subject, inviting the reader to enjoy her eccentricities through the amused eyes of others rather than to suffer her hurts vicariously.

By contrast, Brown (1996) shaped the story of Girl Scout founder Juliette Gordon Low into a continuous narrative that seemed more old-fashioned. It was a factual account, quoting primary sources and incorporating precise details, but it was enlivened by family anecdotes. (This was partly a matter of available source material. Daisy Gordon, unlike poor Calamity Jane, came from a secure clan with the resources to write and archive letters, and even to produce its own biography; one of Brown's major sources was a biography by Gladys Denny Shultz and Daisy Gordon Lawrence.) The 111-page book had 5 full-page black-and-white illustrations by Marie deJohn, and 11 black-and-white photographs in an 8-page center section, but the text dominated the graphics. The subject was sympathetic. Charming and pretty, Daisy weathered her divorce from William Low and found a new direction for her life in the scouting movement; her character was not perfect and her life was not easy, but she died well loved. Daisy would be a more comfortable role model for a middle-class girl than Calamity, and the language and organization of this book combined easily with its material to encourage reader engagement.

Courage was perhaps the most honored trait in these biographies. A few of the women, like Calamity Jane, aviator Bessie Coleman, and jockey Julie Krone, sought physical adventure; some, like Cleopatra, Mary Shelley, and Georgia O'Keeffe, were boldly unconventional in their thinking; some, like Harriet Tubman and Anne Frank, courageously kept their spiritual integrity in spite of oppression; but almost all were characterized as persistent and determined, working hard and steadfastly to achieve their ends. The character "flaw" most readily admitted and forgiven was stubbornness, which reinforced dedication to anything from social reform to athletic achievement. Like shyness in 1946, stubbornness in 1996 was almost more a virtue than a fault; women were now as much honored for their will to succeed as they had then been for their modesty.

Some writers held to the old tradition of summing up their subjects' abstract traits in an introduction or a conclusion: Shephard (1996, 105) found that Maria Montessori had "self-confidence, leadership, and a desire to help others" from an early age, and grew up to become a "caring, determined, and adventurous woman." Others avoided the abstract: Barbara Kramer (1996b) let Toni Morrison's character emerge from an account of her actions and statements. Some traced the way character developed: Cooney (1996) showed how the love and support of her father and her teacher helped Eleanor Roosevelt grow from a child at the mercy of circumstances to a young woman of independence and compassion, and Swain (1996) showed Elizabeth Cady working to construct her own character.

The depth of characterization was limited, however, by the brevity of the books and by their emphasis on subjects' public lives. Character is developed and shown in interaction, and one way to keep a book short and simple is to omit people, as well as events. Thus Mosher (1996a), devoting more space to Nat Turner (who inspired Harriet Tubman) than to John Tubman (who married her), focused on the essential theme of Tubman's courage in fighting slavery. The indices of longer biographies revealed a similar pattern, devoting more space to well-known professional associates than to family or friends. In the case of living subjects, one reason for this could have been protection of family privacy; Toni Morrison taught her children "that there is a part of yourself that you keep from white people—always" (B. Kramer 1996b, 63). In earlier generations, publicity had been considered improper and unladylike; but the celebrities of the 1990s had learned to hide their private lives behind glamorous public images.

A focus on public affairs to the exclusion of private characterization was considered a fault by Arbuthnot in the first edition of *Children and Books* (1947). The eighth edition repeated her comment with only minor editing for gender-neutrality:

> In the past, biographies written for young people failed at precisely this point. They told children about the large affairs in which their subjects played a part but neglected to give any account of the individuals' amusing idiosyncrasies, peculiar bents, and special talents which make them uniquely human (Sutherland and Arbuthnot 1991, 455).

The subjects who hid most effectively behind their public faces may have learned to provide fans with amusing and humanizing anecdotes, which relieved the respectful impersonality of some new biographies.

Illustrations and Graphics

Characterization in these books was also affected by the much greater role of visuals. Criteria for graphics and book design, as for text, had changed less than practice. Illustrations should be authentic: England and Fasick (1987) saw "no excuse for anachronisms when there are numerous reference books." Graphics should be "appropriately juxtaposed to the text" and, above all, "pleasing" (Russell 1991). The experts offered checklists and most demonstrated the application of standards to specific examples, but, like the criteria for texts, their use required tact and discretion on the part of selectors.

Book design varied dramatically—partly, although not entirely, with the age of intended readers. In some of the books for upper elementary and middle school readers, as we have seen, the texts still dominated. Bryant's book on Lucretia Mott was almost two hundred pages long, the sort of paperback book that could fit into a pocket, and had a section of photographs tipped into the center. Little but the clarity of its prints distinguished it from an earlier generation's books.

In picture-book biographies, the balance was reversed, with colorful illustrations engaging the reader's attention and guiding interpretation of the text. Long (1997) reported that historical illustration had developed a wider range of expression in this newly important genre, and could be "impressionistically evocative or realistically grim" or even "complex with esoteric references and layered with subtle meanings"; it was therefore more important than ever to evaluate not only their "craft, composition, and content," documentation, and consonance "with the subject's true spirit," but also their accessibility and appropriateness to young readers. Brodie (1998) felt that illustrations had never been so critical: "It is clear that the criteria for biographies and picture books should be combined when examining this new genre." The six nonseries picture-book biographies of women in 1996 were a distinguished lot. Three (Cooney's of Eleanor Roosevelt, Krull's of Wilma Rudolph, and McCully's of Elizabeth Cady Stanton) were given starred reviews in *School Library Journal*; a fourth (Schroeder's of Harriet Tubman) won the 1997 Coretta Scott King Award for Jerry Pinkney's illustrations. Freeman (2001) named *Eleanor* and *Wilma Unlimited* among the century's seventy-one top nonfiction books for children.

Between the picture-book biographies and those almost entirely dominated by text came books in which substantial print blocks were broken up by numerous design elements, including maps and illustrations, but also subheadings, captions, and sidebars—the sort of design Dresang (1999) called "digital design" or "handheld hypertext." Illustrations—usually photographs or documentary prints—were of different sizes, placed with eye-catching variety on almost every doublespread. Information was distributed among sidebars and picture captions, rather than being almost entirely confined to a continuous narrative. *The Importance of Mother Jones* (Horton 1996), a responsible portrayal of the subversive labor organizer, was one such book; *Victoria and Her Times* (Chiflet and Beaulet 1996), a subversive introduction to a very different little old widow in black, was another.

Horton told the story of Mother Jones more or less chronologically, in double columns, with black-and-white illustrations. Sections filling in historical background interrupted the narrative flow, but perhaps no more than would have been the case in some of the more traditionally formatted books of 1971; the prominent subheadings within chapters made organization more visible. Italicized captions, and boxed quotes from primary and secondary sources, offered brief diversions. In addition to its notes and bibliography, the book supported students with a list of important dates and a three-page index, both of which made it easier to abstract specific details without reading or rereading the text. The illustrations were not in chronological order; Jones was not photographed much until the end of her life, and book designers had to make the most of what was available from any given photo session. The introduction featured a portrait of Jones at a desk, looking up from a book: "Despite Mother Jones's gentle appearance, she was a fierce fighter for the rights of working people" (Horton 1996, 11). In the last chapter, another portrait showed her in the same dress, at the same desk, reading the same book: "At the age of eighty-nine, Jones was arrested for the last time at a worker's rally in Pennsylvania" (Horton 1996, 74). The contrast of fierce captions and peaceful images reflects not only the difficulty of finding good archived images, but also Jones's careful engineering of her persona as a sweet little old hellraiser. "Perhaps it is best to think of Mother Jones as a character performed by Mary Jones" wrote one biographer (Gorn 2001, 4); her image was her most important asset. She had lost husband and children to yellow fever in 1867, started over, and lost her livelihood again in the 1871 Chicago Fire. The new life she constructed on the ruins was outward looking, and the design of this book seems very well adapted to the objective text, which has much action and little interiority.

Oversized and colorful—even garish—*Victoria and Her Times* had a few things in common with *The Importance of Mother Jones*. Each had an index, a bibliography, and a great deal of social history. Both expressed concern for social justice, but in *Victoria*, the expression was often ironic: for instance, on a double-spread about India, the text described war, mutiny, and economic upheaval, while eight reproductions showed British playing polo and shooting tigers; one nearly-nude man sat reading on a porch while an Indian servant fanned him and another rubbed his foot. The passage concluded:

Victoria declares that the British presence in India is "indispensable to national prosperity" and that "the Indians must know that no one has the right to dislike their dark skin and that the greatest wish of

their empress is to see them happy and prosperous" (Chiflet and
Beaulet 1996, 81).

A doublespread on poverty, its text crowded by pictures of starving
ragamuffins, was followed by a doublespread on Victoria's lavish diet,
with a problem on the left ("how much would she have to eliminate if
she wanted to maintain the figure of a young woman whose normal
daily intake was 4,000 calories?") and an upside-down solution on the
right (concluding that Victoria consumed about 7,754 calories a day).
Pictures of Victoria in the book ranged from grotesquely unsympathetic
(the overstuffed cartoon queen clutching her stomach) to sweet (the
dewy young tourist on Albert's arm, with an improbable "I ♥ Paris"
button on her tartan frock); the rapid shifts and playful manipulations
called for an ironically distanced reader, likelier to enjoy a joke at Victoria's expense than to identify with her uncritically. The French authors, Jean-Loup Chiflet (whose name in English means "John-Wolf
Whistle") and Alain Beaulet, clearly intended no excessive respect either to Victoria or to American school curricula.

This was not the story of a developing personality, and chronology
contributed little to its organization. A section on the conquest of Aus-
tralia and New Zealand was followed by one on the Great Exhibition.
Liberal and conservative governments, Romantic painters and brick
architecture, Dr. Livingstone, Jack the Ripper, sewing machines, Oscar
Wilde, underwear, manners, and Prince Albert swirled through the busy
pages; a doublespread outlining Victoria's use of time was illustrated
by a computer screen with whimsical "agenda" icons. By using tiny
print, the book designers squeezed an astonishing amount of information into ninety-six pages, and almost all of it, whatever date was mentioned, was in the present tense. The graphics, too, mixed time. Nineteenth-century reproductions and twentieth-century cartoons were
juxtaposed or blended; one photograph of Victoria was adorned with a
red clown nose ("We are not amused"). Not all the facts were accurate
(Joan of Arc raised the siege of Orléans in 1429, not 1492), but if the
book succeeded in creating "an uncontrollable enthusiasm for the subject matter" as advertised, eager young researchers would correct any
misconceptions they picked up here.

Book design makes its own subtle contribution to young readers'
conceptions of what people are like. Where readers of the fictionalized
but sparsely illustrated biographies of the past might have viewed the
world through the subjects' eyes, identifying with their interior monologues and their reactions to the world around them, a new generation
of readers could look at far more—and better printed—pictures of the

subjects themselves. Like frequent short quotes from contemporaries, the many pictures may have predisposed readers to look at subjects from the outside in, rather than from the inside out.

Also, whether they were intended primarily for curricular or extra-curricular purposes, these digitally designed books were set up for browsing and ready reference as much as for continuous reading. One ingredient in the sports biography formula was the statistical chart, showing, for instance, Gail Devers' best times and rankings (Gutman 1996a, 45) or Julie Krone's career earnings (Gutman 1996b, 45; Savage 1996, 53). Where sports books had statistical tables, biographies of writers and entertainers had bibliographies and discographies (Cary 1996; Sheafer 1996); where sports books had bulleted lists of career highlights, biographies of everybody from Marie Curie to Toni Morrison had chronologies and timelines (B. Kramer 1996b; Pasachoff 1996). These reference lists were obviously useful for keeping events straight, placing them in context, and organizing school reports.

Thus book design, more dynamic and noticeable than in the past, could encourage readers to pick details from text rather than to lose themselves in the story of a life. Perhaps it also encouraged them to imagine character itself as a more fragmentary, less monolithic thing than it might have seemed to earlier generations; or a thing less easily grasped. Design elements in at least three cases deliberately evoked scrapbooks. Raintree Steck-Vaughn's Overcoming the Odds series (Gutman 1996a, 1996b) showed deckle edges on photographs and on the diagonal bars, reminiscent of old-fashioned picture holders, at the bottom of each page. More magnificent was *Anastasia's Album*, with rich, muted colors (Anastasia tinted some of the old black-and-white photographs herself), and a unified book design; ivory margins and thin double lines gave each page a carefully mounted look. Refracted through her many pictures, Anastasia was at once immediately present and poignantly remote.

Pragmatic Criteria: Books in Use

As always, biographies were called on to serve a range of purposes, from curricular support to entertainment. Russell (1991) said they were "among the most popular of nonfiction books for young people," and that just "as there are science fiction buffs, there are biography buffs." Perhaps their most controversial task this year was to provide role models. Some saw this as an extracurricular function (Diggins 1996), while others called for schools to undertake it: "With the trend toward resource-based learning and reading-writing connections, the [school] library seems a natural point of convergence for promoting female role models," argued Harvey-Slager (1992). James Cross Giblin—later the author of an excellent 2002 life of Hitler for young adults—asserted that the goal of juvenile biography was no longer "to establish a role model but rather to provide solid, honest information about a man or woman worth knowing for one reason or another" (Giblin 1997).

Role Models

The term "role model" itself was sometimes limited to the context of career mentoring. The online Role Model Project for girls featured careers, resources, and a Role Model Registry where professional women could share information about themselves and their careers (Womens-Work 1996-1999). Many of the books, too, were work-oriented, showing women in a variety of occupations, from sports and entertainment to teaching and science.

Nevertheless, the call for inspirational role models persisted, and the rhetoric from experts and authors alike echoed the idealism of 1946. A children's literature textbook said the best biographies "speak to the strength and resilience of the human spirit" and "remind us that the life well-lived is its own reward" (Russell 1991); an award-winning biographer hoped that as young people witnessed "the evolution of an ordinary person into a hero or heroine," they would be helped "to recognize the universals implicit in all lives" and "to search for the greatness within themselves" (Bober 1996). There were hints, too, of the view that the self is socially constructed: "Elementary and middle school students are in the process of becoming themselves, and reading about real people can provide glimpses of the kinds of lives they might choose to live" (Huck et al. 1997, 552).

Many commentators, as we have seen, considered most urgent the provision of good models for girls and for members of historically marginalized groups: Harvey-Slager (1992) deplored the numerical disparities between the representation of women and minorities in school biography collections and the presence of girls and minorities in the schools; Ernst (1995) called not only for more representation of women, but for more active representation of women; and Collins (1994) looked for biographies that would "enable black youth to recognize that being black does not have to mean defeat" by allowing them "access to all the many black people who have gone through struggles and overcome adversity."

Women of all backgrounds in these biographies were imperfect. The range of behavior girls might emulate had increased dramatically, as a wider variety of virtues and positive achievements qualified for recognition. While some of these heroines sacrificed themselves for others in the traditional way, others worked hard to advance themselves professionally—with little suggestion that by doing so they were neglecting their families, or that their choices had to be justified by reference to a greater good. Personal ambition was generally acceptable, and if women were dedicated to personal goals, biographers did not seem impelled to blame or excuse them.

Most of these books also seemed very matter-of-fact about things that might have been suppressed fifty years earlier, such as broken or troubled marriages, or battles with substance abuse. Sanford and Green (1996) summed up antiheroine Calamity Jane with a quote: "She swore, she drank, she wore men's clothing. She was just ahead of her time." Twentieth-century politicians and entertainers could hardly avoid negative press; their lives unfolded in the glare of publicity, and whatever had been hashed over in the media could now be mentioned in books for children.

But there were limits. While seemingly open and factual, discussions of personal problems in these biographies were generally brief, taking care to present subjects in the best possible light and not sensationalize their difficulties. A political rival announced Ann Richards' alcoholism at a press conference; Siegel (1996, 74) focused on how Richards, "saddened at having to respond publicly to a private matter," survived the attacks and won the primary. Kruz skimmed lightly over Frida Kahlo's sexual history. Kahlo, whose pelvis was broken in a streetcar accident when she was still in her teens, probably lost as many as five pregnancies to miscarriage or medical abortion (Herrera 1983), and after her husband's affair with her sister, she reportedly had affairs with both men and women (Alcántara and Egnolff 1999). Cruz (1996) said merely that in "all, Kahlo had three miscarriages" (84), and that after Diego and Cristina's affair, "Kahlo herself had a number of love affairs with other people" (33), including Leon Trotsky (51).

The year's two juvenile biographies of poet Maya Angelou, who in her teens had a son out of wedlock, took different approaches. Lisandrelli (1996), writing for young adults, was faithful to Angelou's own account: at sixteen, fearing that she might be a lesbian and longing for a boyfriend to confirm her as a proper woman, she "decided to have sex with a good-looking, popular, and conceited boy in her neighborhood. She approached him. He agreed." Lisandrelli (1996, 49) quoted Angelou's conclusion that the result was nobody's fault but her own: "I hefted the burden of pregnancy at sixteen onto my shoulders where it belonged. Admittedly, I staggered under the weight." Nonjudgmental and brisk, Lisandrelli communicated Angelou's responsible attitude and went on to other issues.

Jayne Pettit, writing for slightly younger readers, shifted any blame from Angelou to circumstance:

> Maya's world was looking brighter, except that she had never had a date with a boy. She wasn't pretty. She was too shy to flirt. And most of all, she was too tall and skinny!
>
> Then, one evening after she had completed her homework, Maya took a walk and ran into a boy from her class. He was friendly and easygoing. Perhaps because of this, the young girl's shyness left her, and moments later they were walking to a friend's place.
>
> The friend answered the door and asked them in. The next thing Maya knew, he was gone. And she and her classmate were alone.
>
> Months later, Maya received her high school diploma. On graduation night, she sat down to write her parents a note. In it, she apologized for bringing disgrace on the family. Maya was pregnant (Pettit 1996, 28).

This passage made minor additions to the account in *I Know Why the Caged Bird Sings*, offering the reader's imagination a familiar context for a young girl's sexual peccadillo. One addition, the simple phrase "after she had completed her homework," made her sound conventionally dutiful; another, "He was friendly and easygoing," suggested that the boy was seducer rather than (as Angelou called him) "seductee" (Angelou 1969, 240). The discreetly elided sexual act was implied by the circumstances and by its result in a way immediately recognizable to knowledgeable readers. The more important omission was Maya's moral responsibility for her decision to seduce a boy, which she herself called aggression. In this version, she sounded like an innocent victim.

Fudged biographical details in these books usually had to do with personal morality. The practice underlined a basic continuity in the genre: subjects were chosen for their historical and cultural importance, but had to be presented as acceptable—if imperfect—role models. American culture in the 1990s permitted children's writers to refer nonjudgmentally to formerly taboo behavior, but the bland objectivity of some of these books masked the same kinds of omissions that writers in the 1940s and 1950s had concealed behind fictionalized passages. Lifestyle was still an issue in the culture wars.

Political Education and the Uses of Truth

Also at issue were politics. A few of the lives in these books were shaped by deep—and usually liberal—political convictions. Mother Jones and Annie Clemenc were labor organizers; Dorothy Day led the Catholic Worker Movement; and Rigoberta Menchú won the 1992 Nobel Peace Prize for her advocacy of the Guatemalan poor. The controversies over symbolism, identity, and manipulations of fact in Menchú's story epitomize the tension between semantic and pragmatic criteria for evaluating nonfiction.

Menchú, a Mayan peasant who had lost most of her family to the Guatemalan government's "rural pacification" campaign, carried on her father's efforts to give a voice to the oppressed native people. She turned out to be an effective speaker and won international attention for the book *I, Rigoberta Menchú*, based on interviews with anthropologist and writer Elizabeth Burgos-Debray (Menchú 1984).

In 1996, Marlene Targ Brill's *Journey for Peace: The Story of Rigoberta Menchú*, passed with little notice. Brill, writing for upper elementary and middle school readers, treated *I, Rigoberta Menchú* as a reliable account, citing it in thirteen of her eighteen endnotes and adapting its basic content for her audience. Reviews were favorable. "Brill's book scores high marks for gender and racial equity, peace studies, and class reports," reported Wilton (1996), although she also noted, "Little is said about the political situation in Guatemala." Rochman (1996) summarized Brill's account, concluding that in spite of the violence to which she was subjected, Menchú had "led her people in nonviolent resistance" and had "given them a voice."

Should Brill have been more critical? In fieldwork during the late 1980s, graduate student David Stoll stumbled on discrepancies in Rigoberta's story. For years, he did not speak about his discoveries on the record, but in 1991 a literary critic made them public at a Latin American Studies Association conference, where they provoked "horrified" reactions: Rigoberta "had become such a powerful and persuasive symbol of indigenous resistance and integrity . . . that a challenge to her credibility, however small, was inconceivable" (Cohen 1999, 50). In 1998—obviously too late for Brill or her reviewers to have seen it— Stoll's own book was published by Westview. *Rigoberta Menchú and the Story of All Poor Guatemalans* was quickly adopted by the right-wing press as ammunition against "multiculturalism, political correctness, and the academic and political left" (Cohen 1999, 48), but Stoll's view was not so simple. He argued that Rigoberta, for political reasons (to bring "international attention to widespread human-rights abuses in Guatemala" and generate "support for the leftist opposition there"), had incorporated other people's experiences into her own story. The things she described had happened; they simply hadn't all happened to her. And although Rigoberta ostensibly spoke for all poor Guatemalans, Stoll contended that her commitment was to the leftist guerilla movement, and left the uncommitted peasants, caught between the guerillas and the government, still without a voice.

The controversy that erupted in the wake of Stoll's book echoed the culture wars attending the National History Standards Project. It raises questions about what constitutes a truthful account of a life. Did Burgos-Debray accurately represent what Menchú told her, or was *I, Rigoberta Menchú* actually a reshaping of native experience by a member of a dominant, colonizing, culture? Can an imaginative synthesis of a whole people's combined experience capture some truths better than strict factual accuracy about one woman's life? Could insistence on the individual perspective be rooted in Western culture? Is the perception of truth culturally determined, and is it a mistake to impose Eurocentric standards of accuracy on the stories of other peoples?

Conclusion

It seems impossible to pursue any of these questions without concern for how their answers will support or undermine political interests. The purposes for which a story is told will always shape or limit the facts used to tell it. But in 1996, if there was tension between strict accuracy and the sensitive presentation of subjects, it was rarely visible either in the books themselves or in the textbook lists of evaluation standards. For all its diversity, the juvenile biography collection maintained a broad consensus, tactfully skimming over potential controversies and respecting the sensitivities of biographees.

Omission is necessary in any biography that takes less than a lifetime to read, and surely in juvenile biographies, which must be short. Facts have to be carefully selected and highlighted, and even if they toned down sensational details, the biographers of 1996 were remarkably open. Cruz may have omitted some of Kahlo's lost pregnancies and affairs, but she evoked the artist's grief by describing her painting of an unborn fetus. Angelou, Day, Franklin, and Montessori had children out of wedlock, and their biographers faced the fact. Overall, these were honest treatments of interesting, if imperfect, lives.

Juvenile biography was still less frank than biography for adults. The rhetorical strategies of the books, and the sorts of things omitted, all pointed to concern for their effects on young readers; as England and Fasick (1987) put it, biographies could serve "the legitimate cause of seeking to show children an appropriate or socially acceptable way to view the world and its peoples." Collins argued that the writing of African American biography for young adults should be guided by reader response and social construction theories, as well as theory on the writing of biography:

> Reader response theory speaks to the power of the act of reading, to what the reader brings to the text, and to what the text brings to the reader. Social construction theory lays to rest the notion of the self as a unified whole, existing within a person. It replaces it with the notion of the self as a creation of relations with others in face-to-face contact, or even through contact with the others in books, plays, dreams, or memory. Finally, critical thought on the writing of biography suggests that a life be written from the inside out, that a parade of facts as substitutes for the life makes for poor biography (Collins 1994, 24).

Reader response or reader reception theories hold that meaning is not a static thing, embedded in the text for the reader to decode correctly or incorrectly, but is something dynamic, created in the mind of a reader who interacts with a text.

Individual reader response tends to be quirky and unpredictable, however, and research on the reactions of children to biographies remained rare. What was available tended to come from the classroom, where children's readings were mediated by creative teachers. Lathlaen (1993) reported on a "Meeting of the Minds" unit: "By coming to know the human factor of each individual and relating it to their own lives, the children better understand the nature of risk, the need for mentorships, and what is required to overcome obstacles, all of which may be addressed by teaching with biography." Duthie (1998) brought the insights of classroom research to her account of how biography and autobiography enriched first graders' understandings of human experience, their developing sense of history, and their social concern. These reports support the idea that children will react to biographies in predictable ways; but the studies are too small and too few to be conclusive.

About the unmediated response of independent biography readers even less is known. As Rosenblatt (1995) pointed out, any given text can be read in more than one way. We might expect novels to be read aesthetically, for pleasure, and cookbooks to be read efferently, for their pragmatic applications; but some will read novels efferently, to pass the test, and cookbooks aesthetically. Still, most texts are structured in ways that elicit somewhat predictable responses from most readers; Iser (1978) has analyzed the gaps and shifts of focus that skilled novelists use to engage their readers in the act of imagination.

In the controversy over Rigoberta Menchú's life story, as in the controversy over the *National History Standards*, semantic issues (whether the truth being told is accurate and objective) and pragmatic issues (how the truth will be used) are clearly at stake. Syntagmatic issues are less prominent; but I speculate that the rhetoric, structure, and illustration of juvenile biographies may have a deeper influence, in the end, than the exact details they give. The old fictionalized narrative style, at its best, invited readers into a subject's life and experience; the biographee was the reader's companion. The new styles, abstracting factual material, offered readers an informational resource; the biography was a reference. Work in either style could meet the standards of accuracy and authenticity, with precise facts and deep, empathetic truths. But the two approaches convey different understandings of human character by their very organization: a human can be a story, more consistent and better shaped than our own, or a constructed set of traits and important acts.

Juvenile Biographies Discussed

Blos, Joan. 1996. *Nellie Bly's monkey: His remarkable story in his own words.* New York: Morrow Junior Books.

Brackett, Ginger Roberts. 1996. *Elizabeth Cary: Writer of conscience.* Greensboro, NC: Morgan Reynolds.

Brewster, Hugh. 1996. *Anastasia's Album.* Toronto: Madison Press Books.

Brill, Marlene Targ. 1996. *Journey for peace: The story of Rigoberta Menchú.* Illus. Rubén De Anda. New York: Dutton/Lodestar Books.

Brown, Fern G. 1996. *Daisy and the Girl Scouts: The story of Juliette Gordon Low.* Illus. Marie DeJohn. Morton Grove, IL: Albert Whitman.

Bryant, Jennifer Fisher. 1996. *Lucretia Mott: A guiding light.* Grand Rapids, MI: Eerdmans.

Cary, Alice. 1996. *Jean Craighead George.* Santa Barbara, CA: The Learning Works.

Chiflet, Jean-Loup, and Alain Beaulet. 1996. *Victoria and her times.* New York: Henry Holt.

Cooney, Barbara. 1996. *Eleanor.* New York: Viking.

Cruz, Bárbara C. 1996. *Frida Kahlo: Portrait of a Mexican painter.* Berkeley Heights, NJ: Enslow Publishers.

Desmond, Alice Curtis. 1946. *Glamorous Dolly Madison*. New York: Dodd, Mead.

Dunlap, Julie. 1996. *Birds in the bushes: A story about Margaret Morse Nice*. Illus. Ralph L. Ramstad. Minneapolis, MN: Carolrhoda Books.

Gourse, Leslie. 1996a. *Mahalia Jackson: Queen of Gospel song*. New York: Franklin Watts.

Gourse, Leslie. 1996b. *Pocahontas, young peacemaker*. New York: Simon & Schuster/Aladdin Paperbacks.

Green, Robert. 1996. *Cleopatra*. A First Book. New York: Franklin Watts.

Gutman, Bill. 1996a. *Gail Devers*. Austin, TX: Raintree Steck-Vaughn.

Gutman, Bill. 1996b. *Julie Krone*. Austin, TX: Raintree Steck-Vaughn.

Hart, Philip S. 1996. *Up in the air: The story of Bessie Coleman*. Minneapolis, MN: Carolrhoda Books.

Horton, Madelyn. 1996. *The importance of Mother Jones*. San Diego, CA: Lucent Books.

Kamen, Gloria. 1996. *Hidden music: The life of Fanny Mendelssohn*. New York: Atheneum Books for Young Readers.

Keller, Emily. 1996. *Margaret Bourke-White: A Photographer's Life*. Minneapolis, MN: Lerner Publications.

Kent, Deborah. 1996. *Dorothy Day: Friend to the forgotten*. Grand Rapids, MI: Eerdmans.

Kramer, Barbara. 1996a. *Amy Tan: Author of* The Joy Luck Club. People to Know. Springfield, NJ: Enslow Publishers.

Kramer, Barbara. 1996b. *Toni Morrison: Nobel Prize-winning author*. African-American Biographies. Berkeley Heights, NJ: Enslow Publishers.

Krull, Kathleen. 1996. *Wilma Unlimited: How Wilma Rudolph became the world's fastest woman*. New York: Harcourt Brace.

Lindbergh, Reeve. 1996. *Nobody owns the sky: The story of "Brave Bessie" Coleman*. Illus. Pamela Paparone. Cambridge, MA: Candlewick Press.

Lisandrelli, Elaine Slivinski. 1996. *Maya Angelou: More than a poet*. Berkeley Heights, NJ: Enslow Publishers.

Lowery, Linda. 1996. *Wilma Mankiller*. Illus. Janice Lee Porter. Minneapolis, MN: Carolrhoda Books.

Lyons, Mary. 1996. *Painting dreams*. Boston: Houghton Mifflin.

McCully, Emily. 1996. *The ballot box battle*. New York: Knopf.

Miller, Calvin Craig. 1996. *Spirit like a storm: The story of Mary Shelley*. Greensboro, NC: Morgan Reynolds.

Mosher, Kiki. 1996a. *Learning about bravery from the life of Harriet Tubman*. New York: Rosen/Power Kids Press.

Mosher, Kiki. 1996b. *Learning about compassion from the life of Florence Nightingale*. New York: Rosen/Power Kids Press.

Mosher, Kiki. 1996c. *Learning about fairness from the life of Susan B. Anthony*. New York: Rosen/Power Kids Press.

Netzley, Patricia D. 1996. *The importance of Queen Victoria*. San Diego, CA: Lucent Books.

Pasachoff, Naomi. 1996. *Marie Curie and the science of radioactivity*. New York: Oxford University Press.

Pettit, Jayne. 1996. *Maya Angelou: Journey of the heart*. New York: Puffin Books.

Pinkney, Jerry. 1996. Illustrator's note in *Minty: A story of young Harriet Tub man*, by Alan Schroeder. New York: Dial.

Rambeck, Richard. 1996. *Oksana Baiul*. Plymouth, MN: Child's World.

Sanford, William R., and Carl R. Green. 1996. *Calamity Jane: Frontier original*. Springfield, NJ: Enslow Publishers

Savage, Jeff. 1996. *Julie Krone: Unstoppable jockey*. Minneapolis, MN: Lerner.

Schroeder, Alan. 1996. *Minty: A story of young Harriet Tubman*. Illus. Jerry Pinkney. New York: Dial.

Sheafer, Silvia Anne. 1996. *Aretha Franklin: Motown superstar*. Springfield, NJ: Enslow Publishers.

Shephard, Marie Tennent. 1996. *Maria Montessori: Teacher of teachers*. Minneapolis, MN: Lerner Publications.

Siegel, Dorothy Schainman. 1996. *Ann Richards: Politician, feminist, survivor*. Springfield, NJ: Enslow Publishers.

Stanley, Jerry. 1996. *Big Annie of Calumet: A true story of the Industrial Revolution*. New York: Crown Publishers.

Strazzabosco, Jeanne. 1996. *Learning about determination from the life of Gloria Estefan*. New York: Rosen/Power Kids Press.

Swain, Gwenyth. 1996. *The road to Seneca Falls: A story about Elizabeth Cady Stanton*. Illus. Mary O'Keefe Young. Minneapolis, MN: Carolrhoda Books.

Yannuzzi, Della A. 1996. *Zora Neale Hurston*.

Other References

Alcántara, Isabel, and Sandra Egnolff. 1999. *Frida Kahlo and Diego Rivera*. New York: Prestel.

American Library Association, Office for Intellectual Freedom. 2004. Challenged and banned books. www.ala.org/ala/oif/bannedbooksweek/chal lengedbanned/challengedbanned.htm.

Angelou, Maya. 1969. *I know why the caged bird sings*. New York: Bantam Books.

Arbuthnot, May Hill. 1947. Chapter 17, Biography. In *Children and books*: 470-501. Chicago: Scott, Foresman.

Belenky, Mary Field, Blythe McVicker Clinchy, Nancy Rule Goldberger, and Jill Mattuck Tarule. 1986. *Women's ways of knowing: The development of self, voice, and mind*. New York: Basic Books.

Berg, Elizabeth. 1996. *The pull of the moon*. New York: Berkeley Books.

Bober, Natalie. 1996. Abigail Adams: Witness to a revolution. *Horn Book* 72 (1): 38-41.

Brodie, Carolyn S. 1998. An evolving genre: The picture book biography. *Ohio Media Spectrum* 50 (3): 23-5.

Campbell, Jay R., Kristin E. Voelkl, and Patricia L. Donahue. 2000. *NAEP 1996 trends in academic progress*. rev. Washington, DC: U.S. Department of Education, Office of Educational Research and Improvement, National Center for Education Statistics. NCES 97-985r. http://nces.ed.gov/nations reportcard//pdf/main1996/97985r.pdf.

Cantor, Norman F. 1991. *Inventing the Middle Ages: The lives, works, and ideas of the great medievalists of the twentieth century.* New York: Quill/ William Morrow.

Carr, Jo. 1982. What do we do about bad biographies? In *Beyond Fact: Nonfiction for Children and Young People*, comp. Jo Carr, 119-129. Chicago: American Library Association.

Cheney, Lynne V. 1995. *Telling the truth: Why our culture and our country have stopped making sense—and what we can do about it.* New York: Simon & Schuster.

Children's Book Council. 2002. 2002 industry sales survey for the years 1999-2001. www.cbcbooks.org/pdfs/IndustrySalesSurveypacket.pdf.

Clark, Roger. 2002. Why all the counting? Feminist social science research on children's literature. *Children's Literature in Education* 33 (4): 285-295.

Cohen, Hal. 1999. The unmaking of Rigoberta Menchú. *Lingua Franca* 9 (5): 48-55.

Collins, Carol Jones. 1994. African-American young adult biography: In search of the self. In *African-American Voices in Young Adult Literature*, ed. Karen Patricia Smith, 1-29. Metuchen, NJ: Scarecrow.

Council on Interracial Books for Children. 1977. *Stereotypes, distortions and omissions in U.S. history textbooks.* New York: Racism and Sexism Resource Center for Educators.

Crabtree, Charlotte, and Gary B. Nash. 1996. National standards for history: Basic ed. See esp. Preface, www.sscnet.ucla.edu/nchs/standards/preface. html and part II, chapter 1, Developing standards in United States history for students in grades 5-12: Significance of history for the educated citizen, www.sscnet.ucla.edu/nchs/standards/dev-5-12a.html.

Del Negro, Janice M. 1996. Review of *Margaret Bourke-White: A biography*, by Emily Keller. *Bulletin of the Center for Children's Books* 51 (1): 18.

DelFattore, Joan. 1992. *What Johnny shouldn't read: Textbook censorship in America.* New Haven: Yale University Press.

Diggins, John Patrick. 1996. The National History Standards. *American Scholar* 65 (4): 495-522.

Diggins, John Patrick. 1997. Can the social historian get it right? *Society* 34 (2): 9-19.

Donelson, Kenneth L., and Alleen Pace Nilsen. 1997. Chapter 7, History and history makers. In *Literature for Today's Young Adults*, 5th ed., 186-221. New York: Longman.

Dresang, Eliza T. 1999. *Radical change: Books for youth in a digital age.* New York: H. W. Wilson Company.

Duthie, Christine. 1998. "It's just plain real!": Introducing young children to biography and autobiography. *The New Advocate* 11 (3): 219-227.

England, Claire, and Adele M. Fasick. 1987. Chapter 9, Biography and history. In *ChildView: Evaluating and Reviewing Materials for Children*, 132-150. Littleton, CO: Libraries Unlimited.

Ernst, Shirley B. 1995. Gender issues in books for children and young adults. In *Battling dragons: Issues and controversies in children's literature*, ed. Susan Lehr, 66-78. Portsmouth, NH: Heinemann.

Feminists on Children's Literature. 1971. A feminist look at children's books. *School Library Journal* 17 (5): 19-24.

Fitzpatrick, Ellen. 2002. *History's memory: Writing America's past, 1880-1980.* Cambridge, MA: Harvard University Press.

Flack, Jerry D. 1996. Review of *Nobody owns the sky: The story of "Brave Bessie" Coleman*, by Reeve Lindbergh. *School Library Journal* 42 (11): 98-99.

Fonte, John D. and Robert Lerner. 1997. History standards are not fixed. *Society* 34 (2): 20-25.

Franklin, Aretha, and David Ritz. 1999. *Aretha: From these roots.* New York: Villard.

Freedman, Russell. 1988. Newbery Medal acceptance. *Horn Book Magazine* 64: 444-451.

Freedman, Russell. 1994. Bring 'em back alive: Writing history and biography for young people. *School Library Journal* 40 (March): 138-141.

Freeman, Judy. 2001. Nonfiction: 71 top books of the century. *Instructor* 110 (6): 20-22.

Fritz, Jean. 1988. Biography: Readability plus responsibility. *Horn Book Magazine* 64: 759-760.

Giblin, James. 1997. Writing biographies for young people. *The Writer* 110 (April): 7-9.

Gilligan, Carol. 1982. *In a different voice: Psychological theory and women's development.* Cambridge, MA: Harvard University Press.

Girard, Linda W. 1988. The truth with some stretchers. *The Horn Book Magazine* 64 (4): 464-469.

Goldberg, Vicki. 1986. *Margaret Bourke-White: A biography.* New York: Harper & Row.

Gorn, Elliot J. 2001. *Mother Jones: The most dangerous woman in America.* New York: Hill and Wang.

Grant, Michael. 1972. *Cleopatra: A Biography.* New York: Barnes & Noble.

Green, Anna, and Kathleen Troup. 1999. *The houses of history: A critical reader in twentieth-century history and theory.* Manchester: Manchester University Press.

Harvey-Slager, Norma D. 1992. Left out, way back, and catch-up: The positions played by women's biographies in four elementary schools. *Journal of Youth Services in Libraries* 5: 385-395.

Hazard, Paul. 1947. *Books, children and men.* 3rd ed. Boston: Horn Book.

Herrera, Hayden. 1983. *Frida: A biography of Frida Kahlo.* New York: Harper & Row.

Holtze, Sally Holmes. 1996. Lyons, Mary E. In *Seventh book of junior authors & illustrators.* New York: H. W. Wilson Company. Updated 1999 in *Biographies* at http://hwwilsonweb.com/login/ (Accessed June 16, 2004).

Hopkins, Dee, and Shirley A. Tastad. 1997. Censoring by omission: Has the United States progressed in promoting diversity through children's books? *Journal of Youth Services in Libraries* 10 (4): 399-404.

Huck, Charlotte, Susan Hepler, Janet Hickman, and Barbara Kiefer. 1997. Chapter 11, Biography. *Children's literature in the elementary school,* 6th ed., 551-576. Boston: McGraw-Hill.

Ink, Gary. 1998. Book title output and average prices: 1996 final and 1997 preliminary figures. *The Bowker Annual Library and Book Trade Almanac,* 43: 521-527.

Iser, Wolfgang. 1978. *The act of reading: A theory of aesthetic response.* Baltimore: Johns Hopkins University Press.

Lathlaen, Peggy. 1993. A Meeting of the Minds: Teaching using biography. *The Reading Teacher* 46 (6): 529-531.

Lechner, Judith V. 1997. Accuracy in biographies for children. *New Advocate* 10: 229-242.

London, Herbert. 1997. National Standards for History judged again. *Society* 34 (2): 26-28.

Long, Joanna Rudge. 1997. Eloquent visions: Perspectives in picture book biography. *School Library Journal* 43 (April): 48-49.

Lynch-Brown, Carol, and Carl M. Tomlinson. 1998. Children's literature, past and present: Is there a future? *Peabody Journal of Education* 73: 228-52, http://vnweb.hwwilsonweb.com/.

Lynch-Brown, Carol, and Carl M. Tomlinson. 1993. Chapter 9, Nonfiction. In *Essentials of children's literature,* 151-170. Boston: Allyn and Bacon.

Menchú, Rigoberta. 1984. *I, Rigoberta Menchú: An Indian woman in Guatemala.* Ed. and introd. Elisabeth Burgos-Debray. New York: Verso.

Nilsen, Alleen Pace. 1971. Women in children's literature. *College English* 32 (8): 918-926.

Orenstein, Peggy. 1994. *Schoolgirls: Young women, self-esteem, and the confidence gap.* New York: Random House.

Oyate. 2005. Books to avoid. www.oyate.org/books-to-avoid/index.html.

Pipher, Mary. 1994. *Reviving Ophelia: Saving the selves of adolescent girls* New York: G. P. Putnam's Sons.

Purves, Alan C., and Dianne L. Monson. 1984. *Experiencing Children's Literature.* Glenview, IL: Scott, Foresman.

Quinn, Susan. 1995. *Marie Curie: A life.* New York: Simon & Schuster.

Readability Calculations. 2003. Dallas, TX: Micro Power & Light Co.

Rich, Doris L. 1993. *Queen Bess: Daredevil aviator.* Washington, DC: Smithsonian Institution Press.

Rochman, Hazel. 1996. Review of *Journey for Peace*, by Marlene Targ Brill. *Booklist* (September): 120.

Rosenblatt, Louise M. 1995. *Literature as exploration*. 5th ed. Foreword Wayne Booth. New York: Modern Language Association of America.

Ross, Catherine Sheldrick. 1985. Young adult realism: Conventions, narrators, and readers. *The Library Quarterly* 55 (2): 174-191.

Russell, David L. 1991. Chapter 11, Biography. In *Literature for children: A short introduction*, 124-132. New York: Longman.

Sadker, Myra, and David Sadker. 1994. *Failing at fairness: How America's schools cheat girls*. New York: Charles Scribner's Sons.

Schene, Carol. 1996. Review of *Margaret Bourke-White: A biography*, by Emily Keller. *School Library Journal* 42 (9): 156.

Schwarcz, Joseph H. 1982. *Ways of the illustrator: Visual communication in children's literature*. Chicago: American Library Association.

Sommers, Christina Hoff. 1995. *Who stole feminism? How women have betrayed women*. New York: Touchstone/Simon & Schuster.

Stoodt, Barbara D., Linda B. Amspaugh, and Jane Hunt. 1996. Chapter 9, Nonfiction: Biography and informational books, in *Children's literature: Discovery for a lifetime*, 250-283. Scottsdale, AZ: Gorsuch Scarisbrick.

Sutherland, Zena, and May Hill Arbuthnot. 1991. Chapter 12, Biography. In *Children and books*, 8th ed., 452-496. New York: HarperCollins.

Van Dijk, Teun A. 1988. *News as discourse*. Hillsdale, NJ: Lawrence Erlbaum.

Vasilakis, Nancy. 1996. Review of *Big Annie of Calumet*, by Jerry Stanley. *Horn Book Magazine* 72: 624-625.

Wagner-Martin, Linda. 1994. *Telling women's lives: The new biography*. New Brunswick, NJ: Rutgers University Press.

Weinberg, Steve. 1992. *Telling the untold story: How investigative reporters are changing the craft of biography*. Columbia: University of Missouri Press.

Weintraub, Stanley. 1987. *Victoria: An intimate biography*. New York: Truman Talley Books, E. P. Dutton.

Wilms, Denise M. 1982. An evaluation of biography. In *Beyond fact: Nonfiction for children & young people*, comp. Jo Carr, 135-140. Chicago: American Library Association.

Wilton, Shirley. 1996. Review of *Journey for Peace*, by Marlene Targ Brill. *School Library Journal* 42 (September): 210.

Witucke, Virginia. 1985. Trends in juvenile biography: Five years later. *Top of the News* 42 (Fall): 45-53.

WomensWork. 1996-1999. Role model project for girls. www.womenswork.org/girls/.

Chapter 5

Pocahontas:
Four Political Fictions

Pocahontas, known to generations of Americans as the heroic girl who saved John Smith's life, has been an iconic figure in juvenile biography for at least two centuries. There have been scores of children's books about her, including numerous spin-offs from the Disney film version of her life. She is a vintage American heroine, and the one woman about whom new juvenile biographies were published in all three years of this study: the d'Aulaires' *Pocahontas* and Seymour's *Pocahontas: Brave Girl* appeared in 1946, when she was the only woman of color represented; Bulla's *Pocahontas and the Strangers* in 1971, when she was one of six; and Gourse's *Pocahontas: Young Peacemaker* in 1996. All four show Pocahontas as a sympathetic and engaging character; however, characterization, plot, and rhetoric change in ways that reflect a growing uneasiness with stereotypes, first of Native peoples, and then of women.

Sundquist (1987) analyzes the stereotyping of Indian women in nineteenth-century American fiction and concludes that their image was closer to that of white women than of Indian men. The men were represented as having good physiques, wilderness skills, stoic expressions, and a tendency to speak broken English, and in captivity narratives both men and women might be stereotyped as ruthless savages. In other contexts, however, Indian women were far more likely to resemble the stereotype of the young, innocent, frail, passive, and often doomed "Angel," a staple of popular fiction at the time. Many stories were roughly based on the legend of Pocahontas, who in the nineteenth century was usually portrayed as an "Angel," although Sundquist notes that this was not the only possibility; she could have been portrayed as "a traitress to her people, . . . betraying and doing harm not only to one

man or a few, but to a whole tribe, and to the generally victimized Indian people at that. Her conversion from her own native religion could
have been judged as inconsistent and proof of a shallow nature, which
is very far from an Angel" (50-51).

The writers who portrayed her were not Indians, however, but descendants and inheritors of the white settlers she aided. This is still true
of the twentieth-century fictionalized biographies for children we exam-
ine here. The "Angel" is above all else "not threatening to manhood"
(Sundquist 1987, 25), and the image of Pocahontas is not threatening to
whites. And for children's writers especially, there is ample space to
develop her character in ways that will either soothe or challenge white
conscience. Even her birth date, 1595, is only approximate, based on
her apparent age when the Jamestown settlers first met her. Her home
life before that, and her relationships with her father and other members
of her people, are open to invention—the little evidence we have comes
from people who had only short glimpses of that life and did not even
speak her language.

The documented facts are scanty. She was the daughter of Wahun-
sunacock, also called Powhatan—the name both of his own people and
of the broader coalition he headed (Shepherd 1998). After rescuing
Captain Smith, she continued to be friendly with him and helpful to the
Jamestown settlers; then she disappeared from the record until 1612,
when she was abducted by Captain Argall and held in Jamestown for a
ransom her father—knowing, no doubt, that she was safe—did not pay.
In 1613, she converted to Christianity. In 1614, she married John Rolfe,
and in 1615 gave birth to a son, Thomas. In 1616, they went to England, where she was received at court, sat for her portrait, and attended
a Twelfth Night masque staged by Ben Jonson. In 1617, just before a
scheduled return to Virginia, she died and was buried at Gravesend. To
fill out book-length accounts of her life, writers must rely "at best . . .
on studies of Powhatan Indian culture" and other contextual sources,
and at worst on "pure conjecture" (Tilton 1994, 7-8). Allen (2003)
agrees that Smith's account is unreliable and archaeological findings
require careful inference, but adds the oral tradition of Native peoples
to the context guiding her interpretation.

This scarcity of primary sources is a common problem for women's
biographers. There have been more children's than adult books about
Nelly Bly, for instance—possibly because fictionalization, a technique
more associated with juvenile than with scholarly biography, helps
make a coherent life story from spotty and unreliable evidence. Although none has a bibliography or notes, all four biographies examined

in this chapter show signs of research and appear to be consistent with the scholarship of their times. Still, all four are fictionalized, and the conventions of fiction help shape their imaginative reconstructions of Pocahontas's life.

Tilton (1994) has traced evolving versions of her story from Smith's 1624 *Generall Historie of Virginia* through the nineteenth century, pointing out how it was used by different generations in shifting contexts. In the eighteenth century, much of Virginia's elite was descended from Pocahontas, and her marriage to Rolfe was more emphasized than her rescue of Smith. Her story gave Virginia a legend to compete with the Massachusetts Pilgrims, and thinkers up to the time of Jefferson occasionally suggested that the Jamestown settlers had missed an opportunity by not following Rolfe's lead, marrying Powhatan's people instead of fighting them. By the early nineteenth century, however, any mixing of races had become controversial, and the image of the child Pocahontas sheltering Smith became more popular than the image of the adult Lady Rebecca cradling her half-English child. As the controversy over slavery intensified, Northern abolitionists used the Pocahontas legend against southerners who professed horror of miscegenation. Her story provided "an interesting analogy to the fate of many African slaves," Tilton points out: "It must be remembered that Pocahontas was also tricked and taken prisoner on board a European ship by whites, and, while not enslaved, she had to learn to live in a foreign world that she was not free to leave" (161).

In the winter of 1607-1608, in "perhaps the most famous incident in the history of Virginia," Smith's head was forced down on two great stones before Powhatan, the chief of the Powhatan confederacy; men with clubs stood ready "to beat out his brains":

> Pocahontas, the king's dearest daughter, when no entreaty could prevail, got his head in her arms, and laid her own upon his to save him from death (Gleach 1997, 116).

Did this actually happen? Scholars have debated the matter for over a century. Massachusetts historian Charles Deane challenged Smith's version in 1860 (Tilton 1994, 164), and Mossiker (1976, 85) also points out that Smith, the sole eyewitness on record, did not publish his account of the episode until "1624, when Pocahontas and Powhatan were no longer around to dispute it." She admits Smith was a braggart, but concludes that circumstantial details tend to support at least the objective details of his story. Rountree (1990) disagrees, on the grounds of both historical and anthropological evidence; she points to Smith's suspicious history of being rescued from peril by fair ladies of high rank, and finds it unlikely that Powhatan would have feasted Smith before ordering his execution.

Beyond the question of Smith's factual accuracy, however, there is the question of his understanding. Mossiker (1976, 81) suggests that Pocahontas, either spontaneously or at her father's request, was exercising a woman's right to adopt a captured enemy as compensation for a lost kinsman, and that what Smith described was actually an initiation ceremony in which he faced, not death, but "only a simulation of death." Gleach (1997, 121-122) analyzes the episode in the context of other ritual events during Smith's captivity and in the light of Powhatan culture, history, and strategic interests; he concludes that Powhatan's "intention at the end is clearly to have the English settle in his territory, as his subordinates." The Powhatans "adopted the English . . . in good faith," but "Smith and the colony never recognized" the meaning of the ritual sequence.

The meaning the English did perceive was probably, as Mossiker (1976, 82) says, closer to the meaning of ancient stories that pitted "the lover against the father. . . . Hate the Alien Father and Love the Alien Daughter is another way to say it. . . ." The story proposed by Gleach makes Pocahontas her father's agent in establishing friendly relations with the English on terms favorable to the Powhatans. Smith's construction of the same events, "a story with undertones of miscegenation and overtones of racial conciliation" (71), encourages us to admire her loyalty to Smith and his English companions, mediating on their behalf, bringing them food, and protecting them from her father's hostility.

1946: Ingri and Edgar Parin d'Aulaire, Flora Warren Seymour

The year 1946 saw the publication of two juvenile biographies of Pocahontas. One, by Ingri and Edgar Parin d'Aulaire, was a picture book. It had many doublespreads in full color, as not all picture books did in those days when color separations had to be done expensively by hand. The d'Aulaires, European immigrants to the United States, were much admired for their unique use of lithography in children's books and had won the 1940 Caldecott Medal for their *Abraham Lincoln*. The other book, by Flora Warren Seymour, was part of the Childhood of Famous Americans series—those little orange books with their silhouette illustrations, published by Bobbs Merrill for independent readers only a little older than the picture-book crowd. According to the *Library Journal*'s review, Seymour was the "first woman member of the Board of Indian Commissioners" and was "said to know her material thoroughly" (Andrus 1946); she also contributed a biography of Sacajawea to the Childhood of Famous Americans series. (Seymour's board credential suggests that she was an outside and not disinterested observer of Native peoples, and would not go far to establish her reputation for expertise today.) Both books showed Pocahontas as a warm, sympathetic character, encouraging readers to identify with her views.

The d'Aulaires' book was generally well received. "The text is good and so is the color lithography," said Skinner (1946)—although she cautioned, "some of the pictures of Pocahontas lack dignity and make her look something less than the Indian princess she was." The *Booklist* reviewer, too, had reservations about the "'un-Indianlike' and even distorted" illustrations (Anon. 1946), but *Library Journal* recommended it and *Horn Book* praised its "soft colors" and "dramatic episodes" (Jordan 1947). Arbuthnot (1947, 482), discussing the artistry of the d'Aulaires in *Children and Books*, called it "a gay book and the most winning story of them all." It was "a well-loved story" (Jordan 1947), although "perhaps not previously well known" to younger children (Webb 1946).

The illustrations contain elements that suggest that the d'Aulaires had researched their book with some care. The use of tattoos (although the d'Aulaires show them as geometric, rather than floral designs) and Powhatan's hair, shaven on one side and worn long on the other, are documented in the literature, and the dancing girls on page 31 mimic the poses of dancers in a 1585 water color by John White, whose drawings of the Roanoke Indians are the closest thing we have to a visual record of life among the Powhatans and their neighbors. A few of the drawings are touchingly realistic: Pocahontas as a small child caressing her stern father, or an older girl, weeping as she goes to warn the English of his planned treachery.

But realism often yields to symbolism in these pictures. Powhatan first appears framed by a moonbeam as he emerges from an abstract forest. One hand holds his tomahawk ready and the other reaches out a necklace and feathers to Pocahontas, who runs from the lit house to welcome him and seize his gift. Behind him in the moonbeam are the staring, bodiless heads of many braves, perhaps representing the thirty tribes over whom he is said to rule. Such cartoon crowds may give the impression that all Indians are alike. In the rescue scene (d'Aulaire and

d'Aulaire 1946, 22-23), Powhatan is flanked by nine braves, all scowl-
ing, all holding their folded arms high against their chests; behind them
stand nine women in white feathered cloaks, watching with consterna-
tion as Pocahontas, also in a white feathered cloak, rushes to place her
head between Smith's head and the medicine men's clubs. Their nearly
uniform ranks suggest the formal structure of the ceremony she is dis-
rupting by her precipitate action—but, combined with the eerily painted
faces of the medicine men, they also suggest unwelcome stereotypes of
Native people.

The English are also visually lampooned. The "sick and hungry"
settlers are shown plaintively clutching their heads, their stomachs, or
their feet, or wailing in bed despite John Smith's best efforts to "cheer
them up." A row of English visitors watches aghast, eyes popping and
mustaches curled, as Pocahontas and her friends dance out of the
woods. An Englishman stands on tiptoe, straining to place a crown on
Powhatan's unbowed head. Yet the kinetic energy and humor of the
d'Aulaires' Indians, combined with the abstraction and stiffness of
some of the drawings, can too easily be interpreted as condescending
toward the Indians. A picture set in London shows Powhatan's "trusted
brave" notching a stick, trying to count all the English: "The Indian
notched and notched, but the faster he notched the more people popped
up. It was the deuce how many men there were in England" (38).

The d'Aulaires' prose, like their art, is stylized. They give Pocahontas's life the cadences of folklore:

> In the dark woods of Virginia, where dusky owls hooted over the
> treetops and prowling beasts howled at the moon, there lived a stern
> old Indian chief. . . . He had a little daughter who was the very apple
> of his eye. She was as sweet and pretty as he was ugly and cruel
> (d'Aulaire and d'Aulaire 1946, 9-11).

To children familiar with fairy tales, this rhetoric signals a remove from
the mundane to a world in which Pocahontas can be simply "good" and
Powhatan mostly "bad." Later in the story, Pocahontas visits a "village
chief and his wife" who are "ugly and cruel" people, and help an English captain kidnap her in exchange for a copper kettle. The formulaic
label, "ugly and cruel," could be seen as racist, but contemporary juvenile biographies of the Tudors and Stuarts also called enemies of their
protagonists "cruel" and "ugly," attributing their actions to personal
malevolence rather than political strategy or religious conviction. In
books for the young, views held by cruel, ugly individuals were generally wrong and did not require serious consideration.

Maintaining a folkloric storytelling voice, the d'Aulaires tell how Pocahontas listened to her grandmother, who knew how to make "healing drinks and ointments" and "pots of clay and mats of sweet-smelling grass," and also how to propitiate mischievous spirits and praise good ones. "Oh, it was much that Grandmother knew":

> In all the world there was only one who knew still more about spirits and magic than Grandmother, thought Pocahontas. That was Powhatan's medicine man. He knew secret magic ways to find answers to every question (d'Aulaire and d'Aulaire 1946, 17).

This child's-eye build-up of infallible adult knowledge is punctured when the settlers arrive and throw Powhatan's folk into confusion. "His medicine man . . . juggled and conjured to try to find out what kind of magic the palefaces practiced, but he could not make it out." Faced with genuine novelty, traditional knowledge proves inadequate, and the Indians appear childish and timid as they wait to make sense of the newcomers. The tone moves from light irony toward broader sarcasm; young readers in a scientific age are licensed to scoff at magic and to regard adults who think guns are "magic sticks" with knowing condescension. Pocahontas looks wise by comparison when, in a moment of childish insight, she decides that the "palefaces [look] just like her corncob doll" and can "not be evil, for corn [is] the Indian's best friend." Unlike the other children, she is "not the least bit afraid" of John Smith; she sees "no evil" in his strange blue eyes.

The d'Aulaires treat this perception as more valid than her father's concerns about the English "acting as though they owned his land." When the medicine men finally announce "that the spirits had told them the white man's magic was evil, the prisoner must die," Pocahontas saves Smith's life, and secures Powhatan's favor, at least temporarily, for the struggling colony. She saves his life a second time when, angry at Smith's continued demands for corn, Powhatan plans to have him killed. Pocahontas "did not want to take sides against her father, but she could not let him kill her white friend." Much is omitted from this account. Powhatan's demand for guns is not mentioned, and we are not told that most of the Jamestown settlers died even before that first winter. The urgent survival issues are suppressed, and as the issues become personal, the conflict of interest between peoples is trivialized.

Seymour's book, with its episodic structure, resembles contemporary children's adventure stories more than folklore. It, too, introduces Pocahontas as a privileged pet—not just of her father but of the whole village. The first chapters are devoted to life before the English. Again, whites are introduced from the Indians' point of view, but Seymour's Indians are responsible adults, not childishly superstitious. They speak different languages, and recognize differences between Spaniards and Englishmen. They are not intimidated by paleface "magic" but curious, eager to appropriate new technologies. They have a culture of their own, and Seymour shows some appreciation of its details, even as she casts her heroine in opposition to it. "Playful Girl" is inventive within her culture; she has the idea of using poles with wind-blown streamers to frighten birds from the crops. At the same time, she questions everything from gender-specific chores (why can't she keep hunting rabbits, instead of learning to cure their pelts?) to the reasons for fighting the "pale-faced men" or executing the captive Smith, and is told again and again, "It is the custom of our people" (Seymour 1946, 56). She is tender-hearted and drawn to the new, and her questioning is made to seem more reasonable than consistent adherence to custom; but Seymour does not portray the Powhatans as acting wholly without reason.

Early in the book, Pocahontas hears the story of Don Luis, who had been kidnapped by the Spanish in 1560 and returned with a Jesuit mission in 1570. "Instead of helping convert the Powhatans," writes one often-cited authority, "Don Luis reverted to savagery" (Woodward 1969, 43); Shepherd (1998) states that he led an attack on the mission in 1571, and the Spanish retaliated later that year by killing thirty Powhatans. Seymour's version, as told by old Aunt Teemo, avoids any invidious reference to "savagery," but stresses that Indians can learn good things from the foreigners. Don Luis slowly remembered his native tongue and "began to like the feeling of air on his bare skin, as he had felt it when he was a boy." The "medicine men" chanted to help him "forget the strange things he had learned," Teemo continues:

> But there was one thing he remembered and taught our people. He said it was better for the villages whose language was the same to be friends. So, because of what he told us, your father Powhatan is treated like a chief when he goes to other villages (Seymour 1946, 26-27).

Aunt Teemo does not hint that Don Luis might have urged unification to resist the white men, or that Powhatan's empire-building involved war against the Kecoughtan, the Chesapeake or the Chickahominy. Pocahontas and the reader are taught to see her father's authority resting on a peaceful consensus.

Seymour was evidently familiar with current scholarship on Native custom. Pocahontas knows, for instance, that women may adopt prisoners, a custom widely documented among the woodland peoples (Jennings 1975). Her "Aunt Jappy" takes a captive boy to raise in place of a lost son, and Pocahontas secretly decides to adopt "an older one, not one I have to take care of," for herself (Seymour 1946, 54). Meanwhile, she plays with "Captive Boy," teaches him her language and learns his, and is the unwitting cause of his escape when the two of them run off to see the captive Smith. This invented episode foreshadows her rescue and teaching of Smith, and at the same time gives a motive for Aunt Jappy's betrayal of Pocahontas to Captain Argall: she does it not just for the copper kettle, but because, years later, she still resents the loss of a boy she would have raised in place of her own. Thus Seymour explains events by the interplay of custom and personal motives, leaving strategic considerations in the background.

Also left in the background, or omitted entirely, are details that Seymour must have known but probably considered unsuitable for explanation to a young audience, including religion and marriage customs. Powhatan is said to have had as many as a hundred wives in his lifetime, and approximately a dozen at any one time; he kept each one until she had borne him a child, then dismissed her and took another. Rountree (2001) speculates that Pocahontas spent her early years with her mother's family, in the home of a stepfather or grandparents. Seymour's version is safer: Pocahontas's "own mother had died when she was a baby," and she was looked after by many "aunts and elder sisters" (23). The reader's attention is not caught by any contrast between the values of Powhatan's extended family and those of a nuclear family in the United States, and so Powhatan's moral authority as father is not undermined by the questioning of hard-to-explain cultural differences.

In the central episode, however—the rescue of Smith—Powhatan presides over a "cruel" customary ritual that is stopped only by his fatherly indulgence of Pocahontas's intervention. Pocahontas "knew what it meant when men came in with three great flat stones," and she "could not bear to think of it." She calls out for Powhatan to prevent it, but "her girl's voice was not strong enough to be heard in the midst of the shouts of triumph from the warriors." Unable to get her father's attention any other way, she puts her own head between the prisoner and the warriors' raised clubs:

> Her father looked at her a long time in silence. He could see how excited and eager she was.
>
> "Very well," he said at last. "Since you wish it, his life will be spared. We shall adopt him as a member of our tribe" (Seymour 1946, 84-89).

Seymour discounts Powhatan's opposition to English settlement, attributing it to uninformed acceptance of tradition, and allowing him to set it
aside on the whim of a favored child. His people's relations with the
English are shown as personal, not political or strategic: Powhatan
keeps a truce with the English after Pocahontas's marriage to John
Rolfe, but his heir, "Pocahontas' cruel old uncle" Opekanko, who
"loved to brag about the many men he had killed in battle" (179), later
attacks them. Hostilities between the Powhatans and the settlers are thus
caused by an individual's aggressive nature, rather than the conflicting
interests of two populations.

Pocahontas bases her support of the settlers on instinctive trust and
affection rather than abstract reasoning: they treat her like a princess;
she believes Captain Smith is less likely than her own father to harm
her; and she doesn't "like all this fighting and hurting" (135-136). Seymour gives her the individual virtues of pacifism, faithfulness (to the
English), and courage, and frames her story—as did the d'Aulaires—in
the context of English rather than Powhatan history. Pocahontas is a
good Indian because she is on our side. In the final chapter, her cousin
Chanco keeps the promise he made her and warns the English of a
Powhatan raid; Seymour portrays Chanco's loyalty, along with the
many descendants of her son Thomas, a statue in Jamestown and a
painting in the U.S. Capitol of her baptism, as Pocahontas' legacy. Her
death is passed over lightly, not mentioned until we have been reminded
that over three centuries have passed. Young readers are invited to identify with her as a warm, lively girl, constantly questioning established
custom—while the seeming completeness of her personal story reinforces the twentieth-century status quo, deflecting any questions they
might have about the justice of the English cause.

1971: Clyde Robert Bulla

Twenty-five years later, Clyde Robert Bulla cast the story as a tragedy.
He had published his first book in 1946; by 1971, he was known among
children's librarians and teachers as a writer whose "unaffected simplicity" and "satisfying style" made his work accessible to "the bright child
who is a retarded reader" (Arbuthnot 1964, 654). Griese (1971) argued
that Bulla's simplicity was deceptive, and could lead critics to overlook
his "adroitness in managing plot," his rounded characters, his strong but
unobtrusive themes and the poetic openness of his style. *Pocahontas*

and the Strangers exhibits both artistic craft and research. The research brings political history to the foreground; Bulla says more than Seymour about actual military actions and negotiations between Powhatan and the English. In this context, Pocahontas is shown as a lively, inquisitive girl whose stubborn sympathy for her people's enemies traps her in a painful cultural conflict.

Bulla establishes her character in the first scene: she is impulsive and rashly altruistic, angering her brother Nantaquas when she frees a snared eagle. Later, she persists in helping John Smith and the Jamestown English against the clear wishes of her father, Powhatan. In the end, she marries John Rolfe, is treated as something between a celebrity and a side show in England, and dies there, murmuring in her last delirium, "Let the bird go free, Nantaquas" (Bulla 1971, 176).

Bulla's third-person narration is restricted, with unusual consistency, to Pocahontas's viewpoint; no other person's thoughts are given, even her own fictionalized introspection is kept to a minimum, and the narrator expresses no judgment. The reader is left to infer motives and feelings from action and dialogue, and the dialogue constantly reminds us of the limits of knowledge. Pocahontas is irrepressibly curious, but almost every conversation she has with her father or her brother includes at least one attempt to squelch her. Her father has "never punished her," but is likely to "set her outside as if she were a puppy" when she tries to listen to the men's conversation (Bulla 1971, 14). Nantaquas, repeatedly warning her against the English and debating her interpretations of their behavior, cuts off argument with lines like, "You cannot understand these things. You are only a foolish girl!" (39). Other women in the story are not strong role models. Pocahontas's mother waits and defers to men, and urges her to do the same. Old Hapsis, weary of bloodshed, wants to flee at first word of the English. Tassana, the wife of Japazaws, is "plump and pretty" and "like a child" (124), shallow enough to betray Pocahontas for that copper kettle. The governor's daughters, Mary and Betsy, dress Pocahontas and show her off like a doll. To be "only a girl" in this book is to be insignificant.

Smith takes a different attitude; he seems interested in what Pocahontas has to say, and she in turn believes in Smith. "And you believed him?" asks Nantaquas (76). "You believed him?" asks Powhatan (90). "Why should I not believe him?" Pocahontas asks Nantaquas, and he tells her, "These palefaces are not truly our friends" (76). Mostly through dialogue, Bulla gives far more detail than Seymour about negotiations and acts of war between the Powhatans and the settlers. It becomes clear to the reader, if not to Pocahontas, that the two populations cannot easily coexist and that Powhatan has reason to distrust Smith. Yet, Pocahontas trusts him. "And you have not forgotten your promise?" she asks, reminding him that he will take her to England one day. "What promise?" he asks (87), and then makes a quick recovery. Her trust does not falter. The warnings of Namontack, who has been exhibited in England, and Old Hapsis, who remembers earlier settlers, make no more impression than those of her father and brother. "Are you wiser than your father?" asks Hapsis. "In this one way I may be," says Pocahontas (47).

Bulla withholds editorial comment, and the reader is free to believe that Pocahontas is wiser than her kin or that she is stubbornly wrong, misled by her heart. For, without making an explicit claim, Bulla implies that Pocahontas has fallen in love with Smith at first sight:

> Pocahontas felt warm. She felt happy. The paleface had looked at her. She was almost sure he had smiled.
>
> She wanted to smile back. She wanted to hear his voice (Bulla 1971, 44).

While her father and brother consider the English and especially Smith as a threat to their people, Pocahontas sees them only as interesting and even lovable persons. Perhaps, the reader may decide, Nantaquas is right, and as a girl she should be content to operate in the private realm she understands. Or perhaps his relentless teasing is merely a convention of mid-twentieth-century children's fiction, the provision of something familiar—a benign sibling rivalry—to help young readers identify with the characters.

Throughout the first part of the book, Pocahontas struggles to be heard. She is so eager for communication that Nantaquas can make her happy by breaking his angry silence to tell her she talks too much. It is talk, even more than food, she carries between Jamestown and her father's house. She risks death to be heard when she places her head between Smith's and the clubs, and again when she warns him of her father's planned ambush. Only when Tom Savage brings word of Smith's death does she fall silent: "She did not speak again for many days" (Bulla 1971, 121).

As the second part begins, Pocahontas is a young woman, visiting cousins and friends by the Potomac. She is merry and popular, though she still feels sad when she remembers Captain John Smith, and she makes every effort to elude Captain Argall's kidnapping. Her motives are still personal and intuitive: "She did not like the captain. His smile was mocking, and his eyes were too bold" (125). Taken to Jamestown against her will, she tries to escape and maintains some emotional distance from the English, although she is polite and quick to learn their ways. Only when her father's inability to ransom her leaves her feeling abandoned does she accept the proposal of gentle, attentive John Rolfe, which results in a new kind of silencing.

As her husband, Rolfe discusses her wishes and his decisions in her presence as if she is not even there. He prevents her from visiting Powhatan with their son, and volunteers her for a visit to London. Pocahontas now seems timid and shy, and Rolfe tells her how to act: "You must smile, Rebecca. . . . When our friends are here, you must look as if you are happy" (165). When Smith, not having bothered to let her know he was still alive, drops by unannounced for a casual visit, Rolfe seems astonished by her speechless anger: "Rebecca," he says, "if you know this man, speak to him" (172). Pocahontas, repeatedly hushed by all the men in her life, retreats into silence.

Bulla's use of simple vocabulary and avoidance of authorial comment on feelings could be admired for its accessibility to young readers or criticized as stereotyping Indians; he gives their speech the easy cadence of an oral culture, but seems to enjoy the naiveté of words and phrases like "firestick" and "great canoes" and "palefaces." Powhatan and his men appear reasonable in their responses to the settlers; they are neither vilified nor infantilized by the plot. Yet Bulla does not plead their cause openly; their struggle is only the background for the more personal story of an individual girl, and with her removal to England, it seems to fade into the past as well as the distance. Or perhaps Pocahontas herself is a symbol for her people, and her fate, imprisoned in English clothes and customs, foreshadows theirs—charming, intuitive, and in the end irrevocably lost.

1996: Leslie Gourse

The Childhood of Famous Americans series is now published by Simon & Schuster, in red, white, and blue Aladdin Paperbacks with brightly colored illustrations on the front and line drawings inside. The new *Pocahontas*, by Leslie Gourse, matter-of-factly includes sensitive details that were omitted from Seymour's version. Powhatan's polygamy is quietly acknowledged when Pocahontas talks with two of her father's wives about the captive they expect to feast later. Native religion enters the story when Powhatan attributes Jamestown's misfortunes to the god

Okeus, who "punishes men for breaking moral laws" (Gourse 1996, 82)—as Smith has done, by promising guns and then failing to deliver them. Pocahontas is ill for months before her death; three of the Indians who went with her to England die of respiratory illnesses, and her own death is an integral part of the story, not tucked into an afterword.

There are limits to this openness. For instance, Gourse notes that a young brave named Kocoum wanted to marry Pocahontas; according to Rountree (2001), they were married, and it is not clear whether Poca-hontas's extended absence after her kidnapping constituted a divorce. Gourse (1996, 108-109) avoids the question of bigamy by saying merely that "Pocahontas considered marrying him. But when she thought about how routine her life would be, it made her very sad." This does not directly contradict the record, since it leaves open the question of whether or not the marriage occurred; but the fictionalized thought may introduce a greater inaccuracy by attributing to Pocahontas a rather modern, individualistic attitude toward marriage and routine.

Overall, however, the tone of the book is frank, and the relations between Pocahontas and her father also suggest that Algonquian parents are open to their children's questions and ready to answer them respect-fully. Bulla's Powhatan shoos his daughter away, and she gets most of her news from her brother; Nantaquas doesn't appear in Gourse's ver-sion, but Powhatan takes time to talk with his daughter, walk with her through the village, and explain the special responsibilities of leader-ship. When she wonders if she can become a chief in her own right, he takes the idea seriously, and counsels her:

> You must pay attention to the needs of the people, as I do. You must
> think about what they need to be strong. You are the daughter of the
> chief. You must observe what everyone is doing and keep them cou-
> rageous. Your job in life is a spiritual one (Gourse 1996, 29).

Even when they repeatedly disagree about Smith, her father seems to be grooming Pocahontas for future responsibilities. He keeps her with him in the council of elders that plans to ambush Smith, and afterward says, "I understand you are sad because you and Captain Smith are friends. But you must understand something, too. Trouble will befall us all if I let his lies continue. . ." (98). This kindness makes her betrayal of the plan more problematic. In the 1946 accounts, it seemed to be at least partly justified by the ignorance, if not ugliness and cruelty, of the Powhatans. In Bulla's 1971 narrative, it was the action of an impulsive girl who seemed incapable of understanding the interests of her people. But Gourse's Pocahontas, made privy to her father's reasoning, warns his enemy with "a heavy heart" (98). When Smith, recognizing the gravity of the betrayal, invites her to stay in Jamestown for her safety, she refuses: "All my blessings have always come to me from my father and our great people" (100).

Pocahontas is much closer to her father in this account than in the earlier three books, where he favors her but does not take her ideas so seriously. Their closeness makes unnecessary many of the minor characters, like Grandmother and Aunt Teemo and Old Hapsis, who in the earlier books told Pocahontas about their people's lore and history, or Rawhunt and Nantaquas, who gave her news of her father's intentions. Gourse names fewer Native individuals and fewer women, but more of the distant English, like Lord de la Warr and Governor Percy. If taken as a statement about the relative importance of groups, this might seem inconsistent with the evident feminist and multiculturalist intentions of the story, but it is completely consistent with the trend in juvenile biographies toward more journalistic accuracy. Gourse is a journalist, writing magazine and newspaper features as well as books, and although this book is fictionalized, she has stopped short of naming the fictional characters. She also slips in occasional details that, while useful for establishing historical perspective, are awkward in context: for instance, Pocahontas must "tell her father how far she had trekked on this bright day in April, 1607" (Gourse 1996, 40), and since the third-person narration is limited to her point of view and she has not yet learned English, her knowledge of the date is anachronistic.

Gourse's tone is somewhat inconsistent, possibly because she has practiced resistant reading on one or more of her main sources. Much of the information she works into her narrative could have come from Grace Steele Woodward's *Pocahontas*, originally published in 1969, widely cited, and reissued in 1995 as part of *Three American Women*. Woodward celebrates Pocahontas as an intelligent and creative individual who rose above her background to negotiate the success of the Jamestown colony, but references to a Powhatan "culture of dark superstitions and devil worship, . . . easy cruelty and primitive social accomplishments" (Woodward 1969, 8) mar her text:

> She rose, surely and dramatically, above the ignorance and savagery of her people, whom the Jamestown colonists termed "naked slaves of the devill." Her story is one of growth—cultural, intellectual, and spiritual (Woodward 1969, 6-7).

Gourse echoes Woodward in suggesting that first Powhatan and later the Virginia Company used Pocahontas as an emissary because of her intelligence, her gift for language, her comfort with different people and her natural poise and dignity. In Gourse's version, the Jamestown elders ask Pocahontas to lobby Virginia Company officials for funds, and it is she, rather than Rolfe, who first hears and accepts the plan. "I'm sure John would like to see his brother in England," she says, and when he comes home, he asks, "What does my wife say?" (Gourse 1996, 142).

Where Gourse most differs from Woodward is in her earnest effort to treat the Powhatan culture with respect. To do so within the conventions of biographical fiction for children, while at the same time honoring Pocahontas for her part in that culture's eventual extinction, requires a difficult balance. Gourse points to the problem in her final paragraph:

> Indians would come to regret that Pocahontas had helped the English to survive, because their endurance spelled the end of Indian rule in North America. But Pocahontas had wanted everyone to live together in peace with respect for one another's cultures and spirits. The goals of Pocahontas still inspire people today (Gourse 1996, 175-176).

Conclusion

An editor's note in Gourse's 1996 *Pocahontas* states that each book in the Childhood of Famous Americans series "is faithful in spirit to the values and experiences that influenced the person's development." Little is known about Pocahontas's life, and much of that little comes from the self-serving record of John Smith, "whose contemporaries often found him insensitive to any negative effects that his self-absorbed behavior had on people" (Rountree 2001, 25) and whose understanding of Algonquian languages and customs was at best partial. It is hard to know how close any of these fictionalized accounts comes to the facts, yet each clearly reflects the values and experiences of its own time.

War-weary children's book editors and librarians in 1946 embraced the idea that children's literature could help advance world peace and demolish prejudice. Less was said about genuine cultural conflict and clashes of interest between peoples, but juvenile biography, like genre fiction, often seems to have functioned as a way of reconciling the irreconcilable. By putting the life of Pocahontas in the foreground, writers were able to celebrate friendship between individuals while masking the nature of the conflict between their nations; both the d'Aulaires and Seymour justified her cooperation with the colonists on the grounds of Powhatan ignorance and mindless adherence to custom.

In 1971, pressure from groups like the Council on Interracial Books for Children was raising the sensitivity of teachers, children's librarians, and publishers to the stereotyping of minority groups. Bulla's writings were said to display "empathy for the special problems of minority groups" (Griese 1971, 774); his 1954 *Squanto, Friend of the White Man*, was highly regarded. Careful not to belittle the intelligence of Powhatan and his councilors, Bulla resolved the story's contradictions by making Pocahontas a tragic figure, snared by her own fatal inability to see beyond her love for Smith to her nation's interests.

By 1996, when Gourse's *Pocahontas* replaced Seymour's in the Childhood of Famous Americans series, children's writers tried hard to avoid sexist as well as racist stereotypes. Gourse's Pocahontas is a strong and intelligent agent, negotiating between her father and Smith, and later between the Jamestown colonists and the Virginia Company. Her father is an admirable, if somewhat romanticized, spokesman for the history and culture of his people; he moves easily from geopolitical strategy to the tender, therapeutic counseling of his daughter: "Pocahontas, tell yourself that the sky is blue, the grass is green, and the rivers run clear, and you can see the fish. Then you will find peace" (Gourse 1996, 106). Whether or not this is an accurate reflection of Powhatan values and experience four hundred years ago, the family dynamics are not fully believable. If Pocahontas and Powhatan are both strong, intelligent, and loving individuals, deeply committed to their people, Pocahontas's motives for supporting the English are hard to explain. Perhaps the inconsistencies can only be resolved by pushing the envelope further, as Allen (2003) has recently done. In her magical *Pocahontas: Medicine Woman, Spy, Entrepreneur, Diplomat*, we see not a traitress, a dupe, or a victim, but a "Beloved Woman," a person of great spiritual power, whose activities advance a new world order foreseen by her people.

In 1990, Beverly Slapin and Doris Seale published the first edition of *Through Indian Eyes*, including an essay on "How to Tell the Difference" between accurate, respectful portrayals of Native lifeways and unacceptable words and pictures that "would embarrass or hurt a Native child" or "foster stereotypical thinking in a non-Indian child" (Slapin and Seale 1998, 179). The d'Aulaires' flippant treatment and Seymour's emphasis on "our custom" as the justification for Powhatan's hostility toward the settlers would be unacceptable by Slapin and Seale's criteria. Bulla's version, although he certainly showed "the ways in which Native peoples actively resisted the invaders," would also be criticized: he was guilty of language that might be construed as "early jawbreaker," and he did not show women "as the integral and respected part of Native societies that they really are."

But even Gourse, careful to avoid negative stereotypes, does not answer one central question satisfactorily: "Are Native heroes only the people who, in some way or another, are believed to have aided Europeans in the conquest of their own people?" Pocahontas has been a heroine for whites, believed to have aided the English against her own people. Public library catalogs list dozens of children's books, films, and other materials about her; in Rhode Island, one of the most commonly held is still the d'Aulaires' *Pocahontas*. By contrast Oyate (2004), a Native organization with an extensive online catalog of educational resources and trade books, lists no Pocahontas books.

Biographies of her add gender balance and cultural diversity to library shelves, and soothe white conscience by implying that peace is obtainable at little cost. The same apparent betrayal that makes her an impossible heroine for her own people makes her a difficult role model for contemporary white children. If she is to be an attractive character, what she did has to be explained and justified; but most of us would not want the justification to be so compelling that our own children would imitate her, trusting the words of strangers over their parents. Fictionalized biographies for children are made to negotiate such tensions between known facts and acceptable interpretations.

In reviewing such biographies, we look for factual accuracy and freedom from stereotyping. We often do this by matching the text to lists of known facts or stereotypical tendencies. Yet even in the most accurate and carefully researched text, the fictional biography's conventional bias toward unified, harmonious interpretations is a bias toward illusion. A consistent narrative is a world of its own, and the selected facts, arranged to create a whole, obscure whatever portion of reality has been omitted. More than any possible stereotypical passage, the genre's conventional bias toward unified, harmonious interpretations works against the young reader's full consciousness that Captain John Smith and his Jamestown colony represented a genuine danger to the Powhatans.

References

Allen, Paula Gunn. 2003. *Pocahontas: Medicine woman, spy, entrepreneur, diplomat.* New York: HarperSanFrancisco.

Andrus, Gertrude. 1946. Review of *Pocahontas, Brave Girl*, by Flora Seymour. *Library Journal* 71 (November 1): 1546.

Anon. 1946. Review of *Pocahontas*, by Ingri and Edgar Parin d'Aulaire. *Booklist* 43 (December 15): 120.

Arbuthnot, May Hill. 1947. *Children and books*. Chicago: Scott, Foresman.

Arbuthnot, May Hill. 1964. *Children and books*. 3rd ed. Glenview, IL: Scott, Foresman.

Bulla, Clyde Robert. 1971. *Pocahontas and the strangers*. Illus. Peter Burchard. New York: Scholastic.

D'Aulaire, Ingri, and Edgar Parin d'Aulaire. 1946. *Pocahontas*. Garden City, New York: Doubleday.

Gleach, Frederic W. 1997. *Powhatan's world and colonial Virginia: A conflict of cultures*. Lincoln: University of Nebraska Press.

Gourse, Leslie. 1996. *Pocahontas: Young peacemaker*. Illus. Meryl Henderson. New York: Aladdin/Simon & Schuster.

Griese, Arnold A. 1971. Clyde Robert Bulla: Master story weaver. *Elementary English* 48 (7): 766-778.

Jennings, Francis. 1975. *The invasion of America: Indians, colonialism, and the cant of conquest*. New York: W. W. Norton & Company.

Jordan, Alice M. 1947. Review of *Pocahontas*, by Ingri and Edgar Parin d'Aulaire. *Horn Book* 23 (1): 34.

Mossiker, Frances. 1976. *Pocahontas: The life and the legend*. New York: Alfred A. Knopf.

Oyate. 2004. Our catalog. www.oyate.org/catalog/index.html.

Rountree, Helen C. 1990. *Pocahontas's people: The Powhatan Indians of Virginia through four centuries*. Norman: University of Oklahoma Press.

Rountree, Helen C. 2001. Pocahontas: The hostage who became famous. In *Sifters: Native American women's lives*, ed. Theda Perdue, 14-28. New York: Oxford University Press.

Seymour, Flora Warren. 1946. *Pocahontas: Brave girl*. Illus. Charles V. John. Indianapolis: Bobbs-Merrill.

Shepherd, Ken. 1998. Powhatan. In *Gale encyclopedia of Native American tribes*, ed. Sharon Malinowski and Anna Sheets, 262-267. Detroit, MI: Gale.

Skinner, Mildred C. 1946. Outstanding picture books, 1946. *Library Journal* 71 (October 15): 1408-1409.

Slapin, Beverly, and Doris Seale. 1998. *Through Indian eyes: The Native experience in books for children*. Los Angeles: American Indian Studies Center.

Sundquist, Åsebrit. 1987. *Pocahontas & Co.: The fictional American Indian woman in nineteenth-century literature; A study of method*. Atlantic Highlands, NJ: Humanities Press International.

Tilton, Robert S. 1994. *Pocahontas: The evolution of an American narrative*. New York: Cambridge University Press.

Webb, Marian. 1946. Review of *Pocahontas*, by Ingri and Edgar Parin d'Aulaire. *Library Journal* 71 (December 1): 1717.

Woodward, Grace Steele. 1969. *Pocahontas*. Norman: University of Oklahoma Press.

Chapter 6

Conclusion:
Dressing the Role Models

Although Elizabeth Tudor's vast wardrobe and pale makeup had stuck in my mind since childhood, I was surprised by how much space the older biographies devoted to them. Elizabeth, I thought, was a special case: a role model no girl ought to imitate too closely. By lavishing attention on her personal presentation, biographers could cover up the omission of more substantive matters. Levin (1994) persuaded me that Elizabeth's self-presentation *was* a substantive matter. For a queen without a large standing army, the appearance of power was essential.

Even then, it did not occur to me that appearances would be a major theme in juvenile biographies of other women. It should have. These books were full of women who loved clothes, women who disdained them, women who longed for what they couldn't afford, women who used fashion as protective coloring, women who changed dress as they moved into new communities, and women whose costumes declared their unique identities, separating them from their communities. And there was an audience of girls, presumed to care deeply about looks and clothing. Consciously or not, authors reached out to readers by emphasizing this interest they shared with biographees.

All of the texts in 1946 and 1971 at least mentioned clothes and appearances, and for the few 1996 texts that did not, illustrations filled the gap. In the older books, subjects or other main characters were usually described by the third page of text, often in fictionalized vignettes that helped readers visualize these women and their world. Descriptions were usually short, and more evocative than detailed. Writers seemed to expect that readers would share their sense of what a long glove or a perky hat could mean.

In the gaps between what was written and what was implied, we see the writers' assumptions about their readers' own knowledge of and interest in fashion. Codes too important to question were barely mentioned; who could doubt that men's and women's clothes were different, or that feminine beauty is to be admired? The author's silence implied the reader's competence and sophisticated complicity in the arrangements of her own time—and to some extent, it created what it implied. The reader was invited to identify with subjects, to experience their pleasure in being admired or their anxiety about being too ugly for acceptance. Imagining herself in the subject's place, smiling, standing up straight, enjoying a new dress or worrying that somebody would notice her shoes, a reader took an easy first step to identifying with and internalizing the subject's values and achievements. Reading these books was like playing a kind of moral and intellectual dress-up.

Interwoven with the theme of dress and appearance was another, less commonly made explicit, which also had deep implications for the experience of identity: the theme of publicity, fame, or celebrity. By 1996, publicity was usually assumed to be desirable, if not for its own sake, then as a tool. But well into the twentieth century, many people considered it shameful for ladies' names to appear in newspapers between their birth announcements and their obituaries. Elizabeth Blackwell suffered when her 1847 entrance into medical school was written up: "Like all nice young ladies, she dreaded such notoriety" (L. Kerr, 1946), and women in the nearby town ostracized her because of it. Certainly there were nineteenth-century women who enjoyed publicity, but more who shrank from it. Even in 1946, women in the aviation industry spoke slightingly of "publicity" and "glamour" as motives for flying (Knapp 1946); and the least sympathetic subject to reviewers that year was Florence Nightingale, who used her celebrity to threaten Lord Panmure with publicity if he did not make reforms.

A biography, however benign and unsensationalized, is still a form of public notice. Few subjects were completely private individuals; almost all had come to the world's attention in their lifetimes, willingly or unwillingly. That fact alone could have made them imperfect role models for girls in the 1940s. To be conspicuous, whether in dress or in the newspapers, set a woman apart; and in the biographies of 1946, a third noticeable theme was the importance of belonging. In a poignant memoir published that year, Ruth Smith tells how conscience had wrenched her from the little Kansas community where she grew up and driven her into the fight against racism. By reaching out to the excluded black minority, she effectively excluded herself from the easy and familiar life of white privilege, and must have been alienated from at least some of her old family and friends. Yet her language shows her deep reluctance to accept divisions. She rarely uses the first person singular, speaking instead as part of a corporate group, one of "we children" or "we Kansans" (Smith 1946). It is not her individual story she wants to tell, but a national story. She wants to be, not prominent—not an outsider—but just another anonymous member of a more inclusive community.

These three themes—clothes, publicity, and community—wove through biographies in 1946, 1971, and 1996. What was said or hinted about them varied from book to book, of course. Subjects differed in their need and tolerance for publicity. Generations differed in their sense of the desirable balance between individual rights and community responsibilities, and authors differed in their sense of what needed to be made explicit. By 1996, many had grown up with the assumption that women had as much responsibility to themselves and their own gifts as to others. Young readers undoubtedly craved belonging as much as ever, but community life had changed and so had the fashions that would help them fit into it.

This last chapter is a reflection on how three generations of books, refracting different images of notable women who are separated from their readers by varying distances in time and space, may offer different kinds of resources for the construction of identity. Reader response theory reminds us that the books themselves cannot determine what meanings their readers will take from them. Anybody who spends time with children and books knows that young readers are capable of unexpected insights and brilliantly creative misunderstandings—and that they come to these books with expectations already formed by family traditions, schools, television, and other media, so they do not find or create their meanings in a vacuum. I have not attempted an empirical study of children's responses to biographies. In this chapter, however, I sketch in a little of the history of fashion—the clothes girl readers wore, the clothes biographees wore, and the contrast between them—as a reminder that many overlapping contexts can affect meaning.

1946: Dreams of Belonging

The biographies of 1946 were about women who had lived in or before the nineteenth century. The girls who first read them had been born and learned to read during the Great Depression and World War II. They knew older women who had once submitted to the constricting fashions of the Edwardian era, with "light, airy dresses" worn over corsets and multiple petticoats designed to mold the body into an "S-shape"—or to the briefly popular hobble skirt, which pinned a wearer's legs together from knee to ankle, so that she could take only tiny steps (Presley 1998; my own grandmother, in her teens, broke her tailbone when she absent-mindedly attempted a high kick in a hobble skirt). But well before these girls were born, hems had risen, waists had loosened, and gently reared ladies had appeared in public wearing the least restrictive clothes West-ern fashion had permitted in centuries. The 1920s had seen the passage of the Nineteenth Amendment, guaranteeing American women the right to vote. They had also seen flappers, beauty pageants, and public bath-ing. By the 1940s, movie star Katherine Hepburn could look aristo-cratic in soft shirts and loosely tailored trousers. The voluminous dresses that elegant ladies had worn less than fifty years earlier now belonged to fantasy; girls could expect to wear such things in real life only on rare occasions—formal dances or weddings—marked off from everyday life.

Indeed, patriotic war brides had worn businesslike little suits in-stead of long white gowns at their weddings. Fabrics had been rationed. Silk and nylon went for parachutes, not stockings. Skirts were cut short and sleek, using only a yard or two of fabric, far from the "more than thirty yards" a lady's skirt took in Scarlett O'Hara's heyday (Knibiehler 1993). Some of the 1946 girl readers, like Ann Richards and Wilma Rudolph—born in 1933 and 1940 respectively—had worn clothes sewn from flour sacks or feed bags (Siegel 1996; Krull 1996). Almost imme-diately after the war, yardages increased, and advertisements showed women at work in their kitchens in dresses with puffed sleeves and bouffant skirts, the impracticality of which paid tribute to the miracu-lous labor-saving devices around them.

Description of the clothes worn by biographical subjects was a familiar literary convention and served more than one function. It was informational; where illustrations were few and sketchy, description could help readers visualize past lives. It was used to evoke character, and of course to elicit reader interest and sympathy for the subject. Pri-mary sources often told what subjects wore and how they (and their acquaintances) felt about it; but at the same time, the authors' own atti-tudes pervaded their accounts, and fashion commentary carried social-izing messages.

This last function was clear in two books of biographical sketches published for girls in 1946, both of which emphasized the femininity of the modern working women they profiled: Knapp's *New Wings for Women* and Stoddard's *Topflight*. Brownmiller (1985, 235) reminded a later generation that, although "a total surrender" to femininity "has stopped women point-blank from major forms of achievement," still, "a judicious concession here and there has been known to work wonders as protective coloration in a man's world and as a means of survival." Girls of the 1940s hardly needed the reminder:

> A Seattle newspaper article warned women not to "go berserk over the new opportunities for masculine clothing and mannish actions." Women workers at the navy yard were told to be "feminine and lady-like, even though you are filling a man's shoes." At Boeing Aircraft, the Women's Recreational Activity Council offered courses in proper dress, makeup, poise, and personality to help women workers maintain their "FQ" (Femininity Quotient) (Colman 1995, 67).

In Canada, personnel manager Ethel Colwell helped design "smarter appearing, more practical work outfits" for women in the aviation industry, where the "miscellany of female work clothing being worn" was often "impractical and dangerous" (Knapp 1946, 124). Safety may have been the primary concern, but femininity was served by making even utilitarian overalls look more stylish.

The balance between women's capacity to do men's work and their unruffled femininity was a recurring strand in *Topflight* and *New Wings*. Unlike the year's full-length biographies, these were more journalistic than fictionalized. Knapp built each *New Wings* sketch around an interview with a woman in some branch of the aeronautics industry; *Topflight* included profiles of women in more varied careers. Intended to give girls "inspiration and many helpful suggestions" for careers that were relatively new to women, both books "faithfully set forth the difficulties of achievement as well as its rewards" (Stoddard 1946, viii).

Writers and interviewees repeatedly mentioned feminine tact as a way of overcoming difficulties, and quick descriptions that introduced characters generally paid homage to their femininity: novelist Alice Tisdale Hobart, for instance, had "silvery hair . . . under a smart little hat" and "clothes characteristically expressive of a certain odd blend of sophistication and unspoiled simplicity" (Nourse 1946, 111). Authors often accentuated the contrast, either between a subject's inner strength and outward fragility, or between low expectations of her as a woman and her impressive competency in a man's work. Margaret Bourke-White, "this slip of a girl," had dared blast furnaces and bombarded rooftops to shoot her dramatic photographs (Raymond 1946, 169). Aviators were especially poised and charming in the face of heavy work, masculine opposition, and danger; one test pilot, after bailing out of a burning Hellcat, went to a party "just as calm" as if she did it every day (Knapp 1946).

In these twentieth-century vignettes, feminine delicacy was camouflage. Girl readers were shown that women should look smart and wear their trim uniforms with grace. Their eyes should twinkle with friendly laughter; their voices should be low, their manners unassuming. They should set the people around them at ease. But all these genuine charms should merely sheathe a woman's deeper strength and potential for heroism. Women should be modest, but capable of anything, and authors relished anecdotes in which petite heroines succeeded at man-sized tasks and amazed their detractors. Such stories afforded a romantic enjoyment of disguise and revelation, a pleasure in the suddenly discovered capabilities of the underrated.

The year's full-length individual biographies featured mostly middle class nineteenth-century women. Poor women of the time made do with scantier dress; Little Nell's worn shoes and thin clothes exposed her to cold and damp. For subjects like Nightingale and Potter, born into prosperous families, work outside the home was considered unthinkable, and if elaborate clothes limited their range of motion, that seemed too normal to require comment. Others, like Madison and Greenaway, might need to contribute to household finances, but through genteel occupations; they did not wear slacks and tunic, like a woman coal miner (Higonnet 1993, [293]).

Nineteenth-century ladies' fashions were famously unhealthy and uncomfortable, good for little but to enforce the era's ideal of feminine submissiveness. In the first half of the century, a stylish costume could weigh upwards of thirty pounds—the later hoops and crinolines, substituted for padding, actually lightened the load. Tight-laced corsets impaired women's circulation, digestion, and breathing, and long skirts trailed on the filthy streets, collecting dirt and germs (Torrens 1997). George Sand rebelled by simply adopting men's clothing. Others called for reform of women's dress, trying to disarm criticism by modeling their new fashions after children's or Turkish women's clothes rather than men's. In the United States alone, these included "women's rights activists, Seventh-Day Adventists, hydropathists or water-cure doctors, health reformers, members of the National Dress Reform Association (NDRA), Strangite Mormons, and utopian communities" like the Oneida Perfectionists (Fischer 1997). In France, an 1832 engraving mocked a woman follower of Saint-Simon in a short skirt over dainty pantalettes (Higonnet 1993, 270); in 1851, United States feminists drew national derision when they tried to popularize a similar costume (Fischer 1997; Torrens 1997).

In girls' biographies, however, the physical inconvenience of ladies' clothes was rarely discussed. The subjects were not dress reformers, but pioneering workers who had made their names in occupations previously barred to women, and some at least had felt the best hope of success lay in being inconspicuous. Elizabeth Blackwell was typical in her disapproval of "women fanatics . . . wearing trousers as they traveled about the country crying 'Votes for women!'" (L. Kerr 1946, 176)

The books did allude frequently to the ways in which dress signaled a woman's place in her world. Madeleine de Verchères, the appealing aristocrat who in 1692 successfully defended her family's fort against a week-long Mohawk siege, first appeared in "Indian moccasins and a skirt of coarse homespun woolen no better than that worn by the poorest girls in New France" (E. Brill 1946, 2). Even in their parents' absence, however, fourteen-year-old Madeleine made her two younger brothers dress for dinner, confirming and communicating their identity as aristocrats. They lived "in a wild new country," and Indian wars had disrupted trade with "Old France"; but seigneurs like Madeleine's father treasured old ways along with their old tablecloths and threadbare jackets. The shabby finery symbolized pride, responsibility, authority, and courage rather than economic prosperity; it set the de Verchères apart from both the Indians and the peasant *habitants*. When the Indians captured almost all the settlement's men, Madeleine had only her brothers and an elderly retainer to help protect the women and children. She used a soldier's hat both symbolically (to assert her leadership) and instrumentally (held above the stockade on a stick, to check for the presence of snipers). Yielding both hat and command when the siege lifted, she resumed her customary place in the world she had defended.

Dolly Madison and Pocahontas, subjects of two books each in 1946, married out of their birth communities; and for each, the transition from one community to another was clearly signaled by a change of dress as well as name. Pocahontas "was dressed all in white, like an English girl," for her baptism as Rebecca (Seymour 1946, 164); later, going to England with John Rolfe and their baby, "she [seemed] in every way like an English wife and mother" (167). The young Dolly Payne's transformation from Quaker to First Lady also involved a cultural discontinuity. As a girl, she craved bright colors and vain ornaments forbidden by her religion; she was dressed to communicate her family's faith. Desmond (1946) and Morgan (1946) both used an anecdote about her loss of a secretly treasured bauble to underline her difficulty in conforming. In marrying James Madison, she cut herself off from her church and stepped into a role that required her to shop. Much as she enjoyed her Empire gowns and colorful turbans, they reflected more than personal taste. As wife of Jefferson's Secretary of State, and later as First Lady, she dressed to communicate a new nation's power and sophistication.

The books on pioneering workers showed that they, too, made fashion decisions to reflect and reinforce their community standing. Nineteenth-century society had settled what prosperous wives and daughters should wear, but professional women were a new category. Professionalization itself was new—the professional occupations were not, but to practice them now required credentials and formal education, so that in some cases women were disqualified from jobs they had traditionally done. Higonnet (1993, 253) notes that "women in the artisan classes had worked for centuries in family workshops," learning their skills at home; "the onset of capitalism" forced women "to enter a public labor market and apply for jobs their mothers and grandmothers had inconspicuously inherited." Ulrich (1990) documents the displacement of midwives by doctors early in the late eighteenth and early nineteenth centuries. Nineteenth-century women who entered professions or lectured in public often seem to have aimed for a dignified plainness in dress; their economic situations may have enforced the plainness, but they also may have hoped, by their modesty, to avoid challenging male egos or attracting ridicule. Leading feminists quickly retreated from dress reform when the Bloomer costume was used to discredit their political objectives.

Kerr's use of description in her portrait of Blackwell was in many ways typical. Blackwell dressed plainly. Setting off to teach and save money for medical school, she refused to pack her lavender bonnet because it was "too fancy" (L. Kerr 1946, 66). She wore basic black for her medical school graduation and to a party in London, where she felt "quite self-conscious among the shining ball costumes" (105). But Kerr emphasized her good looks, and the possibility that she could have married. A boy at her New York City clinic was surprised to find that she was the "lady doctor":

> "You are?" he cried. "But you can't be, ma'am. I thought you'd have your hair cut like a man—I thought—"
>
> Elizabeth laughed good-naturedly. "No," she said. "I manage to look pretty much like other women. What can I do for you?" (L. Kerr 1946, 141)

The tone recalls the year's sketches of woman pilots: an understated pride in the ability to accomplish things and still retain one's femininity. The lurking suggestion that a professional woman must take care not to be seen as a sort of masculine monster was real, even in the twentieth century; Kerr hardly needed to explain it, but her dismissive treatment implied that it was a delusion of unschooled boys, a thing of the past.

Kerr portrayed Blackwell as a woman who sacrificed her chances of love and her feminine sensibilities to pursue a mission. This was the usual story told of Florence Nightingale, until Strachey (1918) undermined it by claiming that Nightingale only sacrificed what she disliked and did what pleased her. She was unable to escape a life of long, leisurely dressing rituals, visits, balls, and chaperoned travel until the age of thirty-two. Even after she won her father's reluctant support for her career plan, her mother and sister were opposed to it with a violence that bordered on hysteria (Huxley 1975). The intensity of their feeling suggests the "horror or visceral intolerance" which, according to Bourdieu, is provoked by "the tastes of others . . . because each taste feels itself to be natural" and rejects "others as unnatural and therefore vicious" (Bourdieu 1984, 56).

It is natural to accept the values of one's family and peers—attributing to the rules of one's social milieu almost the same inevitability as the laws of nature. As a socialite, Nightingale wore Parisian fashions that would have made heavy labor virtually impossible; such clothes, accepted as natural, made work unnatural. As a nurse, she adopted "unadorned, extremely simple" dress (Nolan 1946, 158). Her new costume, although constructed with less art than her old, may have seemed unnatural to her family because it called into question tastes and ethics that lay at the foundation of their social world. The "unnaturalness" of Nightingale's life seemed problematic in Nolan's account, not only because Nightingale did not marry, but because she was alienated from her family. Nolan, who must have disliked family dissension, treated their battles with an understatement that made Florence's rejection of them appear unfair—and then questioned whether Florence "perhaps . . . had not in her nature the longing for affection and warm personal relationships which most women know" (1946, 168-169). The tone was heavily ironic.

Irony has been called "a sophisticated form of hostility" (Hutch 1997), and juvenile biography, like juvenile fiction, is normally a sympathetic genre. Schwenke Wyile (1999; 2001) has shown how the relationship between narrator and focalizing character can be manipulated to engage or ironically distance readers of juvenile fiction; the mechanism is the same in biography. Irony opens up a distance between narrator and subject, so that the subject becomes, not the focus through which a reader is encouraged to view the world, but rather the focus of the reader's critical gaze. Nolan's tone stripped Nightingale of sympathy, leaving her bare to cold admiration; the deviation from genre standards echoed Nightingale's own deviation from social norms.

Blackwell and Nightingale were forced by their work to appear in public—to maintain dignity in the face of hostility and derision—in an era when women were supposed to live private lives. Nightingale, in the end, became a recluse. So did Emily Dickinson, whose white dresses seemed to reinforce her withdrawal from society; Gould (1946), a friendlier biographer than Nolan, did not emphasize what Dickinson's privacy cost others.

The year's latest-born subjects, illustrators Kate Greenaway and Beatrix Potter, also had reclusive tendencies; Greenaway was painfully shy, and Potter, although she became a tough businesswoman, always guarded her privacy. Their avoidance of the public arena was convenient in subjects for juvenile biography in 1946, when women were asked to leave the factory for the kitchen; both Greenaway and Potter created small worlds, private shelters for the imagination, and the clothes they drew figured more prominently in their biographies than the clothes they wore. Children in Greenaway's pictures dressed unfashionably in shepherd smocks and high-waisted gowns, eighteenth- and early nineteenth-century styles that lingered, in country districts, into her childhood. Her Valentines and books made her style suddenly popular in the nurseries of Europe and America; the French called it "*Greenawisme*" (Newcomb 1946, 86). Her pastoral landscape was sweet and orderly, unthreatening, always under control.

Superficially, Beatrix Potter had much in common with Greenaway; she too wrote and illustrated small books that became great nursery favorites. But Potter's imaginary world was never so tame as Greenaway's. True, she painted clothes with loving patience (the elegant embroideries in *The Tailor of Gloucester* were copied from museum pieces); but she also drew animals with a lively expertise based on years of sketching pet mice and lizards. From Peter Rabbit's first popped buttons, the clothes were subject to loss and damage, as their wearers were prey to angry farmers, hungry owls, and tricky foxes. Potter's vision was not so much pastoral as comic, with order menaced, disrupted, and restored.

Her own life, for many years, was uneventful. She was stranded in wealthy but neglected childhood until her midthirties; rather like Nightingale a generation earlier, she longed for education and work but was blocked by her family. Her efforts to teach herself scientific illustration and produce a book on fungus were disappointed, and her grief at the death of her first fiancé, publisher Norman Warne, could not even be mentioned at home in the face of her parents' disapproval. In Lane's reticent account, her very clothes symbolized captivity:

> She submitted patiently to the starching and brushing and tying up with ribbons, the lacing of boots and the carrying of muffs, which was a part of well-to-do childhood. . . . It was something to escape from, when one should be old enough, a part of that stagnant life which went on in the drawing-room. . . (Lane 1946, 17).

She escaped only when the unexpected success of her books made her financially independent, so she could buy her own land, live apart from her parents, and meet people. Married at forty-seven, she spent thirty contented years as Mrs. Heelis of Sawrey, a farmer and a respected sheeptrader. The books ceased. Her eyes were no longer good enough for watercolor miniatures, but perhaps more important, she no longer needed to create and dominate an imaginary world, having finally achieved a satisfactory share in the control of her own. In old age, wearing "her usual rag-bag attire with a sack on her head and shoulders" while tending lambs in a storm, Mrs. Heelis was amused to be taken for a tramp (157). Like Peter, she had wriggled out of bourgeois constraints to become completely herself. Lane's narration kept a certain amiable distance, respecting Potter's privacy; the irony was lighter than Nolan's, however, and never turned against the subject.

Lane used clothes to evoke the repression of Potter's girlhood and the liberation of her old age, but there was little in this crop of books to connect fashion constraints with the repression of women in general. In Harper's partial biography of her grandmother, Martha Jane St. Clair developed fashion sense as she came of age and found her role in life. At fifteen, she moved with her family to Punxsutawney, where they ran an inn. To her chagrin, she made her "first appearance" there in an old dress and "horrid stout shoes." She was the oldest daughter in a large family—her mother's adjunct, a dependable sewer-on of her brothers' buttons and darner of her sisters' stockings. But she had one wildly impractical dream, inspired by a circus rider who stayed at the inn. She longed to ride a white horse while wearing a red silk dress, "only three or four inches below her knees," with matching pantalettes. She found just the right pattern while poring over an 1851 issue of *Godey's Lady's Book* with her friend Jennie Campbell. Harper did not mention Amelia Bloomer's attempt to popularize Turkish trousers that year, nor did she say much about the outlandishness of a circus rider as a fashion ideal for a good middle-class girl. Jennie, Martha Jane's sole confidante, was scandalized by the color alone:

> Why, Martha Jane St. Clair! Red! Of course you would look beautiful
> in it, with your fair skin—I don't know why mine won't be fair! But
> red might be rather—rather— You'd have a brightish red? (Harper
> 1946, 39)

Jennie promised not to tell, and Martha saved her money. She would
need at least six yards of silk, and the price of silk rose to three dollars
a yard; Martha Jane never managed more than ten dollars at a time. It
was impossible, and not only because of the money.

Dress tied Martha Jane securely to her community. It was a major
part of her work and her social life; she and her friends socialized over
their mending. They admired one another's clothes, appreciating both
craft and fashion, but their important audience was male: Jennie, imagining a "perfectly celestial" dress, explained that it would make a handsome man fall in love with her.

Martha Jane knew the dress code. Still, she misconstrued it at least
once. The new school teacher awarded her a locket as a recitation prize;
but when she wore it to a dance, he frightened her with arrogant inti-
macies, claiming she had led him to expect a warmer welcome. Only
then did she remember her mother's words: "No lady accepts jewelry
from a man she's not engaged to." She fled the dance in terror, and her
father removed her from school for the rest of the year (82-83).

Conway (1998, 40), tracing "the romantic life plot" in nineteenth-
and twentieth-century autobiographies, said that the romantic heroine
was "essentially passive, someone acted upon rather than her own
agent." Martha Jane actively conformed herself to womanly ideals.
Early on, she thought, "I hate being the oldest daughter. I have to give
up everything to everybody!" (Harper 1946, 18). She joined the church
to subdue her inner rebellion: "I want to quit being angry at the children
and rebellious at Father and Mother, and quit being afraid and quit hat-
ing" (97-98). She loved Jennie's brother George, but made no direct
effort to capture his attention. Yet, she took moral action repeatedly,
risking her beauty to nurse an immigrant family through smallpox and
using her silk money to serve the needs of others.

Jennie betrayed her friend's longing for red silk to George, of all
people: "For all she's been baptized and is maybe going to be a teacher
to the heathen, Martha Jane's not so demure as you'd think, George"
(126). In spite of this or because of it, George fell in love, waited years
for her father's consent, and married her in the end. Her bridal gown
and trousseau were prepared in a triumphant communal frenzy of dress-
making. Better yet, George gave her a white colt, and her new in-laws

added a riding habit of dark red wool, its lining and fitted jacket of bright red silk.

Harper didn't use the word "compromise," but the riding habit was a brilliant one. Its conventionally fashionable lines hinted at neither the circus nor the feminists. It was a costume Martha Jane could actually wear in public, in the real world. But that red silk expressed her new family's affection for Martha Jane, the dreamer, not so demure as she appeared; it seemed to promise a life within which she could become fully herself, while at the same time being integrated into a healthy community. Martha Jane was not yet so self-assured as the women pilots of 1946, who played femininity like a game; but, like them, she was assimilating her society's codes, accommodating herself to her assigned role, and finding ways to enjoy the process. To a generation of second-wave feminists, her willing accommodation would seem problematic. In 1946, it still seemed natural and healthy. Martha Jane, although merely a private individual, shared essential virtues with the year's other subjects: modesty, moral strength, and a commitment to others. The reader who identified with her was encouraged to regard self-interest as a temptation and to engage responsibly in communal life.

1971: Insecure Liberations

Twenty-five years later, juvenile biographies were still narrative, still as a rule friendly to their subjects, and still not very likely to question the dress code. None of the twenty-six books failed to mention its subject's looks and her clothes, although a few put off the description until after the first chapter. On the surface, little had changed; but overall, these books did not convey the same confident feeling that femininity was a harmless game. A new generation of active feminists was questioning gender expectations long taken for granted.

Even grandmothers in 1971 wore knee-length skirts. For teenagers and younger women, the Sears catalogue advertised miniskirts, polyester tunic-and-pants sets, and ankle-length ruffled peasant skirts (Causey 2004); the stylized body language of models, even when wearing ankle-length dresses, suggested athleticism and physical freedom. Barbie dolls had their own bellbottoms, fur collars, disco boots, and peasant dresses (Doll reference 2004). What most girls wore, much of the time, were blue jeans and t-shirts. Girls in 1971 were more likely to see the fashions of previous generations on television than to find them moldering in attic trunks.

Television was a major force in 1971, and certainly had the power to influence young people's identity formation. Commercialized images of beauty in movies and magazines were nothing new. Martha Jane Sinclair and Jennie Campbell, in 1851, had dreamed of making themselves over to match the glamorous images in *Godey's Lady's Book*. But the small screen was a daily presence, bringing celebrities into the intimacy of almost everybody's living room. If nothing else, it drew the gaze, and while girls watched its flickering surface, they were not looking at family or friends or neighbors—at living people who could respond to them.

In the quest for beauty, as Brumberg (1997) points out, girls now relied on diet and exercise to sculpt themselves into the proper shape. The proper shape was emaciated, so control of the body was in some ways more tyrannical than in the days of whalebone corsets: "in 1967 a teenage British model named Twiggy, ninety-two pounds on a five-foot-seven-inch frame, with no breasts and hips to speak of, was promoted as the body type" all women should desire (Brownmiller 1984, 48). Clothes exposed imperfections. Naomi Wolf (1997, 39) recalls the anxieties of adolescence in the San Francisco Bay area between 1968 and 1971, when she and her friends tried to negotiate how much midriff they had to bare in order to fit in without looking "slutty," or "what was just naked enough and what was too naked."

The year's biographies were not obviously influenced by either television or the quest for beauty. They were in some ways more daring than either the 1946 or the 1996 books. Subjects included women who not only divorced, practiced free love, and gave birth out of wedlock, but also developed and defended radically challenging ideas. There were substantive treatments of anarchist Emma Goldman, who taught birth control, conspired to assassinate the chairman of the Carnegie Steel Company (the attempt was unsuccessful), and after foreswearing violence was finally deported for draft protests in 1918; of the Pankhursts, who used every weapon from tea parties to rock-throwing to hunger strikes in the fight for women's suffrage; and of Ida Tarbell, whose documentation of the rise of Standard Oil and John D. Rockefeller's business practices led to the passage of antitrust laws. These were serious books, imbued with the social conscience of the late 1960s and early 1970s, and they were not meant to be about appearances. Yet the descriptions, most of them brief, hinted at a growing insecurity about looks, even as several of the books showed a new openness in discussing the uses of publicity.

In many of the 1971 biographies, subjects' complexions and sizes were described before clothes. In one fictionalized opening scene, a night watchman announced the loss of a two-year-old girl with "Blue eyes! Rosy cheeks! Light-brown hair" (Bobbé 1971, 5); in another, an artistic girl painted her own "wide-apart gray eyes" and "rather large nose" but could not get "the total effect" right (Wilson 1971, 4). Shulman, who did not fictionalize her account of Goldman's childhood, noted that her "blue eyes and blonde hair" were "so unusual in a Jewish child"—and so unlike her parents—that her father twitted her with not being his daughter (Shulman 1971, 2).

Being lost, being unable to draw one's own face, not fitting into a family—all three introductions associate looks with at least minor insecurity. The year's biographees (with rare exceptions like Empress Josephine, Emmeline and Christabel Pankhurst, and Maria Tallchief) were not famous beauties. In the lives of women like Susan B. Anthony and Golda Meir, beauty hardly seemed to be the point. But over and over again, we read that they were pretty:

> To her surprise, Nellie Bly found Emma no wild terrorist or seductress but a pretty, intelligent woman without a trace of frivolity. "She sacrifices her looks for books," wrote Nellie Bly, amazed (Shulman 1971, 97).

Nellie Bly herself was "a pretty girl, about five feet five inches tall, with brown hair and brown eyes" (Graves 1971, 13) and a famous smile; when she investigated marriage agencies by pretending to look for a husband, the agent was surprised to hear that "such a pretty girl" needed his help (52). Marie Curie, who "had always thought she was plain," turned "into a lovely young woman with delicate features framed by a halo of unruly yellow curls" (McKown 1971, 11). Golda Meir at fourteen was "a lovely girl with clear, fair skin, naturally curly chestnut hair, and deep-set, clear gray eyes" (Morris 1971, 15); "when she smiled," her "firm, almost stern look was replaced by a joyful sweetness" (Mann 1971, 40).

Passages on the subjects' prettiness, and their shyness or insecurity about their looks, seemed to court the sympathy of girl readers, who by implication were insecure about their own looks. These heroines were attractive, but not threateningly beautiful; girl readers could easily want to be like them, or to have them as friends:

> Pablita was a slender, bright-eyed, young woman with shiny, black hair and a pretty, wide smile. She liked to laugh and to talk with her friends, but in a group she was shy (Nelson 1971, 34-35).

Often it was the subject's smile that was "pretty," and phrasing echoed the kind of faint praise that had likely failed to reassure many girl readers about their own looks. Jane Addams, for instance, "feared that she was ugly" because she was small, thin, and "had been born with a curve in her back"; people "who saw her . . . friendly smile" called her pretty, "but she didn't believe them" (G. Keller 1971, 7).

The insecurity of biographical subjects had less to do with their actual looks than with the friendliness of their beholders. The family of Mary Anne Evans (later known as George Eliot) thought her distressingly "plain," "awkward," "dowdy," or even "freakish" (Vipont 1971, 18, 31); her legendary ugliness shadowed her development as a woman, and was a major theme in Vipont's biography. Yet in photographs she appears no homelier than Julia Dent (later Mrs. Ulysses S. Grant), whose father called her "the prettiest girl in Missouri" in spite of her plain features and crossed eye (Fleming 1971a, 9). Dent grew up as a good-natured, self-confident charmer, and became a popular First Lady. A century later, Betty Marie Tallchief considered herself "so plain," "too fat," and—worst of all—"not Russian" (De Leeuw 1971, 37); she was later known as "a great beauty" (135). Standards of beauty were not absolute, but rose from the intersubjective judgments of a community; for a girl, to be lovely (or at least pretty) was to be accepted.

In 1971, many girls' biographies—even the lives of women of color—took blond, blue-eyed norms of beauty for granted. Tallchief's early insecurity may have been at least partly racial; she was not only an aspiring dancer, trying to starve and exercise her body into an approved mold, but also half Osage, making her way in an art dominated by blondes. By referring to them not as white women but as Russians—a specialized group, dominant in the world of ballet but not in all of society—De Leeuw de-emphasized the racial context. Charlotte Forten, like Jane Addams, worried about her looks, and Douty's biography hit the same note of not-quite-believable encouragement:

> When she was happy like this, with shining eyes and face alight with a smile, people said that Charlotte Forten was really quite pretty, especially since her slender figure was graceful, and she held herself straight and proud (Douty 1971, 33).

But Forten, an African American woman at a white school in Massachusetts before the Civil War, had "adopted white standards for beauty that caused her to think of herself as unattractive when by all accounts she was a pretty woman" (Stevenson 1988, 33). Her loneliness and insecurity, like George Eliot's, were reinforced by the aesthetic standards of those around her, and like Eliot, she responded by persistently developing her character and intellect to achieve a more meaningful inner beauty. Although Douty (who based her book on Forten's journals) is sensitive to all this, she presents it as an individual rather than as a general problem.

These books meant well. Biographies had more multicultural subjects, and there were fewer in which people of color figured only as stereotyped foils to benevolent whites. But writers had not internalized diverse standards of beauty. Fuller (1971, 19) described the fifteen-year-old daughter of Phillis Wheatley's new owner as blond and "extremely pretty"; Phillis herself merely grew "healthy" in the Wheatleys' care, with a "dark complexion . . . as smooth as a chestnut shell" (18). Later, at a party in England, she was granted a qualified beauty:

> Phillis astounded and charmed all the guests with her honest and humble manner. She looked beautiful in a cream-colored gown that complemented her dark skin (Fuller 1971, 53).

Both beauty and acceptance were aided by humility; Wheatley did not stridently object to what Fuller called her "heritage of slavery."

The year's biographical subjects were also diverse in class, and for some, clothing was labor. Susan B. Anthony had a taste of it at the age of twelve, substituting for a sick worker in her father's textile mill (Peterson 1971). Goldman worked a long series of grueling subsistence jobs, including several in corset factories, a glove factory, and an overcoat factory; did piecework at home knitting shawls and sewing blouses; and, while in jail, ran the prison sewing shop (Shulman 1971). Compared to Martha Jane's hectic but social domestic labor, factory jobs were demeaning and ill-paid, and working women themselves were often poorly dressed. Golda Meir struggled throughout most of her life. When she was in her teens, she went to live with her sister, who made three significant promises:

> First, you'll have all the opportunities to study; second, you'll have plenty to eat; third, you'll have the necessary clothes that a person ought to have (Mann 1971, 38).

In the 1930s she had "only two dresses," one to wear while the other was in the wash, and buying a new "dress or a blouse constituted a problem which could not easily be solved" (Mann 1971, 93). Like the image of Abraham Lincoln splitting rails, the image of Meir's frugality was part of her political iconography.

In two partial biographies of girls who witnessed major eighteenth-century events, description of clothing contributed to historical scene-setting. Biographers of Anne MacVicar and Patsy Jefferson focused attention on what they saw more than how they looked. MacVicar, the child of a British soldier in the French and Indian War, catalogued the populations she encountered. English colonists in Carolina dressed "in silks or velvets if well off, in homespun if not" (Bobbé 1971, 10); her first Indian was "tall, half-naked and copper-skinned," with feathers in his hair, bands on his arms, and "fringed soft leather" on his legs (11); French *voyageurs* wore "gaudy shirts" (59); and the children of Dutch colonists in upstate New York were "bunchy," with their quilted bonnets, layered skirts, and breeches that looked "*stuffed*" (16-17). Allies signaled loyalty by adopting articles of each other's costume: the Mohawk King Hendrick's "light-blue coat with silver buttons" was a gift of the British king (42), while Sir William Johnson's "Indian fringed tunic and leggings" (47) betokened his Indian sympathies. Anne observed it all, and used costume as one index to the way communities worked.

For Patsy Jefferson, too, clothes served as an accessible code, supplementing her father's talk and allowing her to glimpse the way things worked in France. She was quick to notice the Marquise de Lafayette's simple "dark silk dress with a lace fichu" (Kelly 1971, 35) and the iconic "white and gold silk brocade" of the queen, who looked "so sweet and pure" that Patsy could hardly believe "the tales about her" (88). Clothes could suggest innocence (Patsy saw nuns taking the veil; 46), or its opposite (Abigail Adams was shocked by the "bold" costumes of dancers, "made of the thinnest gauze and with such short petticoats" that high jumps revealed "their garters and undergarments"; 61). Clothes could indicate a place in the hierarchy, like Patsy's school uniform of "rich red silk" (50), or the "waistcoats of cloth of gold, heavily plumed hats," and wide gold bands worn by nobility in meeting in the Estates General (107). They could, like the tricolor in a hat, be the "symbol of revolution" (127). But throughout the book, Jefferson warned his daughter against confidence in appearances. Marie Antoinette was not so innocent as she looked.

Neither was Josephine Bonaparte; but Mossiker (1971), author of a more probing look at the Bonaparte marriage for adults, veiled her faults in this juvenile biography. Here, description served primarily to enlist sympathy for Bonaparte and to display her as an alluring image. She was a plump teenager whose first husband found her "neither grand enough nor elegant enough" to socialize with his friends (Mossiker 1971, 38); but she developed into "the slender, sleek and shapely, the exquisite and graceful creature" (45) who captivated Napoleon. At her coronation, "resplendent in diamonds," she wore "a diamond bandeau in her hair" and "a gown and court cape of white satin embroidered in gold and silver," and didn't look older than twenty-five (Mossiker 1971, 110).

Josephine's story ended in sorrow; but until the last act, Mossiker shaped it into a fairy tale, shining with the promise of love and security. The structure of the biography—a near-static series of beautiful, tragic tableaux—intensified the effect, focusing reader attention on the heroine's individual qualities and blurring her social and historical context. The black and white drawings, too, were almost without background. The biographies of MacVicar and Jefferson prompted to readers to identify with the protagonists and explore the world through their observant eyes; the biography of Josephine encouraged readers to identify with the protagonist and to gaze at her mirrored self, almost as if the purpose of the world was to provide a setting for her glamour.

Josephine was portrayed as an image to be seen—what Wolf would call a "Barbie," whose "life force consisted of a filled suitcase." Barbie was static; there was a limit to what you could play with a doll whose character was defined only by her image, but the image swayed girls' aspirations. Wolf suggests the limits of biographical subjects as role models: "Between a sexless Marie Curie and a hot-pink Barbie or Brandi or Kiki, even with the ambivalence we felt about their sexiness and thus about our own, there was no contest" (Wolf 1997, 16-17); girls wanted to be Barbie.

Barbies, however, were rare in these books; most subjects were actively engaged in their worlds, and few stood still long enough to become icons. Marie Curie, not so sexless as Wolf imagined, "shunned publicity as though it were a disease" (McKown 1971, 77); her protective students hid her from reporters at the Sorbonne (62-64). McKown did not mention it, but after Pierre Curie's death, Marie was vilified in the press for her affair with a fellow scientist, Paul Langevin, who was married (Quinn 1995). McKown (1971) did refer to Langevin more than once, and acknowledged interviews with his son, daughter-in-law, and granddaughter; but she said nothing about the affair. Instead, she introduced the bride who wore a "sensible navy blue suit" because it could be worn again later (31); the woman who owned just a single evening dress and whose daughters had to insist on her buying new clothes for a tour of America; the "unobtrusive, middle-aged woman with the work-worn hands" (69). This was a carefully constructed image, a shield against the hostile gaze of the French press; and it was important because, in spite of everything, Curie needed publicity for her work. Wolf and her friends, agonizing over how to be just naked enough and not too naked, might have understood Curie's predicament, if they'd ever suspected she had one. They didn't. Curie's biographies, like her plain dark clothes, functioned as protective coloring.

For other subjects, too, unobtrusive fashions were a defense. In 1851, when mobs heckled Elizabeth Cady Stanton, Susan B. Anthony, and Lucy Stone for wearing bloomers in public, women were not even supposed to speak in public; the costume merely compounded their offense (Faber 1971; Peterson, 1971). Subsequent reformers usually dressed to be inconspicuous. Elizabeth Blackwell lectured in "a plain but well-tailored, dark dress," and maintained a "dignified and kindly" manner (Heyn 1971, 57); Jane Addams wore a "freshly ironed, frilly blouse with a high collar and a smooth woolen skirt to her ankles the way rich ladies of the time did" (G. Keller 1971, 27). Golda Meir's immigrant father announced, "In America, young lady, you will dress like everyone else!" (Mann 1971, 24). For Mary Cassatt, even high fashion could be camouflage: as her sister Lydia advised, "It's more conspicuous to be different than to follow the trend" (Myers 1971, 10).

The appearance of normal femininity underscored women's solid connections with their communities, and might make it a little harder for opponents to isolate them from public sympathy. Thus Nellie Bly, covering a National Woman's Suffrage Convention, excoriated many of the delegates for their deficiencies in dress:

> I never could see any reason for a woman to neglect her appearance merely because she is intellectually inclined. It certainly does not show any strength of mind. I take it rather as a weakness. And in working for a cause I think it is wise to show the men that its influence does not make women any the less attractive (quoted in Kroeger 1994, 282-283).

Unmarried and widely considered homely, Susan B. Anthony had little defense when the press "sneered at her appearance," calling her "an angular, sour old maid," and warning, "If all woman's righters look like that, the theory will lose ground." She simply had to ignore the insults, bear herself "with dignity," and dress conservatively in "a dark silk gown with a collar of white lace" (Peterson 1971, 65-66).

Emmeline Pankhurst, by contrast, had unusual advantages. She was a widow who, like Curie, was carrying on the work of a loving and beloved husband. She was the mother of four. And she was beautiful. Noble (1971) emphasizes her willingness to use beauty for strategic effect in the campaign for suffrage. Emmeline, "in her cultured and ladylike voice," would introduce herself as "a hooligan" (120); or she would place herself on a stage between a young cotton-mill worker and a stout, bustling working-class woman so that every woman "in the audience could identify with one or the other on the platform" and "feel that this was her crusade" (54). Emmeline's hunger strikes in jail were made effective by the incongruity between jail itself and her elegant fragility; and she delighted in the way her looks confounded people's expectations of suffrage workers:

"What do you expect?" she would ask them as they admired her dress or told her she was beautiful. "A frump? Some old creature who is doing this work because her mind is twisted?" (Noble 1971, 73).

Of course, that was the image feminists had to combat.

In the biographies of 1946, fine clothes and feminine daintiness often seemed to be a game, a transparent disguise for womanly strength. Now, several books hinted that femininity was more than a game—that it was a tool, like Bly's million-dollar smile that charmed a millionaire (Graves 1971), or a necessary concession, a way to deflect attention so that serious work could be done. In telling the story of Shirley Chisholm, however, Nancy Hicks recaptured some of the old playfulness. Chisholm, the first African American woman elected to the United States Congress, "attractive without being pretty" and "always immaculately groomed" (Hicks 1971, 11), was a small woman, and Hicks repeatedly contrasted her looks to her character:

To look at her you might think she is a nice librarian. . . . Do not be fooled! (11).

Who was this small, frail woman with the big mouth? (78).

So Shirley Chisholm rose and went to the microphone, very composed, very quiet. She was wearing a white dress and looked angelic, more like a schoolteacher than a political power (113).

Chisholm needed that mouth. She had to brave more than one hostile audience, and she did so with courage, wit, and a strong awareness of her own role as "a historical person at this point" (19).

Hicks, a *New York Times* reporter, focused on Chisholm's public image, skimming over her childhood with its hand-me-downs and home-sewn clothes, and quickly arriving at her newsworthy career. Her outfits were described as they would be in a newspaper: her "dramatic black-and-white cape and the high spiked heels she never tired of," her "green knit suit and her ever-present high heels" (74), her "blue brocade dress with a little jacket" (116).

But Chisholm was no Barbie doll. Her ensembles were the 1970s equivalent of Blackwell's plain dark dresses or Cassatt's shirred silk: costumes that fit into their milieu, commanding only the right amount and the right kind of attention. She was deeply rooted in her community, and dedicated to the service of its people. The zesty enjoyment of display in this book rose partly from the knowledge that what looked frivolous was only a tool, used to advance a serious purpose. All this was smoothly continuous with 1946, but as the journalistic biography of a living subject, Hicks's book also looked forward to 1996.

1996: Managing the Image

In 1996, ten of fifty-one new biographies—almost 20 percent—did not say anything about their subjects' looks or clothes. They didn't need to (all ten were profusely illustrated), and they had scant room for description (eight were short books for the early grades). Other picture-book biographies said only a few words: a fellow slave told Tubman that she needed a bandanna (Schroeder 1996); Nellie Bly, tired of her practical blue travel dress, envied "the Japanese women in their bright kimonos" (Blos 1996). Still, almost all the books reviewed for fourth grade and up did at least mention their subjects' appearances, and there were continuities as well as differences in what they said.

In twenty-five years, hems had gone up and down more than once. Women who worked in offices had worn pantsuits in the 1970s, skirted versions of men's suits in the 1980s, and relatively unadorned black or gray outfits in the 1990s (Goldstein 1999). The 1980s look was popularized by John T. Molloy, whose 1977 best-seller, *The Women's Dress for Success Book*, followed a 1975 version for men; his advice was based on surveys showing that "women who wore business suits were one and a half times more likely to feel they were being treated as executives—and a third less likely to have their authority challenged by men" (Faludi 1991, 175). A decade later, the fashion industry declared the look dead, and urged women to adopt working clothes with more individuality (Minsky 1987).

One constant was blue jeans. Another was dieting: no matter what clothes were in fashion, they always looked better on thin bodies. According to the news, anorexia and other eating disorders were epidemic; but it was not always easy to see where recommended disciplines (like rigorous exercise and calorie-counting) crossed the line and became problematic. Although it is hard to pin down any causal relationship between anorexia and the media, Lager and McGee (2003) argue that "women are socialized by images of models who are typically 23 percent below the average weight for their height" (283), and girls' dieting is considered normal: "body obsession is part of enacting the feminine gender role" (288). Some anorexics also became addicted to self-injury, a phenomenon that gained publicity in 1996 when Princess Diana con-fessed to practicing it (Austin and Kortum 2004).

Framing "women's body image issues" as "a result of patriarchal perceptions of how women should look, which often oppress and mar-ginalize women as objects of male desire" (288), Lager and McGee had ample precedent in the years between 1971 and 1996. To name just three examples, Susan Brownmiller's *Femininity* (1984), Susan Fa-ludi's *Backlash* (1991), and Naomi Wolf's *The Beauty Myth* (1991) all explored ways "images of beauty are used against women," and all were issued in paperback editions labeled "national bestseller." Schol-ars had raised women's awareness of femininity as a social construct to new levels. These ideas were in the air, and hints of them surface in the juvenile biographies.

Some writers still used both beauty and insecurity to endear their subjects to girl readers. The adolescent Juliette Gordon Low, in a hu-morous letter to her mother, underlined her anxiety with a portmanteau word: "My nose is getting 'trenormous,' much bigger than yours ever was! I am so disgusted!" (Brown 1996, 29). There were a few subjects whose unattractiveness was poignantly linked to outsider status. Elea-nor Roosevelt's rejecting mother considered her ugly (Cooney 1996). After her mother's death, Mahalia Jackson was raised by an aunt; her father had remarried and did not want her around his new family or his barber shop—possibly, Gourse (1996a) suggests, because of her looks.

Relatively fewer subjects were called "pretty," however, and those few were often either confident about their looks or not particularly interested. Mother Teresa was "a pretty, loving girl with large brown eyes" (Mohan 1996, 10); baby Victoria, according to her proud father, was "a pretty little Princess, as plump as a partridge" (Netzley 1996, 19); some "even thought" Marie Curie was "a beauty" (Pasachoff 1996, 9); Mary Shelley was "still quite beautiful" after a bout with smallpox (Miller 1996, 98); and one observer compared Dorothy Day to the famed actress, Greta Garbo (Kent 1996). The formula was used more inclusively than in the past; African American pilot Bessie Coleman was a "pretty, petite youngster" (Hart 1996, 13). But authors did not seem so eager to reassure readers that self-doubting protagonists were "really quite pretty." Perhaps this was partly because ambitious women were no longer so quickly suspected of being too masculine, so the reassurance was less needed. More probably it was because the biogra-phies were no longer so liberally fictionalized; the novelistic conven-tions used to elicit readers' identification with subjects were simply less used.

At the same time, the "warts and all" creed led to more frequent negative comments about subjects' looks. Sometimes these were related to health. Malnutrition, for instance, was a threat to beauty. The Gordon children, at the end of the Civil War, "were very thin and pale and had boils and dull hair" (Brown 1996, 14); their grandparents went into feeding mode at the first sight of them. Some girls worried about being too small and thin—worries that were implicitly countered in descriptions of Frida Kahlo (Cruz 1996), Fanny Mendelssohn (Kamen 1996), and Lucretia Mott (Bryant 1996) as strong and energetic in spite of being small.

For the girls who read these books, obesity was a greater threat. This, too, could of course be caused by ill health. Athlete Gail Devers suffered from fluctuating weight because of Graves disease (Gutman 1996a). As a bow-legged child, Mahalia Jackson probably had rickets, and cured herself by learning to eat well. As an adult, "she was unaccustomed to weighing under 200 pounds," and in spite of her doctors' approval "felt that she had lost her health" when she got down to 160 (Gourse 1996a, 107). But weight could be a cause as well as an effect of ill health, and if subjects were not responsible about keeping themselves fit, the writers of 1996 were likely to mention it. "In spite of being extremely overweight," Maria Montessori "insisted she was in good health" at the age of eighty (Shephard 1996, 102).

Biographers in 1971 had not said much about weight. True, the middle-aged Emma Goldman was showing her "spreading pounds" at a time when the public imagined her to be a dangerous seductress; Shulman (1971, 163-164) noted this mainly because of what it said about the public's imagination. Julia Grant, in her forties, showed her agility by jumping over a porch railing when Ulysses teased her about "getting plump"; Fleming (1971a, 133-134) seemed more interested in the amicable tone of their marriage than in Julia's weight. Even when subjects were decidedly stout, earlier generations of biographers tended to ignore it. Streatfield (1958, 14) called Victoria "podgy" at the age of five, but made no reference to her shape later on.

A generation later, some biographers were still quiet about women's figures. Swain (1996, 25) called Elizabeth Cady Stanton "more than a little plump," and went on to talk about her sense of humor; Sheafer (1996) let photographs tell the story of Aretha Franklin's rising and falling weight, with no help from the text. But others said more. Netzley (1996, 42) regarded Queen Victoria's weight as a psychological problem: after Albert's death, "the joy ebbed from [her] life." She became careless about grooming, and "gained weight but refused to go on the walks Melbourne suggested." Chiflet and Beaulet

(1996) looked at it as a caloric problem. In the eyes of 1996, what she ate daily at royal banquets represented a failure of self-discipline— ironic for a woman so dedicated to duty as Victoria. Similarly, Calamity Jane was an alcoholic, and Sanford and Green's 1996 portrayal of her was unflattering; they made jocular allusions to her homeliness and thick waist, twice describing her as "real tall and built like a busted bale of hay" (8, 26). Whether it was brought about by (forgivable) depression or by (unforgivable) lack of discipline, weight gain in these late twentieth-century accounts of nineteenth-century women seemed more of a problem to be solved than a part of their identities to be accepted.

Race, on the other hand, was a given, and racial issues were treated with greater awareness than in the past. Girls of color were still hurt by internalizing white standards of beauty, but now at least some of them had given voice to the pain, and writers described their feelings sympathetically. Amy Tan "once spent a week sleeping with a clothespin on her nose trying to change her Asian appearance because she thought it set her apart from other children" (B. Kramer 1996a, 8). Later, her mother gave her a fashionable miniskirt, but said:

> You want to be the same as American girls on the outside. But inside you must always be Chinese. You must be proud you are different. Your only shame is to have shame (B. Kramer 1996a, 21).

Maya Angelou's childhood insecurity about her looks was intensified by racism. Pettit (1996, 9) noted that "neighborhood children tormented her about her big size and hair that stuck out in every direction." Lisandrelli (1996, 18) went further. Dreaming of "having long blond hair and light blue eyes" like the "sweet little white girls," she imagined that an evil spell had turned her into a "too-big Negro girl" (Lisandrelli 1996, 18). Reading nineteenth-century British novels made her believe there was "something of beauty" in her "beyond the physical" (29), but inner beauty wasn't enough. She didn't believe her brother when he told her "she was pretty." Her voice was too deep, her "breasts were underdeveloped," and she "worried about her sexuality, too" (48). To reassure herself, she seduced a boy and became a teenage mother. Two things distinguish this story dramatically from older accounts of adolescent anxiety: the sexual explicitness, and the recognition that Angelou, an African American, was measuring herself by inappropriate standards. Charlotte Forten had done the same (Douty 1971), but neither she nor her biographer had analyzed it so clearly.

Gourse (1996b) used the old feminine love of adornment to bridge cultural distances. In Powhatan Virginia the women gossiped as they painted "colorful designs on their bodies," each in her own style (15);

in Stuart London, Pocahontas went shopping with the "wives of the Virginia Company owners" and bought "a perky little hat to set atop her hair" (152). When one of the women expressed "amazement" at the Indians' "deerskin costumes," Pocahontas said they looked "normal" to her. "You must see the world," she urged the Londoner; "That's a great education" (153). The scenes were fictionalized and not strictly accurate; for instance, Powhatan women probably had tattooed designs, not just painted ones, on their faces as well as their legs (Allen 2003, 68). Yet, after generations of white characters condescending to people of color in children's books, Pocahontas's airy superiority here was rather pleasing. Multicultural sensitivity was clearly a priority, and writers were more aware than ever that standards of beauty could indeed be cultural constructs.

In some of the biographies, the conventional idea of beauty was mildly spoofed. The impish Grand Duchess Alexandria stuck her tongue out or crossed her eyes for the camera (Brewster 1996, 23, 47). Shannon Miller and her sister Tessa "put on makeup" to play "beauty," but they also dressed up "as nerds" and clowned for their parents (S. Green 1996, 19). When a young man bet the future Elizabeth Cady Stanton that she couldn't "go for a carriage ride with him and keep quiet," she sent a "dressmaker's dummy wearing a very large hat" in her place (Swain 1996, 26). Swain made it a story about winning a bet, but it raised a serious question: if a woman had to dress well and keep quiet, how was she different from a mannequin? Even the loveliest court dress could be an ordeal, as Elizabeth Cary found in the seventeenth century (Brackett 1996). Juliette Gordon Low, in "a white satin dress with a train six yards long, white gloves, and three plumes in her hair," grew so tired in Queen Victoria's long receiving line that she set her "bouquet on the bustle of the lady in front of her, who unknowingly carried it through all the rooms" (Brown 1996, 41-42).

In biographies of women who could barely afford the clothes they needed—like Mahalia Jackson, shivering for want of a coat in Chicago (Gourse 1996a), or Anne Frank, outgrowing her clothes in the Secret Annex (Katz 1996, 46)—comments about dress were usually just quick factual details. Mothers sewed for their daughters, sometimes using feed sacks (Krull 1996; Siegel 1996), and damaging a carefully sewn dress was a disaster (Cary 1996). Emily Keller (1996) scrutinized the self-presentation of Margaret Bourke-White, who carefully alternated her accessories so clients wouldn't notice how few outfits she really had; but here, too, the focus was on individual necessity rather than implications for gender equity.

Some of the books, however, communicated a more explicit awareness of how femininity could limit women. Obviously, dress could restrict physical activity; for Margaret Morse Nice, having to wear a long skirt made it hard to catch and mark baby robins for ornithological study (Dunlap 1996). Generations after the suffragists abandoned bloomers, violating the code still carried penalties. Women crossdressers on the western frontier were called "Calamity Janes" after Martha Jane Cannary, who wore men's clothes when she worked as a bullwhacker or scout; according to Sanford and Green (1996), her costume risked fines and "outraged" other women.

More controversial than freedom of motion was the psychological freedom associated with crossdressing. For young Fannie Mendelssohn, being "dressed in her prettiest dress" was part of being a spectator, not being "allowed to conduct an orchestra" (Kamen 1996, 12). By 1993, when Julie Krone became the first woman jockey ever to win the Belmont Stakes, her racing silks did not shock the public; but wearing them was not enough to gain her acceptance in a "man's world" (Gutman 1996b). She struggled "to fit in with the men at the track" by not wearing makeup, not combing her hair, and not smiling. "She walked and talked like a boy. She even spat like one" (Savage 1996, 33).

One woman who felt that beauty was used against her was Maria Montessori, who before her pioneering work in education had already won recognition as Italy's first woman physician. After an 1896 conference at which she spearheaded a resolution calling for women to "get equal pay for equal work," the newspapers described her as "lovely looking—dark eyes, a Mona Lisa smile, a frilled collar, and a strand of pearls setting off the face framed with soft curls." She wrote to her parents, "My face will not appear in the papers any more and no one shall dare to sing my so-called charms again. I shall do serious work" (Shephard 1996, 32-33). She was "plump but strikingly beautiful" in her thirties (53), "motherly looking" later on (72), always fond of "frivolous hats" (100), and "captivating" even in her seventies (95), although more for her manner by that time than for her looks.

If Montessori had a love-hate relationship with the press, she was in good company. Where the biographies of 1946 had favored private women and artists who could work in their own homes, the 1996 crop included many whose work required them to present themselves to the gaze of strangers. Publicity was an important tool, whether they sought funding for education and research (like Montessori and Curie), political reform (like Mott and Stanton), or record sales (like Jackson and Franklin). At the same time, to see one's own image distorted in the press could be like looking in a fun-house mirror, and even after the old prejudice against women's names and faces appearing in public had faded, many found it painful. Franklin complained that *Time* had misrepresented her in a feature article, among other things painting her "as a woman trapped by the blues" when in reality, "I am Aretha, upbeat, straight-ahead, and not to be worn out by men and left singing the blues" (Franklin and Ritz 1999, 123). Collaborator David Ritz said that journalists had "mythologized," inventing "a character who bears little resemblance to the real Aretha" (Franklin and Ritz 1999, xii).

Celebrities developed coping mechanisms, learning to live in the public eye without giving much away, and biographers seemed willing to cooperate. In earlier years, writers had distanced much-publicized subjects like Nightingale (Nolan 1946) and the Pankhursts (Noble 1971) with irony, approving their contributions to nursing and women's rights, but seemingly uneasy with their tactics. In 1996, skill in self-presentation and the manipulation of public images was rather admired than otherwise, from Cleopatra, who had herself delivered to Caesar in a rolled-up carpet (R. Green 1996), to Aretha Franklin, who was "every inch the 'Queen of Soul'" at her 1994 concert in the White House Rose Garden (Sheafer 1996, 8).

The prevailing tone now was journalistic, and admiration was balanced with objectivity, if not neutrality. Writers were careful not to say anything that could not be supported, and relied for many of their facts—and graphics—on the public media. In one Character Building Book, subject Gloria Estefan appeared in seven photographs, all copyrighted by AP/World Wide Photos: four times with a microphone, once with President George H. W. Bush, once at an awards ceremony with her husband, Emilio, and once being wheeled out of the hospital (Strazzabosco 1996). She was on view; even as she embraced Emilio, her smile was toward the camera. The sweet openness of her expression implied a genuine connection with her fans, but it was a glittering kind of intimacy that could mask her private life.

The use of publicly available photographs was typical, and was not limited to celebrity biographies. As in the past, women and their families had at least partial control over what information about them would be available, and biographers made good use of what they could find. It is instructive to look at the year's treatments of two women, union organizer Mother Jones and artist Frida Kahlo, who crafted their self-presentations for quite different purposes.

As a child, Mary Harris Jones, the daughter and granddaughter of Irish rebels, was driven from her homeland by the potato famine. She lost her husband and four small children to the 1867 yellow fever epidemic in Memphis. She built a new life for herself as a seamstress in

Chicago, only to have it destroyed by the 1871 fire. After these losses, she reinvented herself as "Mother Jones," an iconic figure in the American labor movement. Probably born in 1837, she claimed to be one hundred years old in 1930, the year of her death. Indeed, the "only information available about her younger self comes directly from Mother Jones and what she either could recall or chose to reveal" in "a few dismissive paragraphs" of her autobiography (Horton 1996, 14).

With so little personal narrative of her childhood and early years, Horton (like Jones herself) fell back on exploiting the piquant contrast between her outward fragility and tenacious will:

> . . . Mother Jones was disarmingly sweet and gentle looking, almost grandmotherly in appearance. She favored Victorian dresses trimmed with lace and often wore fresh violets tucked into the bonnet on her head. Reporters covering her speeches seemed always to comment on her snow white hair, her twinkling, bright blue eyes, and her petite, five-foot size. But although she may have looked frail and dainty, when she opened her mouth there was no doubt about her strength (Horton 1996, 11).

Jones reputedly "did not care what others might think" (12). Yet much of her life was devoted to influencing public opinion, and she used her image to do it. Exaggerating her age may have helped; people were distressed when a woman in her eighties was thrown into solitary confinement in a military prison, and the publicity won sympathy for labor goals. Because her activities had more to do with tactics than with overarching strategy, an earlier biographer presented her as a "supernumerary" who in the end achieved only a "negative kind of greatness" (Fetherling 1974, vii, 211). Gorn (2001), however, argued that her real legacy went beyond any tangible results of her campaigns: a common working woman, expected "to go silently through life," she had the courage to create "a unique voice" (303). Horton admitted that Jones "was usually impatient with theory," and was perhaps "a doer rather than a thinker" (Horton 1996, 79-80), but concluded that she deserved recognition for the "inspiration, encouragement, and moral support" she gave workers, the money she raised, the publicity she arranged, and the difference she made in "countless ordinary lives" (83). In trying to assess the value of Jones's life, biographers were considering how real a contribution her image made to the cause of labor.

Mother Jones was never young, and never a private individual. The youth of Mary Harris Jones was overlaid by the elderly image, and her autobiography skimmed over personal loves and losses. Horton's book was illustrated in black and white, with thirty-one photographs, thirteen period prints, and a map. Jones appeared in just eight of the photographs, once with President Coolidge, once addressing a crowd, and six times in posed stills. The other illustrations provided historical context, showing child laborers, notable men, the Irish troubles, the Chicago fire, and various strikes.

Frida Kahlo, by contrast, was a photographer's daughter; there were family pictures. More, she was the wife of a muralist, and herself a prolific painter of self-portraits. Unfortunately, all twenty-two pictures in Cruz's biography—even four reproductions of Kahlo's paintings—were in black and white. There were eleven photographs of Kahlo (twice shown marching in demonstrations, and once in a hospital bed painting her own body cast), three of other people without her, and four of places that had significance in her life. Series format may have dictated the lack of color and inclusion of news photos, which seemed at odds with Kahlo's own profoundly intimate visual record. In one of the works reproduced here, "My Grandparents, My Parents, and I (Family Tree)," she painted herself as an egg about to be fertilized, a fetus curled against her mother's white dress, and a naked child. In another, "The Two Fridas," the Frida who had been rejected by her husband sat stoically formal in a white gown of her own, blood dripping onto its skirt as she snipped a vein from her open heart with a pair of embroidery scissors.

Just over half her paintings were self-portraits, memorializing again and again the effects of her life's two great catastrophes: the streetcar accident that broke her body, and Diego Rivera, the womanizing genius who broke her heart. Her calm, unsmiling face, with its single brow winging over her dark eyes and sometimes a faint shadow over her full lips, gazed steadily at the viewer above a body torn open to show the destruction of its spine ("The Broken Column") or its heart ("The Two Fridas"). In spite of her communism, she admitted that her art was not "revolutionary" or "militant" (Alcántara and Egnolff 1999). It was deeply personal. She used herself as material for her art, and she used art in presenting herself. Still, her political commitments were integral to the identity she expressed. The long Tehuantepec costumes she liked to wear concealed her polio-withered and streetcar-battered right leg, but they also expressed her proud solidarity with indigenous Mexican culture (Block and Hoffman-Jeep 1999); Cruz (1996, 64) noted that "Tehuana women are known for their personal strength, beauty, and independence"—certainly traits that Kahlo incorporated into her own persona. Kahlo was born in 1907, but, like Mother Jones, she claimed a different date: 1910, when the Mexican Revolution began (Cruz 1996, 15).

Both Kahlo and Jones are recognizable icons today. Jones became a "folk hero": songs and plays were written about her, an investigative journal was named for her, and her image has adorned T-shirts (Horton 1996). Kahlo has been called "an industry" and "a cult figure" (Bemrosse 1996); she has inspired watches, mouse pads, operas, and novels (Mencimer 2002). One can point to similarities in their lives: both had socialist and labor commitments; both transcended great suffering; both deliberately invented their own images, and their self-presentations included the symbolic use of clothes. But they were women of different generations and temperaments. Jones, looking outward, agitated for political and economic support to ease the suffering of the poor, and was called the most dangerous woman in America. As a role model for girls, Kahlo might be more dangerous still—and, in spite of her mustache, more attractive. Looking inward, she painted mythic connections between her own suffering and the world's; some of her self-portraits could be surrealistic representations of self-injury. Cruz (1996, 87) quoted a friend who "thought that Kahlo considered her paintings as a 'private diary,'" never intending for them to be seen. But a few were exhibited in Paris in 1939, where some found them "too shocking to be shown in public" (82), and Kahlo had a solo exhibition in Mexico in 1953, when she was so ill that she presided over the opening in her four-poster bed.

Conclusion

At least since 1946, children's literature textbooks had insisted that juvenile biography was more open and factual than ever before. But surely neither Jones nor Kahlo would have made a welcome subject then. Their politics were suspect. There was too little record of Jones as anything but an old woman, and too much record of Kahlo's sexual history. Both were too outspoken in public.

That they could be portrayed in 1996 was partly because old social taboos had been broken. These books suggested no lingering sense that women belonged in the home, or that they should always defer to men. Youngsters could be allowed to read that Mother Jones sided with the socialists who "saw labor problems in the context of a class struggle" (Horton 1996, 79), or that Kahlo "had three miscarriages" (Cruz 1996, 84). Thus, the books were seen as more honest than their predecessors because they could include lives, and aspects of lives, that had once been off limits.

Still, they avoided sensationalism. Horton (1996, 79) placed Jones's activities within the broader context of the American labor movement, but she did not go so far as to discuss Marx, and she emphasized that "Mother Jones herself was not interested in discussing or debating theories." Cruz (1996) did not mention the likelihood that Kahlo may have lost more than three pregnancies, some of them to medical abortion (Herrera 1983).

Their scholarly apparatus, too, gave these books an air of respectability; they looked safe. Each had an index, two bibliographies, endnotes, and a chronology or timeline. Horton's book also had sidebars and subheadings within chapters. It was easy to imagine the use of these biographies in school units. Teachers could work them into thematic units, assign students to locate specific types of information for reports in them, and mediate lively discussions; active learners would discover how these women's lives were connected to broader social and historical trends. With plentiful graphics and short quotations voicing a range of contemporary views, these two books were fairly representative of the year's biographies for older children: lively and competent, they presented worthwhile objects to the reader's view. The new biography introduced history from more diverse viewpoints, questioned orthodox Western values, and made use of the methods of social, intellectual, and cultural as well as political history.

Saul (1993) has suggested that librarians, who focus on the child's unmediated encounter with a book, are more concerned with its accuracy, style, and quality than teachers, who expect to mediate the child's encounter. Extending this perception, one might also expect that biographies of Mother Jones or Frida Kahlo would have seemed more dangerous if they had been fictionalized. The old biographies were sometimes hard to distinguish from the historical novels of their time, and, like novels, they usually invited readers to identify directly with their subjects. Subjects were almost always attractive characters, who could be trusted—with rare exceptions like Florence Nightingale and Emmeline Pankhurst—to form reliable views of their worlds. They seemed to be designed for solitary, unmediated reading.

By 1996, however, even brightly illustrated sports and celebrity biographies invited dipping and browsing; the experience of unmediated reading had changed. The interruption of narrative, the provision of multiple viewpoints, and the increased prominence of graphics must all affect the reader's relationship to the subject as a potential role model. Identity, according to some thinkers, is rooted in narrative. It is "the story we tell of ourselves and . . . also the story that others tell of us" (Sarup 1996, 3); it draws on "a life story that is itself created and constantly recreated" (Lifton 1993, 30); it "forms a trajectory of development from the past to the anticipated future" (Giddens 1991, 75). But for Ott (2003), narrative is only one approach to identity construction. Using television's Simpsons as his text, he argues that the identity of Bart's sister, Lisa, is rooted in narrative; the identity of his father, Homer, in indiscriminate consumption; and Bart's own identity in strategically appropriated and generally rebellious images. Bart is "easily appropriated for use in creating an oppositional identity" because "his identity privileges image over narrative" (Ott 2003, 69).

The newer biographies often introduce their subjects as images. They do not, of course, promote the formation of rebellious "oppositional identities"; but they often do rely on the description of striking contrasts to promote reader interest at points where earlier biographies would have been apt to use anecdote instead. Contrast in itself may be conducive to a more critical scrutiny of what is being presented; and the collage-like selection of publicly archived graphics and quotations from different witnesses encourages readers to see biographees through the eyes of the world.

This is a fundamental change. Absorbed in an old-fashioned fictionalized biography, a reader could more easily see the world through the eyes of a subject, and critical awareness might be disarmed. Cumulatively as well as individually, the choice of subjects also affected readers' experience. Surely biographers cannot have conspired in 1946 to feature women who rose to wartime challenges and then withdrew into their homes, or in 1971 to emphasize social conscience; but the choices suited the moods of their times, and in 1971, at least, the goals of publishers' series made it clear that biographies of social reformers should sell. In either case, sustained narrative encouraged an emotional involvement that opened readers to the influence of subjects, and sometimes the influence went deep enough to change lives. Lifton (1993, 145) repeats the story of a Southern "cracker" who could not remember where she heard about Harriet Tubman, but took from her the message "that one must live at risk and pursue justice on the basis of a demanding, transformative Christianity."

The novel-like emplotment of many fictionalized biographies carried another message, as well. Subjects were shown struggling to identify and then fulfill their own missions, the special tasks that would give their lives meaning, like Blackwell's dedication to medicine or Dickinson's to poetry. Tracing the seemingly inevitable arcs of their subjects' lives, the books implied that lives are narratives, each with its own unity springing from cohesive character.

Many of the biographies of 1996—not only picture-book biographies, but longer books for older children—were also effectively unified. Yet, their very format was often kaleidoscopic, with important content distributed between main text, captions, and sidebars. Many were organized thematically rather than chronologically. Where information was lacking, biographers adhered meticulously to fact by using phrases like "it was said," or "some people thought," or "legend has it," warning readers not to rely too confidently on guesswork; in the very act of suspending judgment on the facts, a reader would be further distanced from the subject. Identification was less complete. Where visual records were lacking, the use of publicly available images from libraries or news archives also lessened the intimacy between reader and subject. Thus, book design in 1996 was more likely to engage the reader as a critical observer, rather than a vicarious participant.

At the same time, biographees chosen in 1996 were often engaged in work that brought them before the media. In 1946, the more recent a subject's life, the more likely she was to live it out of the public eye. In 1971, three of the four living subjects—Golda Meir, Shirley Chisholm, and Maria Tallchief—worked before the public gaze; but biographers of Meir, Tallchief, Cassatt, Velarde, and others suggested that they had paid heavily for working away from their homes and families. Now, it seemed to be more easily assumed that women *should* be able to have it all. The old assumption that women could not do men's jobs seemed to call for more explicit attention in 1996, as if young readers might never have heard of it. What could now be assumed without mention was that personal ambition was acceptable.

Book design and the public nature of many subjects' work combined to give a new impression of the relationship between women and their communities. For a Martha Jane Sinclair, or even a Dolly Madison, the relationship appeared to be almost seamless; a reader who identified with almost any subject in 1946 was also identifying with the community in which she was embedded. The examples of Jones and Kahlo warn against sweeping generalizations about the biographies of 1996: the labor movement was essential to Jones's identity, as Mexico was to Kahlo's. But the very style of the new books, with their constant attention to facts and specifics, made their community identifications seem more conscious and deliberate, less organic.

Such differences cannot be absolute. The genre's shift from fictionalized texts and illustrations to a more journalistic stance do not prevent young readers from identifying with biographees in the newer books, and even the most skillfully fictionalized older biography do not force readers to identify with its subject. Many readers may identify more easily with subjects in the newer books, if only because they represent so many more ethnic groups and ways of life. In all three years, the best juvenile biographies could function to introduce history, provide inspiring role models, and stimulate young readers to further interest in their subjects.

No book, however excellent, entirely captures a subject; but many of these books, even those that are less than excellent, communicate enough so that chance readers might sense kinship and look for more. The ultimate outcome of such encounters must be as unpredictable as subjects and readers are quirky and individual. The advocates of biography have always expected it to serve noble ends, helping young readers develop an identity, or an abiding interest in history, or a capacity for empathy. But with luck a good biography, like a good friend, may be an end in itself.

Juvenile Biographies Discussed

Blos, Joan. 1996. *Nellie Bly's monkey: His remarkable story in his own words.* New York: Morrow Junior Books.

Bobbé, Dorothie. 1971. *The New World journey of Anne MacVicar.* New York: G. P. Putnam's Sons.

Brackett, Ginger Roberts. 1996. *Elizabeth Cary: Writer of conscience.* Greensboro: Morgan Reynolds.

Brewster, Hugh. 1996. *Anastasia's Album.* Toronto: Madison Press Books.

Brill, Ethel C. 1946. *Madeleine takes command.* New York: McGraw Hill.

Brown, Fern G. 1996. *Daisy and the Girl Scouts: The story of Juliette Gordon Low.* Morton Grove, IL: Albert Whitman.

Bryant, Jennifer Fisher. 1996. *Lucretia Mott: A guiding light.* Grand Rapids, MI: Eerdmans.

Cary, Alice. 1996. *Jean Craighead George.* Santa Barbara, CA: Learning Works.

Chiflet, Jean-Loup, and Alain Beaulet. 1996. *Victoria and her times.* New York: Henry Holt.

Cooney, Eleanor. 1996. *Eleanor.* New York: Viking.

Cruz, Bárbara C. 1996. *Frida Kahlo: Portrait of a Mexican painter.* Berkeley Heights, NJ: Enslow Publishers.

De Leeuw, Adele. 1971. *Maria Tallchief: American ballerina.* New York: Dell Yearling.

Desmond, Alice Curtis. 1946. *Glamorous Dolly Madison.* New York: Dodd, Mead.

Douty, Esther M. 1971. *Charlotte Forten: Free Black teacher.* Champaign, IL: Garrard Publishing Company.

Dunlap, Julie. 1996. *Birds in the bushes: A story about Margaret Morse Nice.* Minneapolis, MN: Carolrhoda Books.

Faber, Doris. 1971. *Lucretia Mott: Foe of slavery.* Champaign, IL: Garrard Publishing Company.

Fleming, Alice. 1971a. *General's lady: The life of Julia Dent Grant.* Philadelphia: J. B. Lippincott.

Fleming, Alice. 1971b. *Ida Tarbell: First of the muckrakers.* New York: Thomas Y. Crowell.

Fuller, Miriam Morris. 1971. *Phillis Wheatley: America's first black poetess.* Champaign, IL: Garrard Publishing Company.

Gould, Jean. 1946. *Miss Emily.* Boston: Houghton Mifflin.

Gourse, Leslie. 1996a. *Mahalia Jackson: Queen of Gospel song.* New York: Franklin Watts.

Gourse, Leslie. 1996b. *Pocahontas, young peacemaker.* New York: Simon & Schuster/Aladdin Paperbacks.

Graves, Charles. 1971. *Nellie Bly: Reporter for* The World. Champaign, IL: Garrard Publishing Company.

Green, Robert. 1996. *Cleopatra.* New York: Franklin Watts.

Green, Septima. 1996. *Going for the gold: Shannon Miller.* New York: Avon Camelot.

Gutman, Bill. 1996a. *Gail Devers.* Austin, TX: Raintree Steck-Vaughn.

Gutman, Bill. 1996b. *Julie Krone.* Austin, TX: Raintree Steck-Vaughn.

Harper, Martha Barnhart. 1946. *Red silk pantalettes.* New York: Longmans, Green.

Hart, Philip S. 1996. *Up in the air: The story of Bessie Coleman.* Minneapolis, MN: Carolrhoda Books.

Heyn, Leah Lurie. 1971. *Challenge to become a doctor: The story of Elizabeth Blackwell.* Long Island, NY: Feminist Press.

Hicks, Nancy. 1971. *The Honorable Shirley Chisholm: Congresswoman from Brooklyn.* New York: Lion Books.

Horton, Madelyn. 1996. *The importance of Mother Jones.* San Diego, CA: Lucent Books.

Kamen, Gloria. 1996. *Hidden music: The life of Fanny Mendelssohn.* New York: Atheneum Books for Young Readers.

Katz, Sandor. 1996. *Anne Frank.* Chelsea House Publishers

Keller, Emily. 1996. *Margaret Bourke-White: A Photographer's Life.* Minneapolis, MN: Lerner Publications.

Keller, Gail Faithfull. 1971. *Jane Addams.* New York: Thomas Y. Crowell.

Kelly, Regina Z. 1971. *Miss Jefferson in Paris.* New York: Coward, McCann & Geoghegan.

Kent, Deborah. 1996. *Dorothy Day: Friend to the forgotten.* Grand Rapids, MI: Eerdmans.

Kerr, Laura. 1946. *Doctor Elizabeth.* New York: Thomas Nelson & Sons.

Knapp, Sally. 1946. *New Wings for Women.* New York: Thomas Y. Crowell.

Kramer, Barbara. 1996a. *Amy Tan: Author of* The Joy Luck Club. Springfield, NJ: Enslow Publishers.

Krull, Kathleen. 1996. *Wilma Unlimited: How Wilma Rudolph became the world's fastest woman*. New York: Harcourt Brace.

Lane, Margaret. 1946. *The tale of Beatrix Potter: A biography*. New York: Frederick Warne.

Lisandrelli, Elaine Slivinski. 1996. *Maya Angelou: More than a poet*. Berkeley Heights, NJ: Enslow Publishers.

McKown, Robin. [1971]. *Marie Curie*. New York: G. P. Putnam's Sons.

Mann, Peggy. 1971. *Golda: The life of Israel's prime minister*. New York: Coward, McCann & Geoghegan.

Miller, Calvin Craig. 1996. *Spirit like a storm: The story of Mary Shelley*. Greensboro, NC: Morgan Reynolds.

Mohan, Claire Jordan. 1996. *The young life of Mother Teresa*. Worcester, PA: Young Sparrow Press.

Morgan, Helen L. 1946. *Mistress of the White House: The story of Dolly Madison*. Philadelphia: Westminster Press.

Morris, Terry. 1971. *Shalom, Golda*. New York: Hawthorn Books.

Mossiker, Frances. 1971. *More than a queen: The story of Josephine Bonaparte*. New York: Knopf.

Myers, Elisabeth P. 1971. *Mary Cassatt: A portrait*. Chicago: Reilly & Lee.

Nelson, Mary Carroll. 1971. *Pablita Velarde*. Minneapolis, MN: Dillon Press.

Netzley, Patricia D. 1996. *The importance of Queen Victoria*. San Diego, CA: Lucent Books.

Newcomb, Covelle. 1946. *The secret door: The story of Kate Greenaway*. New York: Dodd, Mead.

Noble, Iris. 1971. *Emmeline and her daughters: The Pankhurst suffragettes*. New York: Julian Messner.

Nolan, Jeannette C. 1946. *Florence Nightingale*. New York: Julian Messner.

Nourse, Ray Tyler. 1946. Interpreter of East and West: Alice Tisdale Hobart. In *Topflight: Famous American women*, ed. Anne Stoddard, 111-130. New York: Thomas Nelson & Sons.

Pasachoff, Naomi. 1996. *Marie Curie and the science of radioactivity*. New York: Oxford University Press.

Peterson, Helen Stone. 1971. *Susan B. Anthony: Pioneer in woman's rights*. Champaign, IL: Garrard Publishing Company.

Pettit, Jayne. 1996. *Maya Angelou: Journey of the heart*. New York: Puffin Books.

Pinckney, Jerry. 1996. Illustrator's note in *Minty: A story of young Harriet Tubman*, by Alan Schroeder. New York: Dial.

Raymond, Margaret Thomsen. 1946. Girl with a camera: Margaret Bourke-White. In *Topflight: Famous American women*, ed. Anne Stoddard, 163-178. New York: Thomas Nelson & Sons.

Sanford, William R., and Carl R. Green. 1996. *Calamity Jane: Frontier original*. Springfield, NJ: Enslow Publishers

Savage, Jeff. 1996. *Julie Krone: Unstoppable jockey*. Minneapolis, MN: Lerner.

Schroeder, Alan. 1996. *Minty: A story of young Harriet Tubman.* New York: Dial.

Seymour, Flora Warren. 1946. *Pocahontas: Brave girl.* Indianapolis: Bobbs-Merrill.

Sheafer, Silvia Anne. 1996. *Aretha Franklin: Motown superstar.* Springfield, NJ: Enslow Publishers.

Shephard, Marie Tennent. 1996. *Maria Montessori: Teacher of teachers.* Minneapolis, MN: Lerner Publications.

Shulman, Alix Kates. 1971. *To the Barricades: The Anarchist Life of Emma Goldman.* New York: Thomas Y. Crowell.

Siegel, Dorothy Schainman. 1996. *Ann Richards: Politician, feminist, survivor.* Springfield, NJ: Enslow Publishers.

Stoddard, Anne, ed. 1946. *Topflight: Famous American women.* New York: Thomas Nelson & Sons.

Streatfeild, Noel. 1958. *Queen Victoria.* New York: Random House.

Strazzabosco, Jeanne. 1996. *Learning about determination from the life of Gloria Estefan.* New York: Rosen/Power Kids Press.

Swain, Gwenyth. 1996. *The road to Seneca Falls: A story about Elizabeth Cady Stanton.* Minneapolis, MN: Carolrhoda Books.

Vipont, Elfrida. 1971. *Towards a high attic: The early life of George Eliot, 1819-1880.* New York: Holt, Rinehart & Winston.

Wilson, Ellen. 1971. *American painter in Paris: A life of Mary Cassatt.* New York: Farrar, Straus & Giroux.

Other References

Alcántara, Isabel, and Sandra Egnolff. 1999. *Frida Kahlo and Diego Rivera.* New York: Prestel.

Allen, Paula Gunn. 2003. *Pocahontas: Medicine woman, spy, entrepreneur, diplomat.* New York: HarperSanFrancisco.

Austin, Len, and Julie Kortum. 2004. Self-injury: The secret language of pain for teenagers. *Education* 124 (3): 517-527.

Bemrosse, John. 1996. Fridamania. *Maclean's* 109 (November 4): 72.

Block, Rebecca, and Lynda Hoffman-Jeep. 1999. Fashioning national identity: Frida Kahlo in "Gringoland." *Woman's Art Journal* 19 (2): 8-12.

Bourdieu, Pierre. 1984. *Distinction: A social critique of the judgment of taste.* Translated by Richard Nice. Cambridge, MA: Harvard University Press.

Brownmiller, Susan. 1984. *Femininity.* New York: Fawcett Columbine.

Brumberg, Joan Jacobs. 1997. *The body project: An intimate history of American girls.* New York: Vintage Books.

Causey, Linda. 2004. A Perfect World. www.aperfectworld.org/page_one.htm (accessed July 28, 2004).

Colman, Penny. 1995. *Rosie the riveter: Women working on the home front in World War II.* New York: Crown Publishers.

Conway, Jill Ker. 1998. *When memory speaks: Reflections on autobiography*. New York: Knopf.

Doll reference: Vintage dolls 1951-1976. 2004. 1971 Mattel Barbie fashions. http://members.tripod.com/ltanis/barbiefash35.htm (accessed July 28, 2004).

Faludi, Susan. 1991. *Backlash: The undeclared war against American women*. New York: Anchor Books/Doubleday.

Fetherling, Dale. 1974. *Mother Jones: The miner's angel*. Carbondale: Southern Illinois University Press.

Fischer, Gayle V. 1997. "Pantalets" and "Turkish trousers": Designing freedom in the mid-nineteenth-century United States. *Feminist Studies* 23 (Spring): 111-140.

Franklin, Aretha, and David Ritz. 1999. *Aretha: From These Roots*. New York: Villard.

Giddens, Anthony. 1991. *Modernity and self-identity: Self and society in the late modern age*. Stanford, CA: Stanford University Press.

Goldstein, Lauren. 1999. What we wore. *Fortune 140* (November 22): 156-158+.

Gorn, Elliot J. 2001. Mother Jones: The most dangerous woman in America. New York: Hill and Wang.

Herrera, Hayden. 1983. *Frida: A biography of Frida Kahlo*. New York: Harper & Row.

Higonnet, Anne. 1993. Images—appearances, leisure, and subsistence. In *A history of women in the West: IV. Emerging feminism from Revolution to World War*, ed. by Geneviève Fraisse and Michelle Perrot, 246-305. Cambridge, MA: Belknap Press.

Hutch, Richard A. 1997. *The meaning of lives: Biography, autobiography, and the spiritual quest*. London: Cassell.

Huxley, Elspeth. 1975. *Florence Nightingale*. New York: G. P. Putnam's Sons.

Knibiehler, Yvonne. 1993. Bodies and hearts. In *A history of women in the West: IV. Emerging feminism from Revolution to World War*, ed. by Geneviève Fraisse and Michelle Perrot, 325-368. Cambridge, MA: Belknap Press.

Kroeger, Brooke. 1994. *Nellie Bly: Daredevil, reporter, feminist*. New York: Times Books.

Lager, E. Grace, and Brian R. McGee. 2003. Hiding the anorectic: A rhetorical analysis of popular discourse concerning anorexia. *Women's Studies in Communication* 26 (2): 266-295.

Levin, Carole. 1994. *"The heart and stomach of a king": Elizabeth I and the politics of sex and power*. Philadelphia: University of Pennsylvania Press.

Lifton, Robert Jay. 1993. *The protean self: Human resilience in an age of fragmentation*. New York: Basic Books.

Mencimer, Stephanie. 2002. The trouble with Frida Kahlo. *The Washington Monthly* 34 (6): 26-32.

Minsky, Terri. 1987. The death of dress for success. *Mademoiselle* 93 (September): 308-309+.

Ott, Brian L. 2003. "I'm Bart Simpson, who the hell are you?" A study in postmodern identity (re)construction. *Journal of Popular Culture* 37 (1): 56-82.

Presley, Ann Beth. 1998. Fifty years of change: Societal attitudes and women's fashions, 1900-1950. *The Historian* 60 (Winter), 307-324.

Quinn, Susan. 1995. *Marie Curie: A life*. New York: Simon & Schuster.

Sarup, Madan. 1996. *Identity, culture, and the postmodern world*. Ed. Tasneem Raja; foreword Peter Brooker. Atlanta: University of Georgia Press.

Saul, E. Wendy. 1993. Mediated vs. unmediated texts: Books in the library and the classroom. *The New Advocate*, 6 (3): 171-181.

Schwenke Wyile, Andrea. 1999. Expanding the view of first-person narration. *Children's Literature in Education* 30 (3): 185-202.

Schwenke Wyile, Andrea. 2001. First-person engaging narration in the picture book: Verbal and pictorial variations. *Children's Literature in Education* 32 (3): 191-202.

Smith, Ruth. 1946. *White man's burden: A personal testament*. New York: Vanguard Press.

Stevenson, Brenda, Ed. 1988. *The journals of Charlotte Forten Grimké*. New York: Oxford University Press.

Strachey, Lytton. 1918. Eminent Victorians: Cardinal Manning, Florence Nightingale, Dr. Arnold, General Gordon. New York: G. P. Putnam's Sons.

Torrens, Kathleen M. 1997. All dressed up with no place to go: Rhetorical dimensions of the nineteenth century dress reform movement. *Women's studies in communication* 20 (Fall), 189-210.

Ulrich, Laurel Thatcher. 1990. *A midwife's tale: The life of Martha Ballard, based on her diary, 1785-1812*. New York: Vintage.

Wolf, Naomi. 1991. *The beauty myth: How images of beauty are used against women*. New York: Anchor Books/Doubleday.

Wolf, Naomi. 1997. *Promiscuities: The secret struggle for womanhood*. New York: Random House.

Appendix A

Biographies of 1946: An Annotated List

Pocahontas (Rebecca Rolfe) 1595?-1616	D'Aulaire, Ingri, and Edgar Parin d'Aulaire. *Pocahontas.* (New York: Doubleday, 1946). n.p. K-3. A fairy-tale rendition, with humorous touches and a happy ending (Pocahontas visits London).
Pocahontas (Rebecca Rolfe) 1595?-1616	Seymour, Flora Warren. *Pocahontas: Brave girl.* Illus. Charles V. John. (Indianapolis: Bobbs-Merrill, 1946). Childhood of Famous Americans series. 192p. G3-5. Pocahontas takes care of little Chanco, plays with Captive Boy, and rescues Captain Smith; a mild, episodic adventure story, with historical afterword.
Madeleine de Verchères 1678 - 1747	Brill, Ethel C. *Madeleine takes command.* Illus. Bruce Adams. (New York: McGraw Hill, 1946). 204p. G6-9. When Mohawks attack the settlement, fourteen-year-old Madeleine successfully defends it for a week with the help of her two younger brothers and one old soldier.
Dolly Madison 1768-1849	Desmond, Alice Curtis. *Glamorous Dolly Madison.* (New York: Dodd, Mead, 1946). 274p. G7 up. A Quaker widow with a crush on Aaron Burr marries James Madison, and gradually learns to love him.
Dolly Madison 1768-1849	Morgan, Helen L. *Mistress of the White House: The Story of Dolly Madison.* Illus. Phillis Coté. (Philadelphia: Westminster, 1946). 248p. G7 up. Although she missed meeting Madison in her adventurous girlhood, Dolly was meant for him all along.

Florence Night- ingale 1820-1910	Nolan, Jeannette Covert. *Florence Nightingale*. Illus. George Avison. (New York: Julian Messner, 1946). 209p. G7 up. Admirable, not likable, she fights her family for the right to be a nurse, and the military bureaucracy for re- sources to save wounded men in the Crimean War.
Clara Barton 1821-1912	Stevenson, Augusta. *Clara Barton, girl nurse*. Illus. Frank Giacoia. Childhood of Famous Americans series. (Indian- apolis: Bobbs-Merrill, 1946). 200p. Gr3-5. Too shy to attend school as a child, she gains courage by helping others and becomes a nurse.
Elizabeth Black- well 1821-1910	Kerr, Laura. *Doctor Elizabeth*. Illus. Alice Carsey. (New York: Thomas Nelson & Sons, 1946). 209p. G6 up. A dying friend's wish for a woman doctor shows her how to do something extraordinary with her life.
Emily Dickin- son 1830-1886	Gould, Jean. *Miss Emily*. Illus. Ursula Koering. (Boston: Houghton Mifflin, 1946). 220p. G8 up. Spiritually troubled and unwilling to accept conven- tional answers, a popular girl becomes a reclusive poet.
Martha Jane St. Clair f. 1850s	Harper, Martha Barnhart. *Red silk pantalettes*. Illus. Betty Morgan Bowen. (New York: Longmans, Green, 1946). 228p. G6-9. The inn-keeper's hard-working daughter dreams of missionary work, a red silk circus costume, a white horse, and her best friend's brother.
Kate Greenaway 1846-1901	Newcomb, Covelle. *The secret door: The story of Kate Greenaway*. (New York: Dodd, Mead, 1946). 162p. G7-8. Supporting her family with nostalgic cards and illustra- tions, a shy artist nurtures a wistful friendship with her mentor John Ruskin.
Beatrix Potter 1866-1943	Lane, Margaret. *The tale of Beatrix Potter: A biography*. (New York: Frederick Warne, 1946). 248p. G8 up. Imaginative and unexpectedly tough, an over-protected Victorian girl becomes first an artist, then a sheep farmer.

Appendix B

Biographies of 1971: An Annotated List

Pocahontas (Rebecca Rolfe) 1595?-1616	Bulla, Clyde Robert. *Pocahontas and the strangers.* Illus. Peter Burchard. (New York: Thomas Y. Crowell, 1971). 180p. G3-5. Curious, trusting, and tragically blind to her own family's interests, a young girl suffers in the clash of cultures.
Phillis Wheatley 1753?-1784	Fuller, Miriam. *Phillis Wheatley: America's First Black Poetess.* Illus. Victor Mays. (Champaign, IL: Garrard, 1971). G3-6. Kind Bostonians buy an eight-year-old, teach her to read, and defend her reputation as a poet; she is humbly grateful to her owners.
Anne MacVicar [Grant] 1755-1838	Bobbé, Dorothie. 1971. *The New World journey of Anne MacVicar.* (New York: G. P. Putnam's Sons, 1971). 128p. G5-7. Following her soldier father to the French and Indian War, an observant child befriends Dutch colonists and Mohawks, reads Milton, and finds a wise mentor.
Josephine Bonaparte 1763-1814	Mossiker, Frances. *More than a queen.* Illus. Michael Eagle. (New York: Knopf, 1971). 150p. G7-9. After the failure of an arranged marriage, she accepts the protection of an ardent young Corsican, but falls in love with him only too late. Ill-starred romance.
Martha (Patsy) Jefferson 1772-1836	Kelly, Regina Z. *Miss Jefferson in Paris.* Illus. Nena Allen. (New York: Coward, McCann & Geoghegan, 1971). 159p. G5-6.

A bright girl watches Paris on the eve of the French Revolution; her father grooms her for a good marriage.

Lucretia Mott 1793-1880

Faber, Doris. *Lucretia Mott: Foe of slavery.* Illus. Russell Hoover. (Champaign, IL: Garrard, 1971). A Discovery Book. 80p. G3-4.

Lightly fictionalized full-life account of a gentle but unstoppable advocate of Negro and woman suffrage.

George Eliot 1819-1880

Vipont, Elfrida. *Towards a High Attic: The Early Life of George Eliot, 1819-1880.* (New York: Holt, Rinehart & Winston, 1971). 147p. G7 up.

Homely and awkward, she yearns for acceptance, and in the end finds love and literary greatness.

Susan B. Anthony 1820-1906

Peterson, Helen Stone. *Susan B. Anthony: Pioneer in woman's rights.* Illus. Paul Frame. (Champaign, IL: Garrard, 1971). Americans All series. 96p. G3-6.

Positive and determined, she maintains a courteous dignity in the face of ridicule as she campaigns against slavery and for woman suffrage.

Elizabeth Blackwell 1821-1910

Heyn, Leah Lurie. *Challenge to become a doctor.* Illus. Greta Handschuh. (Long Island, NY: Feminist Press, 1971). 64p. G4-8.

Three dozen drawings with purple wash, and another three dozen photos and reproductions, illustrate the story of the pioneering woman doctor and medical educator.

Julia Dent Grant 1826-1902

Fleming, Alice. *General's lady.* Illus. Richard Lebenson. (Philadelphia: Lippincott, 1971). 155p. G5-7.

Colonel Dent doubts that Ulysses Grant can support his daughter, but love, courage, and good humor will see them through all the hard times.

Emily Dickinson 1830-1886

Barth, Edna. *I'm nobody! Who are you?* Illus. Richard Cuffari. (New York: Seabury, 1971). 128p. G5-8.

Socially isolated at Mount Holyoke because she resisted conversion, the poet is haunted by "questions of immortality" all her life. Selection of poems in book.

Charlotte Forten [Grimké] 1837-1914

Douty, Esther M. *Charlotte Forten: Free Black teacher.* (Champaign, IL: Garrard, 1971). 144p. G4-6.

Homesick for Philadelphia and her beloved father, a black teen excels at school in Massachusetts.

Mary Cassatt 1844-1926	Myers, Elisabeth P. *Mary Cassatt: A portrait.* (Chicago: Reilly & Lee, 1971). 135p. G5-7. Her father first opposes her move to Paris, then moves the whole family there so she can take care of them; she becomes a great artist in spite of obstacles.
Mary Cassatt 1844-1926	Wilson, Ellen. *American painter in Paris.* (New York: Farrar, Straus & Giroux, 1971). 206p. G6-9. What did Cassatt sacrifice to be a painter? Wilson implies that she was half in love with Degas, and that in old age she bitterly regretted her childlessness.
Emmeline Pankhurst 1857-1928	Noble, Iris. *Emmeline and her daughters: The Pankhurst suffragettes.* (New York: Messner, 1971). 190p. G6-10. A lovely widow with four children carries on her husband's fight for woman suffrage—and her eldest daughter, Christabel, radicalizes the campaign.
Ida Tarbell 1857-1944	Fleming, Alice. *Ida Tarbell: First of the muckrakers.* (New York: Thomas Y. Crowell, 1971). Woman of America series. 165p. G6-9. Her lives of Napoleon and Lincoln boost sales of *McClure's*; her exposé of John D. Rockefeller's Standard Oil Company does even better.
Jane Addams 1860-1935	Keller, Gail Faithfull. *Jane Addams.* Illus. Frank Aloise. (New York: Thomas Y. Crowell, 1971). A Crowell biography. 41p. G2-3. A shy girl with back trouble founds a settlement house in Chicago and works for child labor laws, woman suffrage, and peace.
Nellie Bly 1864-1922	Graves, Charles. *Nellie Bly: Reporter for* The World. Illus. Victor Mays. (Champaign, IL: Garrard, 1971). Americans All series. 96p. G3-5. Undercover reporter with winning smile investigates marriage bureaus and mental hospitals, covers strikes, and circles the globe in less than eighty days.
Annie Sullivan [Macy] 1866-1936	Malone, Mary. *Annie Sullivan.* Illus. Lydia Rosier. (New York: G. P. Putnam's Sons, 1971). See and Read books. 61p. G2-4. Taken from the state poorhouse to Perkins Institution, a blind orphan recovers sight and learns the skills that will open the world to Helen Keller.

Marie Curie 1867-1934	McKown, Robin. *Marie Curie.* Illus. Karl W. Swanson. (New York: G. P. Putnam's Sons, [1971]). World Pioneer Biography series. 96p. G4-6. A tale "of seemingly insurmountable difficulties overcome, of love enduring beyond death," as a great scientist continues her husband's work.
Emma Goldman 1869-1940	Shulman, Alix Kates. *To the Barricades: The Anarchist Life of Emma Goldman.* (New York: Thomas Y. Crowell, 1971). Women of America series. 258p. G7 up. The "most dangerous woman in the world," she supports birth control, free love, peace, and justice for workers; is jailed and eventually deported. Stirring.
Golda Meir 1898-1978	Mann, Peggy. *Golda: The life of Israel's prime minister.* (New York: Coward, McCann & Geoghegan, 1971). 282p. G7 up. Journalistic profile of a contemporary leader shows how commitment formed by early struggle in Russia and U.S. bore fruit in Israel.
Golda Meir 1898-1978	Morris, Terry. *Shalom, Golda.* (New York: Hawthorn Books, 1971). 208p. G7 up. With fewer imagined conversations and anecdotes, more photographs than Mann's account; slightly more emphasis on family sacrifices.
Pablita Velarde 1918-	Nelson, Mary Carroll. *Pablita Velarde.* (Minneapolis, MN: Dillon Press, 1971). 58p. G5 up. Pueblo artist was better educated than most Indian women of her generation, married later and out of the life her art helps to preserve.
Shirley Chisholm 1924-2005	Hicks, Nancy. *The Honorable Shirley Chisholm: Congresswoman from Brooklyn.* (New York: Lion Books, 1971). 118p. G5-9. Journalistic account of an active politician revels in contrast between her petite frame and her "unbossed and unbought" fearlessness.
Maria Tallchief 1925-	De Leeuw, Adèle. *Maria Tallchief: American ballerina.* (New York: Dell Yearling, 1971). Half Osage ballerina overcomes youthful doubts and achieves renown in art dominated by Russian blondes.

Appendix C

Biographies of 1996:
An Annotated List

Cleopatra
69? BC-30 BC

Greene, Robert, *Cleopatra* (New York: Franklin Watts, 1996). A First Book. 64p. G4-6.

Allying herself first with Caesar and then with Antony, the last Greek ruler of Egypt used "charm and wealth" in a fight for power.

Elizabeth Cary
1585-1639

Brackett, Ginger Roberts, *Elizabeth Cary: Writer of Conscience* (Greensboro, NC: Morgan Reynolds, 1996). World Writers series. 95p. G6-10.

Women "didn't have many legal rights" and "were not supposed to be writers." Playwright Lady Falkland converted to Catholicism against her husband's will.

Pocahontas
(Rebecca Rolfe)
1595?-1616

Gourse, Leslie, *Pocahontas, Young Peacemaker* (New York: Simon & Schuster, Aladdin Paperbacks, 1996). Childhood of Famous Americans series. 176p. G. 3-5.

Tutored in leadership by her indulgent father, Pocahontas supports the English colonists and becomes their ambassador to London.

Lucretia Coffin
Mott
1793-1880

Bryant, Jennifer Fisher. *Lucretia Mott: A Guiding Light* (Grand Rapids, MI: William B. Erdmans, 1996). Women of Spirit series. 182p. G7 up.

Although loyal to her family, Mott does not shrink from dangerously controversial stands on the abolition of slavery and women's suffrage.

Mary Shelley
1797-1851

Miller, Calvin Craig, *Spirit Like a Storm: The Story of Mary Shelley* (Greensboro: Morgan Reynolds, 1996). World Writers series. 123p. G7 up.

As a teen, Mary Wollstonecraft Godwin elopes with married poet Percy Bysshe Shelley. Her *Frankenstein* is a surprise success, but tragedies dog her life.

Fanny
Mendelssohn
1805-1847

Kamen, Gloria, *Hidden Music: The Life of Fanny Mendelssohn* (New York: Atheneum, 1996). 96p. G5-8.

Goethe and others thought the child Fanny was as talented as her little brother Felix, but because she was a girl, she was discouraged from publishing her work.

Elizabeth Cady
Stanton
1815-1902

McCully, Emily, *The Ballot Box Battle* (New York: Knopf, 1996). Unp. Gr2-4.

Cordelia's job is to feed Mrs. Stanton's horse. The perks include tagging along to the polls when Mrs. Stanton tries to vote—illegal for women in 1880.

Elizabeth Cady
Stanton
1815-1902

Swain, Gwenyth, *The Road to Seneca Falls*, illus. Mary O'Keefe Young (Minneapolis, MN: Carolrhoda, 1996). Creative Minds series. 64p. G4-6.

When her brother dies, Elizabeth tries to console her father by being as good as any boy; his refusal of her gift helps kindle the women's rights movement.

Victoria
1819-1901

Chiflet, Jean-Loup, and Beaulet, Alain, *Victoria and Her Times*, trans. George Wen (New York: Henry Holt, 1996). W5 Series; Henry Holt Reference. 96p. G6 up.

A flippant pastiche of facts and observations about Victoria and the Victorians, organized more like a website than a chronological text.

Victoria
1819-1901

Netzley, Patricia D., *The Importance of Queen Victoria* (San Diego, CA: Lucent Books, 1996). The Importance series. 128p. G6-9.

The stubborn queen who reigned for sixty-four years learned her job the hard way, learned it again with her beloved Albert, and lived to see the monarchy changed.

Harriet Tubman
1820?-1913

Mosher, Kiki, *Learning about Bravery from the Life of Harriet Tubman* (New York: Rosen, 1996). A Character Building Book™. 24p. G1-3.

Five-year-old Harriet was "put to work in the master's house" and "**whipped** (WIPT)"; but she found courage to escape, to come back and to free others.

Harriet Tubman
1820?-1913

Schroeder, Alan, *Minty: A Story of Young Harriet Tubman.* Unp. K-3.

"If your head is in the lion's mouth, it's best to pat him a little," says her mother; but Minty dreams of freedom and practices her father's survival skills.

Susan B. Anthony 1820-1906

Mosher, Kiki, *Learning about Fairness from the Life of Susan B. Anthony*. (New York: Rosen, 1996). A Character Building Book™. 24p. G2-4.

Anthony knew equality mattered when "most people" didn't believe it; "American women were granted the right to vote" fourteen years after her death.

Florence Nightingale 1820-1910

Mosher, Kiki, *Learning about Compassion from the Life of Florence Nightingale* (New York: Rosen, 1996). A Character Building Book™. 24p. G2-4.

A brief account of her abstract virtues omits the complexities of Nightingale's character, and most of the opposition she overcame.

Mary Harris Jones 1830-1930

Horton, Madelyn, *The Importance of Mother Jones* (San Diego, CA: Lucent Books, 1996). The Importance series. 95p. G6-9.

She lost her husband and four children to epidemic in 1867 and her new livelihood to the Chicago fire in 1871; reinvented herself as a passionate union organizer.

Martha Jane Canary "Calamity Jane" 1852-1903

Sanford, William R., and Green, Carl R., *Calamity Jane: Frontier Original* (Springfield, NJ: Enslow, 1996). Legendary Heroes of the Wild West series. 48p. G4-6.

Orphaned in her teens, she was a beggar, a cook, a washerwoman, a bullwhacker, a nurse and a midwife; she drank, cussed, and "may have loved too many men too well." Was she "just ahead of her time"?

Juliette Gordon Low 1860-1927

Brown, Fern G., *Daisy and the Girl Scouts*, illus. Marie DeJohn (Morton Grove, IL: Albert Whitman, 1996). 111p. G3-6.

A charming, impractical daughter of the Confederacy survives hearing loss, childlessness and an unpleasant divorce before founding the Girl Scouts of America.

Nellie Bly 1864-1922

Blos, Joan, *Nellie Bly's Monkey: His Remarkable Story in His Own Words*, illus. Catherine Stock (New York: Morrow Junior Books, 1996). 40p. G2-5.

Kinetic journalist Nellie Bly races around the world with McGintie.

Marie Curie
1867-1934

Pasachoff, Naomi, *Marie Curie and the Science of Radioactivity* (New York: Oxford University Press, 1996). Science Biography series. 112p. G8 up.

Excluded from the French Academy of Sciences and vilified for her love affair with a married colleague, Curie was controversial in her time. Scientific background and explanations in boxes.

Maria
Montessori
1870-1952

Shepard, Marie Tennent, *Maria Montessori: Teacher of Teachers* (Minneapolis, MN: Lerner, 1996). 112p. G4-6.

The first Italian woman physician and the secret but loving mother of an illegitimate son, she pioneered in early childhood education.

Margaret Morse
Nice
1883-1974

Dunlap, Julie, *Birds in the Bushes*, illus. Ralph L. Ramstad (Minneapolis, MN: Carolrhoda Books, 1996). Creative Minds series. 64p. G3-5.

A wife and mother, with no credentials beyond her master's degree, makes serious contributions to ornithology and conservation.

Eleanor
Roosevelt
1884-1974

Cooney, Barbara, *Eleanor* (New York: Viking, 1996). 40p. G1-4.

In Mlle Souvestre, the headmistress of a British school, orphaned Eleanor finds the mentor she needs to become a courageous and compassionate woman.

Georgia
O'Keeffe
1887-1986

Lowery, Linda, *Georgia O'Keeffe* (Minneapolis, MN: Carolrhoda, 1996). 48p. G2-3.

A twenty-seven-year-old art teacher tears up all her derivative work and starts over, learning how to paint and to be "a genuine Georgia O'Keeffe."

Annie Clemenc
1888-1956

Stanley, Jerry, *Big Annie of Calumet: A True Story of the Industrial Revolution* (New York: Crown Publishers, 1996). 104p. G5-8.

The tall wife of a Croatian miner heads a Michigan picket line, becoming a symbol of the workers' determination. A partial life, rich with social history.

Minnie Evans
1892-1982

Lyons, Mary E., *Painting Dreams* (Boston: Houghton Mifflin, 1996). 48p. G4-8.

Raised by former slaves and sometimes called crazy, Minnie painted her extraordinary dreams to "complete the spiritual task . . . God had given her." Late in life she was discovered as a folk artist.

Bessie Coleman
1896-1926

Hart, Philip S., *Up in the Air: The Story of Bessie Coleman* (Minneapolis, MN: Carolrhoda, 1996). 80p. G5-8.

A penniless black woman occasionally set up "expectations she could not meet" to attract backing for her dream of becoming an aviator and running a flight school; but she still flew further than expected.

Bessie Coleman
1896-1926

Lindbergh, Reeve, *Nobody Owns the Sky*, illus. Pamela Paparone (Cambridge, MA: Candlewick Press, 1996; paperback 1998). Unp. G1-4.

". . . Bessie followed her dream, and in 1921 she became the first licensed black aviator in the world." Her success encouraged others to try.

Dorothy Day
1897-1980

Kent, Deborah, *Dorothy Day: Friend to the Forgotten* (Grand Rapids, MI: William B. Erdmans, 1996). Women of Spirit series. 147p. G7-10.

Passionately alert to injustice and haunted by an early abortion, always questing for God and community, Day helped found the Catholic Worker movement.

Anastasia
Nikolaevna
1901-1918

Brewster, Hugh, *Anastasia's Album* (New York: Hyperion Books, 1996). 64p. G5-8.

Photographs, drawings, and excerpts from letters and diaries document a wealthy and affectionate family's life in the last years of the tsar's doomed regime.

Zora Neale
Hurston
1901-1960

Yannuzzi, Della A., *Zora Neale Hurston* (Springfield, NJ: Enslow, 1996). African-American Biographies series. 104p. G7 up.

An itinerant maid at fourteen, she graduated from Barnard, studied anthropology under Boas, and collected African American folklore. Never secure, she died in poverty, leaving an important literary legacy.

Margaret
Bourke-White
1904-1971

Keller, Emily, *Margaret Bourke-White* (Minneapolis, MN: Lerner, 1996). 128p. G5-10.

She won fame for her photographs of dangerously beautiful factories and bombardments, and developed a compassionate social conscience while covering poverty in the Dust Bowl.

Frida Kahlo
1907-1954

Cruz, Bárbara C. *Frida Kahlo: Portrait of a Mexican Painter*, b/w photos. (Berkeley Heights, NJ: Enslow, 1996). Hispanic Biographies series. 112p. G6-9.

Famous for her marriage to muralist Diego Rivera and her self-portraits with heavy eyebrows, traditional Mexican costume, and complex pain, Kahlo began to paint while recuperating from a near-fatal accident.

Mother Teresa
1910-1997

Mohan, Claire Jordan, *The Young Life of Mother Teresa of Calcutta*, illus. Jane Robbins (Worcester, PA: Young Sparrow Books, 1996). 64p. G4-6
Playful Gonxha, who could "sing like an angel," answered a call to "dedicate her life to the poor, sick, and homeless on the streets of India."

Mahalia Jackson
1911-1972

Gourse, Leslie, *Mahalia Jackson: Queen of Gospel Song* (New York: Franklin Watts, 1996). Impact Biography series. 128p. G6 up.
A malnourished New Orleans girl stunned white audiences with her huge, assured voice: "That song was born in my mouth," she told a would-be coach.

Jean Craighead
George
1919-

Cary, Alice, *Jean Craighead George*. (Santa Barbara, CA: The Learning Works, 1996). Meet the Author series. 136p. G4-6.
Raised in a happy, intelligent family to love pets and the outdoors, Jean Craighead George became a successful writer and single parent.

Maya Angelou
1928-

Lisandrelli, Elaine Slivinski, *Maya Angelou: More than a Poet* (Berkeley Heights, NJ: Enslow, 1996). African-American Biographies series. 128p. G7 up.
Angelou rose to challenges, surviving "to remind us that people are more alike than unalike, that their spirit can triumph and rise over adversity."

Maya Angelou
1928-

Pettit, Jayne, *Maya Angelou: Journey of the Heart* (New York: Puffin, 1996). 80p. G5-8.
Surviving "the pain of abandonment, the anguish of child abuse, and the hatred of racial intolerance," she invites readers to share in "the beauty of creativity."

Anne Frank
1929-1945

Katz, Sandor, *Anne Frank: Voice of Hope* ([Broomall, PA]: Chelsea House, 1996). Junior World Biographies series. 80p. G4-6.
Framing Anne's tragedy as one of many caused by anti-Semitism and prejudice, Katz urges young readers to resist hatred, cruelty, and unfair authority.

Toni Morrison 1931-	Kramer, Barbara, *Toni Morrison: Nobel Prize-Winning Author* (Berkeley Heights, NJ: Enslow, 1996). African-American Biographies series. 112p. G6-9. A summary of Morrison's childhood, education, early career, marriage, and divorce supports discussion of her major novels.
Ann Richards 1933-	Siegel, Dorothy Schainman, *Ann Richards: Politician, Feminist, Survivor* (Springfield, NJ: Enslow, 1996). People to Know series. 112p. G6-9. Only child of a hard-working couple who moved to Waco so she could have a "big-town education," Ann married, became politically active, divorced, struggled with alcoholism, and became governor of Texas.
Wilma Rudolph 1940-1994	Krull, Kathleen, *Wilma Unlimited: How Wilma Rudolph Became the World's Fastest Woman*. New York: Harcourt Brace, 1996. 40p. Younger. Tiny and sickly at birth, crippled by polio at five, and faced with racism and poverty, a determined girl from a loving family became "the first American woman to win three gold medals at a single Olympics" in 1960.
Aretha Franklin 1942-	Sheafer, Silvia Anne, *Aretha Franklin: Motown Superstar* (Springfield, NJ: Enslow, 1996). African-American Biographies. 128p. G6 up. Daughter of a magnetic Baptist leader, mother of two sons by unnamed fathers while still in her teens, "she has recorded fifty-eight albums, released seventeen top-ten singles . . . , and won fifteen Grammys (more than any other female performer ever)."
Wilma Mankiller 1945-	Lowery, Linda, *Wilma Mankiller*, illus. Janice Lee Por-ter (Minneapolis, MN: CarolRhoda, 1996). 56p. G2-4. Her family moved from Oklahoma to San Francisco in 1956 under the government's Indian relocation policy, but Wilma Mankiller returned over twenty years later to become chief of the Cherokee nation.
Amy Tan 1952-	Kramer, Barbara, *Amy Tan: Author of the Joy Luck Club* (Springfield, NJ: Enslow, 1996). People to Know series. 112p. G4-6. Tan grew up in California and in constant rebellion against her mother—a strong, complex relationship that has outlasted her unrewarding freelance work, her failed marriage, and other disasters, giving depth to her novels.

Gloria Estefan
1958-

Strazzabosco, Jeanne, *Learning about Determination from the Life of Gloria Estefan*. (New York: Rosen, 1996). A Character Building Book™. 24p. G1-3.

The child of Cuban immigrants to Miami, Gloria was determined and succeeded, overcoming prejudice, poverty, a language barrier, shyness, and a road accident that broke her back.

Rigoberta
Menchú
1959-

Brill, Marlene Targ, *Journey for Peace: The Story of Rigoberta Menchú*, illus. Rubén De Anda (New York: Dutton Lodestar, 1996). Rainbow Biography series. 64p. G3-7.

Faithful to the memoir that won international sympathy for Menchú's Guatemalan countrymen, Brill does not address subsequent controversy about the facts.

Julie Krone
1963-

Gutman, Bill, *Julie Krone* (Austin, TX: Raintree/Steck-Vaughn, 1996). Overcoming the Odds series. 48p. G3-6

Born to ride, Krone gained respect in a man's world, became top jockey, triumphed at the Belmont, and battled back from severe injury.

Julie Krone
1963-

Savage, Jeff, *Julie Krone: Unstoppable Jockey* (Minneapolis, MN: Lerner, 1996). The Achievers series. 56p. G4-6

Her parents' divorce, her suspension for marijuana, and her slump after a boyfriend's defection shadow a triumphant tale of athletic "work ethic."

Gail Devers
1966-

Gutman, Bill, *Gail Devers* (Austin, TX: Raintree/Steck-Vaughn, 1996). Overcoming the Odds series. 48p. G3-6

A good student who went to UCLA on scholarship, was spotted as Olympic material, and fought back from Graves' disease.

Shannon Miller
1977-

Green, Septima, *Shannon Miller: American Gymnast* (New York: Avon Camelot, 1996). 86p. G3-5.

Small, athletic, modest, and popular, Miller worked hard and won five silver and bronze medals at the 1992 Olympics.

Index

About the Author

Gale Eaton grew up in Maine, surrounded by books, readers, story-tellers, and fog. She majored in English and concentrated in medieval studies at Smith College, and then, urged to do something a little more practical, she earned her MLS at the University of Rhode Island. She enjoyed life as a children's librarian for seven years at the Boston Public Library and another seven at the Berkshire Athenaeum before giving in to the lure of academics again—her Ph.D. in librarianship is from the University of North Carolina/Chapel Hill.

Back at the University of Rhode Island's Graduate School of Library and Information Studies, Professor Eaton now teaches children's literature, information ethics, public library services, and research methods. As Assistant Director and Coordinator of Distance Learning, she also dabbles in administration. She is guided by her father's translation of the alleged family motto, *Vincit omnia veritas*: "Always wink when you tell the truth."